Between the Stops

Between the Stops

The View of My Life from the
Top of the Number 12 Bus

Sandi Toksvig

virago

VIRAGO

First published in Great Britain in 2019 by Virago Press

1 3 5 7 9 10 8 6 4 2

A CIP catalogue record for this book
is available from the British Library.

Hardback ISBN 978-0-349-00637-6
C-format ISBN 978-0-349-00638-3

Typeset in Goudy by M Rules
Printed and bound in Great Britain by Clays Ltd, Elcograf S.p.A.

Papers used by Virago are from well-managed forests
and other responsible sources.

MIX
Paper from
responsible sources
FSC® C104740

Virago Press
An imprint of
Little, Brown Book Group
Carmelite House
50 Victoria Embankment
London EC4Y 0DZ

An Hachette UK Company
www.hachette.co.uk

www.virago.co.uk

To my lifelong friends Troy and Pip, without whom I would never have done anything.

Preface

When I was about seven my father gave me my first watch. It was small, with a thin blue leather strap.

'You wear it on your left wrist,' he explained.

'Why?' I asked.

'Because you are right-handed. All right-handed people wear their watches on their left wrist.'

I took the watch and solemnly strapped it to the 'wrong' wrist, where I have been wearing it ever since. It was a tiny act of defiance, of standing apart. I don't know whether it's a curse or a blessing never to follow the crowd. It is a trait that has dogged me all my life. I'm not saying it's a good thing. It's just part of me. So, this is a memoir, but it isn't like the ones most people write. On the whole, when people look back at their lives, they begin with a sort of clearing of the throat before declaring, 'I was born in ...' I don't think I have it in me to write like that. This is about some parts of my life, but it is also about travelling through London on the Number 12 bus, a red double-decker that meanders for just over seven and a half miles from Dulwich Library in south-east London to the BBC's Broadcasting House in the centre of town. I started taking the bus because it happened to stop outside Dulwich Library, which was near where I was living, and happened to head where I needed to go.

I love London with a passion. The sight of a double-decker still gladdens my heart; you just know you are in London. A single shot of such a bus in a film sets the action firmly in the

UK capital. I have spent a wonderful time catching the Number 12. As I travelled, I have realised a few things – that hardly anyone looks out of the window, and that every one of the stops along the way sparks some thought and is worth exploring. I am history mad and here is one of the greatest cities in the world laid out before me at almost no cost. Sometimes I took the bus even though I had nowhere I was supposed to be. I stopped looking at my phone and started getting off to have a look at unexpected places.

I am over sixty now and travel for free, so I have made great use of my bus pass. Sixty used to be the age some women retired but I have never worked harder. I never thought I'd get to such an age. My father died aged fifty-nine and for some reason I never thought I would outlive his years. It has made me reflective about my life. No bus in London is quick, so I have had time to think – a rare thing these days. Things pop into your head as you travel. I suppose none of us remember the past in order. It's all a jumble of recollections.

I have resisted writing a 'memoir' because I didn't want to create some kind of printed version of the 'selfie', where people don't look like themselves at all. I wanted to look out as much as in, so this is also a sort of love letter to the fact that some of the most fascinating travel is available from the nearest bus stop.

I have been in radio, television and on stage for forty years now. Twice in my life I have endured agonising periods of people shunning me, not talking to me. Now when I am out and about I am sometimes recognised and strangers want to talk to me. It's often wonderful though sometimes unsettling, but on a bus, no one talks to those they don't know. On the Number 12 I am blissfully ignored. It is peaceful. A haven in the midst of bustle, and I need that.

Geek that I am, libraries are my happiest places; in a library everyone is intent on their own discoveries and I soon realised that buses have a similar solitary quality. People on buses don't look at each other. The seats all face forward, and if there is room no one sits next to anyone else. I am also that ageing woman on the bus who no one gives a second glance to and I don't mind a bit. Those who have seen me perform may think it bizarre but there is a vast disconnect between the public show-off and the shy book-reader. Unobserved, I am able to see things differently and looking out on the city, really looking, really seeing, has been a revelation. It's made me think about my life, but it's also made me think about seeking what is forgotten or even hidden in plain sight, just like me on my journey.

I am the middle child of three; the daughter of a Danish journalist and an English mother who was one of the first women to become a studio manager at the BBC. I was born in Denmark, grew up in various African countries so long ago that most of them have changed their names, then America, and finally to boarding school in Britain before settling to live in south-east London. It was a rootless childhood, but from it I learned that everywhere in the world has something to commend it if we just take the time to look.

I loved what I saw from the top deck of the bus (preferably the right-hand seat at the front). It taught me to look again at the familiar and find new pleasures. This is not a journey that begins by heading out into the wild blue but instead starts with a walk under a grey sky to a bus stop. The chapters consist of thoughts that occurred to me as I travelled and about places that appealed to me as I stared out the window. It's not as if all my life flashed before me; but much has resurfaced: the solace of books; the love of my dear departed father; the drama and relief of coming out; finding love; my passion for theatre; my drive for justice; an understanding of a kind of loneliness that will forever haunt me; and how I ended up at sixty years old riding a double-decker bus.

If none of these things appeal to you may I gently suggest that you change seats now. Life is too short to read a book that upsets you. On the other hand, if you're ready, let's get going.

The Beginning

I had a fifth-grade teacher called Mrs Strange. It was 1968. I was ten and living in the small town of Mamaroneck, New York, a seaside suburb on Long Island Sound. Mrs Strange was from Arkansas. Her accent was slow and Southern, and she drawled her way laboriously through all information like sieving it through a mint julep. It never occurred to me to wonder if Strange was her real name or merely a general description. Her hair was pulled so tightly into a bun that it gave her a permanently startled look – as if she'd arrived through a wind tunnel. She looked like Miss Gulch in *The Wizard of Oz*. She once gave me detention for declaring I had seen snow at the Equator.

'*Naht paaa . . . ssible*,' she drawled, '*the Eeequator is hahttt.*'

I had seen snow on top of Mount Kilimanjaro when I was about four, but she said it with such firmness that it had to be so. To this day there must be adults who passed through her care who do not believe there could be snow in Africa. It was an early lesson in my understanding that grown-ups can be wrong. I am a grown-up and have been wrong so many times. Dear God, how it distresses me that on my twenty-first birthday, 3 May 1979, Margaret Thatcher came to power and I was naive enough to think it would be a good thing for a woman to be in charge.

It was Mrs Strange who taught me to do 'joined up' writing. I don't suppose, in the current era of the keyboard being king, that these things matter any more, but she was adamant that I learn to make my letters 'flow'. Indeed, we spent many hours learning to flow. Mrs Strange insisted that the entire class slant their lined paper to the left at a 45-degree angle so that our script lurched away from the centre as if keen to escape. They say your handwriting says a lot about you. I think mine says a lot about Mrs Strange. On reflection, she probably had a leaning to the right about most things.

Mrs Strange is in my mind because recently I had to fill in a form by hand. I realised how little I use a pen to write anything any more. The biro felt unfamiliar and my writing sloped away as if out of control. We moved house, to a suburb of London called East Dulwich, and I decided to join the local library. It's often my first thought when I am anywhere new and unfamiliar. I think if I have access to books, I shall make sense of it all. I'm sure everyone else does just as well having coffee somewhere and trying to make friends. The trouble is I don't have any small talk, so I do libraries where no one talks at all. I thought this one looked nice. Well, nice enough. Built from a Victorian kit. I suspect there was a kit for libraries, one for schools and another for public baths.

The white-haired librarian gave me a form to fill in.

When I handed it back, she looked at my details, then looked again at me and then back at the form.

'You're not her,' she said matter-of-factly. 'You're not Sandi Toksvig.'

I paused, wondering, not for the first time, who I am.

'What makes you say that?' I asked.

She looked at me accusingly. 'You're too quiet.'

'It's a library,' I replied, lowering my voice still further. 'I've done libraries before.'

The truth is I hadn't been in a lending library for years. I have spent many, many years studying and writing in the British Library, which I love, but they don't let you take anything home. I looked around this library; I had forgotten that local branches cover all their books in plastic. It makes them look a bit unpleasant. As if every book might stir something in the reader and cause them to need a wipe-down cover.

I got my library card. They're fancy now, with a bar code and some kind of attachment for your keyring. The last library I borrowed from gave you a paper booklet in which smudged rubber stamps reminded you of all the books you had borrowed. I liked that: a condensed litany of study. The bar code on my new key fob made me feel like produce.

'What kind of books do you want?' the librarian enquired.

'Local history,' I said.

She shook her head and muttered darkly, 'They'll be scattered.'

I wasn't sure what that meant. It's the sort of thing people say at crematoriums, not libraries. She kept staring at me, so I left without any books.

I wish I could see a map of the world where a light trail of my life had been left. I couldn't be more surprised to have ended up in Dulwich or Dilwihs or Dylways or Dullag or however it has been spelled before anyone thought to invent spellcheck. The clerk who filled in my marriage certificate called it Dullwich, which was either a barbed comment or suggests it is still a spelling on the move.

Dulwich is a place of some longevity. Edgar the Peaceful granted Dilwihs to a thane in AD 967. It is hard to imagine that my neat Victorian terraced street was once 'the meadow where dill grows'. I have a pathological horror of suburbia and yet there I was amongst houses so identical that a drunk might never find their way home. Perhaps it will be fine, I thought. I am here for the right reasons. We had landed here because my wonderful wife, Debbie, needed to be near her daughter.

My wife and I are non-birth mothers. We are both the former halves of lesbian couples who had kids, but we are the ones who did not give birth and we have learned something from this. There is the obvious lesson of being beyond the pale for the tabloids, but there is also something more surprising. I have never done a full survey, but it seems to us that it is always the birth mother who gets to choose where the children live. It's a particularly niche piece of lesbian lore.

My three kids are all grown up now, but while they grew I lived near Guildford because their other (birth) mother liked it there. Now we were living in East Dulwich because my wife's ex does. Debbie's daughter is a teenager. I didn't choose to be here, but it is best for her and for my beloved so, in a rather British way, I make the best of it. The place was fine. More than fine. Perfectly nice, in fact, but I settled without choice and that always takes a little adjustment.

It's 2017 and I'm walking up a main road in East Dulwich called Lordship Lane. I don't know the place that I have moved to at all. Debbie has lived here before, so she knows all the shortcuts in the area, whereas I am struggling to recall even the main arteries. Lordship Lane is an ancient thoroughfare which runs north–south from a patch of land named Goose Green to some further suburb known as Wood Vale. Names that seem to say even the local places don't want to be in the suburbs either.

Ahead of me is the library where I am now a member and past that is a small turning called Landells Road, where acres of more identical terraced houses stretch away from me. The only Landells I can think of is Ebenezer Landells. He was the man who created *Punch* magazine, which years later my old friend the brilliant humorist (is that even a job any more?) Alan Coren edited.

Was Landells Road named for Ebenezer? What a marvellous

name. Perhaps I should have been bolder and called one of my children Ebenezer.

I think how much Alan Coren would have enjoyed a trip on the bus with me. Alan passed away in 2007. I miss him, but I like that a street can stir history – both general and my own.

I pass the Plough pub, once well named as it stood amongst the fields but now seeming out of place. At one time it had a window on which someone had inscribed with a diamond 'March 16, 1810. Thomas Jones dined here, ate six pounds of bacon and drank nineteen pots of beer.'

Is his gluttony Thomas Jones's only legacy? It remains impressive, but it seems very little to mark a man's life.

Pubs stand sentry on so many corners of this great city. I think about the Tabard inn, which once stood near Borough High Street, not all that far from here and from which Chaucer sent his pilgrims off to Canterbury. Perhaps I can have a pilgrimage of my own.

Lordship Lane is heavy with car fumes. On this very lane in 1799 I might have seen Byron the schoolboy, with shoulder-length dark, curly hair. He liked to play in the nearby Dulwich Woods and 'chat to the vagabonds' – which sounds jolly, if politically incorrect. When he went to study at Cambridge, he kept a tame bear and used to take it for walks like a dog. I expect he was annoying. The talented can be tiresome and people say he was spoilt and strange.

Byron is on my mind. In his day he was a true star. After he published his poem *Childe Harold's Pilgrimage* he wrote, 'I awoke one morning and found myself famous.'

We're having work done on the house at the moment and as I delivered the morning round of tea to the workmen I chatted with the plasterer's assistant.

'What's your name?' I asked.

'Byron,' he said.

I smiled. 'What a great name! I love that!'

He smiled back. 'Because of the burgers?'

I had forgotten there is a high-street hamburger chain of that name. It was an easy mistake. 'No, the poet,' I explained.

The young lad frowned. 'There was a poet?'

'Yes.'

'What was his name?'

'Uh, Byron,' I said. 'Well, Lord Byron actually.'

'He was a lord as well?' It was my turn to nod. The boy shook his head and let out a sigh. 'He must have been busy.'

Etherow Street / Barry Road

The Number 12 begins its journey to the centre of town at a stop just past the corner of Etherow Street and Barry Road. I am not the first this morning. There is already a middle-aged man waiting. He is blind and carries a white stick. I don't know if he is aware that I wait for him to get on first, but as he steps up to show his pass to the driver he drops a quite large, brightly coloured garland of flowers, a soft plastic Hawaiian lei. It seems entirely out of keeping with either the weather or the transport.

'You dropped this,' I say, holding it out only to realise that he cannot see what I am doing. I place it in his hands, and he takes it, smiling. I want to ask him where he is going, why he carries the garland, but of course I don't. Still, I love that he has it. I should like us all to wear Hawaiian leis in the winter.

The driver sits behind a Perspex screen. I tap my Oyster card against the entrance pad and say a cheery 'Good morning!' but he looks straight ahead. While I have been trying to be both cheerful and helpful two more people have raced to the stop and got on ahead of me. By the time I get upstairs they have taken the window seats at the very front. Every other seat is empty, and I suspect bus etiquette dictates that I don't sit next to either of the two at the front. I am childishly disappointed. It is grey and cold. Everyone is wrapped and hidden in hats and scarves. It is possibly not the time to make friends. I take a seat further back.

I look out at the houses before we set off, thinking that if only the Germans had been better at geography the people of this area might have escaped much death and destruction. During the Second World War, forty-one V1 and three V2 rockets fell on Dulwich, and all down to human error. So much of history turns on a misunderstanding. Mussolini was killed because his driver took a wrong turning. The Nazis propelled flying bombs to this part of London in the mistaken belief that North Dulwich Station was a vital junction. In fact, they made the station their mean aiming point. Many of the stoical locals dealt with this by sleeping in a sort of cage reinforced with iron bars, which they often kept under the dining-room table.

It must have been terrifying. It is said that you could hear the drone of the V1 rockets when they were on their way: the sound from the pulse jet engine could be heard from miles away, but it wasn't the noise that was frightening. The terror came when the sound stopped. That meant the rocket was ready. The fuel to the engine was cut off and the V1 would shed its wings and engine before hurtling to the ground.

The V2 was a different matter. The supersonic rocket made a double-thunderclap sound as it re-entered the atmosphere. There was no other warning and what little there had been served no purpose for it was travelling at 3000mph, several times the speed of sound. The 47-foot rocket fell from the sky and unleashed devastation with its one-ton payload of explosive. It had only been minutes since the rocket had left mainland Europe.

The German scientist Wernher von Braun had led the V2 development team. When the war was over the Americans welcomed him and his scientists to work for the US army and then NASA, where they helped design a series of boosters for the Saturn rocket that took Neil Armstrong to the moon. Twenty-five missiles hit East Dulwich alone and seventy-seven people there died thanks to Wernher von Braun. I expect their descendants watched the moon landing.

I do have a moment where I wonder if I ought to be heading for something a little more exotic. Maybe I'm ready for some gap-year travel. My son Ted has had months off work seeing the world and both my daughters have had gap years. One of them seems to have had several. I am now old enough to utter the sentence 'We didn't have them in my day.'

I don't know if it's the same now, but in the late 1970s anyone applying for Oxford or Cambridge had to do the Oxbridge exam, which usually meant staying on for one more term after A levels. I did just that and when in 1976 I got in to Cambridge, it left me with nine months to fill before I 'went up'. It never occurred to me to bum around Bali or faff about Fiji, and no one suggested it. Instead, desperate to be independent and adult, I worked night and day. I was eighteen. Fresh out of boarding school and so wet behind the ears as to feel permanent dampness.

The day job was being the world's worst telephonist for what on reflection was possibly a rather dodgy solicitor in Bedford Square in central London.

Many a morning would begin with instructions from the senior partner: 'Sandi, if Mr Watson calls tell him I'm not here.'

'But you are here,' I would reply innocently.

The lean lawyer with greased-back hair from the 1940s shook his head at my ignorance before adding, 'And if Mr Everidge turns up, lock the door.'

I sat in a small room by myself just beyond the white double-doored entrance which led out onto a slightly down-at-heel Georgian square. It had once been an elegant and stylish building. Now I sat at a desk with wooden laminate that was peeling off in protest. There was no art of any kind on the walls, just woodchip wallpaper that looked like giant bugs had got trapped under a magnolia cover. It too peeled and curled as it attempted to separate itself from the building. I was about to study law and had had some romantic notion about this being a good place to observe justice in action. In the six months I was there I never saw any kind of action.

My job was to work a small grey switchboard called a PBX, which had a series of plastic switches. Calls came through to me and I would then put them through to the various lawyers. The trick was to remember who was talking to whom, which I managed on an infrequent basis.

'Have you worked one before?' asked the secretary showing me the ropes on my first day.

'Of course,' I replied. I hadn't. I'd never even seen one before. 'But why don't you just talk me through the basics,' I said brightly, 'in case this system is different to the last one I worked.'

The job was mind-numbingly boring. So boring that I took to answering every tenth call with a new accent. After that I began making up places of work that the caller might mistakenly have come through to.

'Up and Plumbing, we're here for all your draining needs. How can I help?'

'Renal and Rectal, we're here for all your draining needs. How can I help?'

No one ever said anything, so it can't have mattered. There was a sweet young clerk with a large beard who hung around me. He was the only person I ever really spoke to. He had dandruff in his beard, and I would watch the flakes drift down as he spoke. I realise now he was flirting with me, but it passed me by at the time. I was never any good at reading heterosexual signals. Possibly sexual signals of any kind.

I think Alan Coren and I got on because we never had a

moment of sexual tension. I met him through a BBC game show in 1996, which seems a long time ago.

'They're doing *Call My Bluff* again,' my agent said, always managing to sound surprised that I might work at all. 'They want you to be a team captain.'

I had never heard of *Call My Bluff*. My growing-up years had not been in the UK until I was fourteen, and hadn't included the show's early incarnation with Robert Robinson et al.

'They want you to meet at Television Centre.'

Alan Coren swept into the dressing room in a tweed jacket and brown fedora. He was a little breathless and a little florid. I had never heard of him either, but I liked him straight away. We began by congratulating each other on having parked our cars. In those days Television Centre had half a dozen parking spaces in what was known as the Horseshoe, the area right at the front of the building. No one but the top stars parked there, and we had both been given spaces. Alan was thrilled. There was a general consensus that we had arrived.

Soon we moved to the Pebble Mill Studios in Birmingham, where we would make the show together. Alan was hilarious, but always in a nonchalant manner. *Call My Bluff* featured four celebrities for each recording and over the six years we worked together Alan and I met hundreds of the great and the good. One afternoon we were in the make-up room waiting to begin when Cliff Richard walked in. We didn't know him well, but Alan had impeccable manners and commented, 'Nice tie!' Sir Cliff looked down and replied, 'It's a Galtieri.' Clearly he had mistaken a terrible Argentinian general for a designer. Alan didn't miss a beat. 'Ah,' he said, 'I wondered what he did after the Falklands.'

Alan and I developed a sort of strange showbusiness marriage. We used to make four programmes a day, four days in a row. We stayed at a fancy hotel and quickly tired of the elaborate menu, so Alan took to ordering burgers for us in his room and we would lie, side by side, on his bed eating and watching television. One night, as he wiped ketchup from a pillowcase, I declared, 'Dear God, Alan, we're almost like an old married couple, except we don't have sex.'

'No, Sandi,' he replied, 'we're exactly like an old married couple.'

The bus blows fumes into Barry Road, named after the great architect Charles Barry and his son (also called Charles, because heaven knows, once you've found a name you like you might as well stick with it) who laid out the Victorian streets I now live in.

'This was all fields, you know,' I mutter to myself.

Clearly, I am the mad woman at the top of the bus. How marvellous!

Charles Barry and son were busy here. The Friern Manor estate had existed since the Middle Ages, but in the late nineteenth century it was sold to the British Land Company and turned into two hundred building plots. Charles Barry was no architectural slouch; he also designed the Houses of Parliament. He and his boy were swift. It took just two years to pave over the green pastures. The railway arrived in 1836 and the new solidly built houses quickly filled with the young families of London clerks.

My happiest early memories involve public transport. When we lived in Copenhagen – I suppose I must have been five or six – every Saturday morning my mother would take me on the bright yellow tram to the centre of town. There was and still is a wonderful department store called Magasin. We would catch the Number 6 and rattle our way there. The narrow tram got its power from overhead cables and the metal rods which rose up from the roof clanked and sometimes sparked as we travelled. I don't remember shopping much, but we would go to the café on the top floor where I would be allowed an open roast beef sandwich with dried onions and a kind of flavoured mayonnaise called rémoulade. I had my mum all to myself and I don't recall being more content.

There used to be a tram in Dulwich which ran in helpful directions, but it is no more. Lordship Lane itself had a railway which would have steamed me straight to Victoria. How furious people such as the great critic John Ruskin were about the trains of the time. He moaned that the slow pace of every day would now descend into infernal noise and hurry. He did not predict the Number 12 bus in present-day traffic. It is no hurry at all.

You never know what people are thinking on buses. I am thinking about being naked. I have been to the Royal Academy Summer Exhibition, where an artist asked if he could paint me. I said yes, only to discover later that he only does nudes, which is probably not for me. Funnily enough, there is a fine painting from the 1870s by the French impressionist Camille Pissarro of a train at Lordship Lane Station. Not a very heroic picture: there is no breath-taking scenery, just a purposeful train and some buildings, but the light is glorious.

Pissarro was half-Danish, just like me, except he was born in the Danish West Indies. Danish West Indies? That sounds wrong on every level. Anyway, Pissarro fell in love with his mother's maid, Julie, but could not marry her as he was Jewish and she was not, she was a servant and he was not, which is how the world randomly divides people. They don't seem to have cared about convention because they ran off and settled in Paris, where they had eight children. They lived happily until Pissarro's studio was ransacked by the invading Prussian army in 1870. Only forty of his fifteen hundred paintings were saved. It is a terrible story. Paintings given to him by Monet were taken and his own canvases were used as butchers' aprons. He fled to Norwood in south-east London, where his mother, and Monet too, now lived. In a letter to a friend Pissarro mentioned that he and Monet had submitted some of their studies for the Royal Academy's exhibition. 'Naturally we were rejected,' he concludes.

Why does anyone ever decide to be an artist of any kind? It is the strangest life to endlessly put your head above the parapet and then wait to be shot down. Camille and Julie did finally marry, in Croydon Register Office. I hope they liked it here.

The bus inches past the corner where once Wright's Dairy Farm kept 186 cows in sheds, lit by gas and ready to send the milk into London twice a day, reaching the city at 5 a.m. and 1 p.m. I love the detail of history. Fourteen people were employed to do the milking, spending seventeen minutes per cow.

I had a great-aunt who was a milkmaid in Denmark. I picture her as ancient, but perhaps she was only as old as I am now. She made lace as a hobby and lived in the heart of Danish farmland in Jutland. She had worked on a farm before she married. She once told me a story about regret. The milkmaids worked every day, but in different shifts. One day there was a great party to which they were all invited, and her friend asked if she might swap shifts so that she could get ready early. She had her eye on a boy and wanted to sway his heart. My great-aunt refused and never got over the pain of her own behaviour. If that were all I had to regret in my life I should be so pleased. When she herself married, she went with her new husband to see the great capital of Copenhagen. They were gone a week and when she returned none of the milkmaids were curious about the big town. All they wanted to know was what it felt like to have a week off.

Goodrich Road

I don't know who gets to name roads. Around here quite a lot of the local roads take their names from pious folk. Thomas Goodrich was Bishop of Ely in the sixteenth century. Hard to know what he had to do with East Dulwich. Born in Lincolnshire, he went to Cambridge University at the age of ten, which seems a tad precocious, but I suppose people didn't live as long then, so you had to get on. He happened to make friends with Thomas Cranmer, who would go on to lead the English Reformation.

Tom Cranmer got Goodrich the gig of helping the King (Henry VIII) sort out the legality of his marriage to Catherine of Aragon. It was the sort of thing that made Henry feel jolly, and pretty soon the Lincolnshire lad found himself heading for high office. Yet another repeat of the lesson that it's not what you know but who you know which helps you get ahead. Goodrich was also an arse-licker, which helped. Once he was bishop, he spent a lot of time telling everyone how great the King was and how God wanted nothing more than for His Majesty to be in charge.

It is on the corner of Goodrich Road that Friern Manor farmhouse once stood, and where the eighteenth-century poet Alexander Pope is supposed to have written his *Essay on Man*. I feel my true geekdom is expressed when I say that I absolutely loved Alexander Pope when I was at boarding school. This particular school was not a fan of the arts. The boarding house had a record player with exactly three singles, and a television set which was switched on to BBC1 from 7 to 9 p.m. on a Saturday regardless of what was showing or how long it lasted. On Thursday evenings we were all allowed to watch *Top of the Pops* on another television in the main school dining room, which was kept in a locked corner cupboard. One year a parent, grateful to the school for containing their child, presented us with a colour television. Enthralled, we watched the music show in living colour for the first time. As Gary Glitter spun round on a silver Catherine wheel and began to sing, I think we all knew the fun was over. The next morning an engineer was called to retune the set to black and white. It had all been far too exciting.

It gives you an idea of how starved I was for entertainment that I thought Pope's satires were hilarious. I can't really imagine why Pope would have been at a farm in East Dulwich. Perhaps he needed a break.

I first began to think about English culture when, at the age of fourteen, I was sent to boarding school in Surrey. Up until then we had been living in America, but I had behaved poorly at three schools in a row. So poorly that each one had asked me to leave. The first was a private school called Riverdale Country Day School for Girls, whose headmistress, Mrs Rochester, said I asked too many questions. She called my parents to her office and told them I was not 'academically minded' and would probably best be suited to an agricultural college. I didn't know what that meant. My father looked at her for a long, hard moment and then began laughing so hard I thought he would pass out. He banged her desk with his hand and gave great gulping laughs as tears of hilarity fell down his cheeks.

'You, madam, are an idiot,' he managed before we left.

I knew what I had done wrong. There was an English teacher

called Miss Coe who sucked the life out of everything we read. She loved to take a sentence, any sentence, and strip it down to its bare bones using a strange technique of drawing stick-like trees with branches of adverbs and metaphors. I couldn't bear it. Whatever book we read she broke it down into this horrible spider's web of clinical appreciation. All meaning and delight in the writing was destroyed with each stroke of her chalk on the board. Opinionated child that I was, I told her so and said I didn't want to do it. That I doubted the writer wanted us to do it. I was gone from the place not long after.

I don't remember why I had to leave the second school. The third was because I had failed to follow the fundamental school rule that you ought to turn up every day. The truth is I found it boring and I don't do well with that. I have learned to deal with hurt, embarrassment, pain of many sorts, but boredom in this world seems unforgivable. I was thirteen and at the beginning of my freshman year at Mamaroneck High School. The town name is an old Algonquin word meaning 'where the fresh water meets the salt'. My father taught me that. The school taught me nothing.

I was given a copy of J. D. Salinger's *The Catcher in the Rye* to read. It's not a vast volume so I went home and read it, arriving the next day fully prepared to discuss my thoughts. It was as the class commenced that I realised that no one else had read it. In fact, the plan was for us to read the book out loud all year, in a rote of disinterested monotones, our fingers tracing one word at a time as we spoke. I abandoned the class. I don't know what I was thinking – perhaps that I would come back when everyone else had read the book.

There were over two thousand students in the school. No one had the same schedule of classes as anyone else and it was easy to get lost in the system. I started skipping other lessons and soon it became a habit of not going to anything at all. I hung out backstage at the large school theatre and no one was any the wiser. Then my parents did a very odd thing that they had never done before. They decided to attend a Parent–Teacher Association meeting and pretty much couldn't find a single teacher who seemed to know me. The game was up, and I was off to be shut up in a British boarding school.

I had never lived in Britain. I had visited my English grandparents, my mother's parents, but, really, I knew nothing about British life. At first, I was excited at the thought of boarding school. I had read a great deal of Enid Blyton and Enid had convinced me that this venture was going to be fun. I never forgave her. She once lived on Lordship Lane. Her house was destroyed by a German bomb, but not, I think, while she was in it.

From the day I arrived at my Surrey boarding school an ache of loneliness established itself inside me and has never truly left. There is a great pool of sadness formed from the curious British notion of abandoning children, particularly the children of the well off, into the care of those least suited to the task.

That first day, when my father dropped me off, I did not recognise myself. I had grown up in American jeans, sweatshirts and sneakers. Now I was stifled in a stiffly starched white shirt with a tie, a light blue blazer trimmed with white and a royal blue pudding-bowl hat made of velvet which suited no one. I had a thick New York accent and no idea what lay ahead. Matron opened the door and I stuck my hand out.

'Hi, I'm Sandi,' I declared with American confidence.

Matron eyed my hand and placed both of hers on her hips.

'I'm Matron,' she sighed.

I nodded. 'Uh-huh. Matron. What is that? Like, your first name?'

She hated me on sight and when the other girls, being as charming as only girls in groups can be, sent me to Coventry (a place I had never even heard of) – that is, they completely ignored me, because of my accent – Matron had no problem with that. For the first six weeks no one in the boarding house spoke to me. I lay in bed at night, miserable, listening to the other girls' breathing. There were six of us, six beds and three tall chests of drawers. No posters or art were allowed on the walls and we were each only permitted three items on the top of the chests of drawers, one of which had to be a family photograph. There were a million rules I didn't understand, which I realise now were aimed at containing any lesbian tendencies. No sitting on another girl's bed. No long-handled hairbrushes. I was fully grown up before I worked out what that particular fear was about.

The beds were no wider than our bodies. The room was small, and we lay so close together that you could touch the person in the next bed by simply opening your arms out wide, but no one ever did. We lay separated in silence. The windows had chains on them to stop anyone opening them more than an inch and the thick floral curtains waved in the breeze. No lights were allowed. It was pitch black. A world of sound in which no noise seemed familiar. The pigeons in the trees made a deep cooing noise that was entirely alien to me. It sounded mournful, even funereal, and to this day it evokes a feeling of desolation which I can hardly bear. I can still feel it weighing down my chest so I can't breathe. I lay there missing my parents and had to believe they would not have done this to me if I had not brought it upon myself. I was filled with self-loathing and for the first time wished I were better at just going with the crowd. I knew I was stuck where I was and if I were ever going to try to blend in then I would have to change, and that change had to begin with how I spoke.

Your accent is a key part of who you are. It tells the world where you come from and so gives a clue to others about your thoughts and attitudes. It is a fundamental thing to decide dramatically to alter your vowels, your consonants, the very shape of your mouth. My parents were three thousand miles away, somehow not understanding my despair, and I could not cope with the isolation from everyone's silence.

One night as a special treat we were allowed to watch *Brief Encounter*. I don't know why. Providing entertainment was not something anyone in the school ever worried about. The film stars two marvellous British actors, Celia Johnson and Trevor Howard, speaking in the most exaggerated clipped 1940s manner. To me with my American twang it sounded as British as one could get and I remember thinking, I'll speak like that. I began mimicking Celia Johnson. It's why, to this day, I think I sound like I'm trapped in a black-and-white film. It has become my accent, but I suspect I lost something of my old self in the process. In Britain, how you speak defines so much about background and class and because of the choice I made lots of people make presumptions about me. If only we'd watched something else that night. Perhaps if the musical *Oliver!* had been on offer I'd sound like the Artful Dodger instead.

A woman gets on the bus speaking in a glorious Irish brogue. Do I presume something about her because of how she speaks? I suspect I think she must be a laugh because Irish is the true rhythm of stand-up comedy. I love the story of the Irish workman who goes to an English building site for a job. The English foreman hears the Irishman speak and immediately makes assumptions.

'Do you even know the difference between a girder and a joist?' he asks pompously.

'Ah, well, yes,' answers the Irishman in his laconic way. 'Goethe wrote *Faust* and Joyce wrote *Ulysses*.'

I'm intrigued by accents. I worry that yet another effect of globalisation is that we'll all end up sounding the same. I read an article about chimpanzees which alleged that Dutch and Scottish chimps have different-sounding grunts for 'apple'.

My first concern was how the chimps from the lowlands of Holland and the highlands of Scotland came to be at an apple fest together in the first place. The more sensational end of the press reported that a group of Netherlands chimps moved to Edinburgh Zoo and adopted the local grunt. Everyone now said 'apple' with a Scots accent. I like this story. It says a lot about the accommodations we make for friendship, but it begs the question – what would have happened if the Scots had gone to live with the Dutch instead of the other way around? Does place outsmart upbringing? I don't know. If I had been more determined, could I have got everyone to speak with an American accent?

Then I read that the conclusion about chimpanzees was in fact a gross exaggeration based on wafer-thin evidence. It was possible that the two sets of apes had always had the same basic call for 'apple' and the Dutch had just made a slight modification in order to fit in. There are countless examples of all kinds of creatures doing just that – birds, whales, dolphins, monkeys and most certainly humans. I suppose all of us, even the chimps, just want to fit in.

Gradually at school I made friends, but I never got used to any of it. Those years were not so much about education as about finding any way to survive. As an adult I look back on four years of what I regard as institutionalised and presumably expensive child abuse. We were cold, we were hungry and, worse, we had the joy sucked out of life. My mother wrote to me each week from New York. She penned her letters on yellow paper sealed in a yellow envelope. In a time of pale blue aerograms, it made me so happy. It was easily the brightest thing in my week, seeing the yellow envelope lying waiting for me when post was laid out in the dining room. The dining room with its Formica tables and not one painting. What kind of place filled with children refuses to decorate the walls with beauty?

Much of British life seemed cold to me. Growing up, suburban

New York State, where everyone's garden ran fluidly into the next, had been a place of freedom. As kids we ran across any lawn and played around any house. Now I lived at a school in suburban Surrey where neighbours might fall out over inches of space and demarcations of ownership in the shape of walls, fences and hedges were everywhere. It is not how I see Britain now, but in those early years life seemed meaner and much more solitary.

Books became my only solace. There was a second-hand bookshop on Guildford High Street called Thorpe's. Once a week, on a Saturday morning, we were allowed into town for forty-five minutes, on the left-hand side of the High Street only. The left-hand rule was strictly enforced. Partly because the Pilgrim Bookshop, which contained the post office and a wide selection of bookmarks with Christian sentiments on them, was on the left and partly, it was rumoured, because some shops on the right-hand side, such as Marks and Spencer, were owned by Jewish people. It seems unfathomable that such a thing might be true. I had never come across casual anti-Semitism before and did not understand it. Clearly, we would not have been allowed to mix with the Pissarros.

Fortunately for me, Thorpe's was on the left and it became my salvation. While the rest of the crocodile of girls dispersed to anywhere sweets or make-up might be purchased, I raced to the bookshop where I discovered dog-eared copies of Thomas Hardy, E. M. Forster, Charles Dickens, Jane Austen ... and I devoured them.

No one else shared my passion until my friend Lorna Hutson arrived in the sixth form. Lorna is now a brilliant professor of English and no one is surprised, for even then she had the most astonishing mind. She shared my tragic love of Alexander Pope. We would sit in prep passing each other dreadful poems about our miserable lives written in Popish style and weep with silent laughter. How pleased she will be when I write and tell her that I was on a bus looking out at the very corner where our beloved poet may well have written his *Essay on Man*. I think of a small play I might write for her.

A Short Play about Alexander Pope at Friern Manor Farm

By Me

It is somewhere around 1729. A farmer and his wife are having breakfast after the morning milking at Friern Manor Farm. They can hear the poet Alexander Pope upstairs in a small bedroom, scratching away with his pen on paper.

Farmer: What's he doing up there, the little fellow?

Farmer's Wife: Not sure. Writing, I think.

Farmer: What's he want to do that at our farm for?

Farmer's Wife: He likes the country. He's no bother.

Farmer: Lucky to be here, I say. It's only a couple of years since we didn't let Catholics come this close to London. *(Pause to pour milk)* Funny-looking fella.

Farmer's Wife: That's not his fault. He can't help being, well ... small.

Farmer: Small? He's no more than four and a half feet, and that funny hump on his back. If he was one of our cows, I'd put him down. I don't like how he wheezes, and his eyes don't look right. Always running and red. *(Pause to drink milk)* What's it called then?

Farmer's Wife: What's what called?

Farmer: The thing he's writing.

Farmer's Wife: 'Essay on Man', I think he said.

Farmer: *(Long pause)* What do you suppose that's about then?

As an adult, my view of Pope has dimmed a bit. The *Essay on Man* proposed that we humans must accept our place in the 'great chain of being' between the angels and the beasts, which sounds like a good way to keep people in their place. It was a piece of work that Pope intended to develop into something larger and hopefully more cheerful, but he didn't live to complete it.

I think about my father who died so young. I was thirty when we lost him. He had so much left to do and I miss him every day. He was splendid. When I finally got my first-class degree from Cambridge all Papa wanted to do was ring Mrs Rochester, who had been so sure that my only hope lay with an agricultural education.

We go past a rather squat block of flats called Halliwell Court. Halliwell? Geri? I doubt it, as it appears to have been built in the 1950s. I have to admit I am no Geri Halliwell expert. I met her once and had no idea who she was. I'm not a great party-goer but once went to Ian McKellen's birthday party because he had been so kind to me when I came out. The party did not go well for me. I realise I ought to pay more attention to people in the public eye. When I turned up at Ian's do someone asked me if I would mind having my photograph taken for *Hello!* magazine, and would I mind if it was with another guest? They turned to introduce me to someone, but I didn't catch the name. He was a nice, slightly older man with sandy hair, a crumpled linen suit and wire spectacles. I thought he looked like Alan Bennett and decided Alan Bennett was the sort of man Ian would know. I don't think the gentleman knew who I was either, but nevertheless we stood arm in arm toasting each other with glasses of champagne as if we were old showbiz friends.

Then I found myself seated next to some woman at dinner, and after forty-five minutes was about to ask her what she did for a living when she was whisked away. Turned out she was Geri Halliwell. I spent the rest of the evening with Monica Lewinsky. I did know who she was. I really liked her, and we bonded over the fact that we both felt out of place at this gathering. How awful that she should be defined in some way by what had happened when she was so young. If the #MeToo movement had been around when she was in the public eye, I wonder if that would have made a difference. Long after the scandal Monica was asked if she had ever thought of changing her name. She replied, 'No one ever asked him, did he think he should change his name?' It is still the case that too many women end up as footnotes in the history of men. The woman at the heart of nearly bringing down a president was at the party mostly ignored.

A week after his birthday party Ian phoned and said what a nice photo there was in *Hello!* of me drinking champagne with David Hockney.

Underhill Road

I've been to register at the local doctor's. It's the second one we've tried. The first, which was around the corner from the new house, had a receptionist who is never going to win any awards.

'What do you want?' she said to Debbie.

'I want to register, please,' declared my unfailingly polite partner. 'We've just moved here.'

The woman showed no sign of helping the conversation forward.

Debbie tried again. 'You have a big sign outside saying "New Patients being accepted".'

The woman looked over her shoulder and then leant forward, whispering, 'I wouldn't come here.'

'Why?' Debbie whispered back.

'You'll never get to see a doctor.'

She seemed honest, for each morning that I pass the surgery en route to my bus I see a long snake of waiting patients standing less than patiently outside the front door sharing their ailments with the environment. We registered further away.

A charming man did my health check.

'I need to check your blood pressure,' he said, placing a fabric cuff around my upper arm and attaching it to a machine.

The machine whirred, and the cuff tightened. The fellow looked at the screen for the reading.

'Nothing,' he said.

'Nothing?' I repeated. He continued looking at the machine and not speaking. 'Does that mean I am dead?' I asked.

'I don't think so,' he replied with no certainty and not a hint of humour, 'I think it's the batteries.'

When I was growing up in Mamaroneck, our local medical man was an elderly fellow called Dr Hunter. Perhaps he wasn't that old but when you're a child, adults can seem ancient. He wore a white coat and chain-smoked, which these days isn't quite the doctorly thing to do. There was not a single moment when he checked my lungs or looked into my ears that he didn't have a cigarette hanging from his lips. I was fascinated by the fact the thing seemed to be glued there, and as he carried out his examination he seemed to forget that he was smoking at all. Astonishingly long chains of ash hung suspended from the tip of his Marlboro. I could hardly speak, so gripped was I waiting for the moment this snake of ash dangling in the air would finally collapse onto the floor. Many a prescription we collected was filthy with the stuff. This was the doctor who pierced my ears when I was twelve. It was unbelievably painful, and I don't think ear-piercing was his expertise as the hole in one ear is much higher than the other. I can really only successfully wear earrings if I slightly tilt my head to one side.

Underhill Road. Named after another sixteenth-century bishop, I suspect. John Underhill. He was chaplain to Elizabeth I and a praelector of moral philosophy, a job which never came up in career discussions at school. Come to think of it, I don't think we had career discussions at school. We were all intended to marry or, in the case of utter rejection, teach.

Round here, the bishops lie cheek by jowl with actors: the next street across is Henslowe Road, most likely named for Philip Henslowe, an Elizabethan theatrical entrepreneur and impresario. Philip had the good fortune to come to London and marry a rich widow called Agnes, a path to be recommended to any child who wants to get on. He made money in pawnbroking and moneylending, which is never nice, but also traded in goat skins – which is at least unusual. He was clearly also a gambler as he owned theatres, starting with the Rose, the first permanent playhouse on Bankside, and then the Fortune Theatre and the Hope. He must have done well for he concluded his life as a Gentleman Sewer of the Chamber for James I. It doesn't sound like fun, but had to be better than the old job of Groom of the Stool, which was literally a royal bottom-wiping job.

A tired-looking man in an ill-fitting suit is bellowing on the phone. He is clearly trying to give his password to someone and thus sharing it with the rest of us. I rather enjoy these little windows into other people's lives. His suit is grey and has shiny patches on the knees where he has rested his briefcase. The bus seems to be his office. He has the look of a travelling salesman, but I don't know if men still ply such a trade. Do men still 'travel in ladies' underwear'?

'Coriolanus!' he shouts.

There is a long pause.

'It's a play by Shakespeare. Shakespeare! Sha— . . . You don't need to spell Shakespeare, just Coriolanus.' The poor fellow looks beaten down and I wonder why he has chosen a play about a brilliant but arrogant Roman general as his password into the world. Perhaps he intends to conquer it in some manner. I like his attitude.

My introduction to Shakespeare was doing *A Midsummer Night's Dream* at school. I played Puck. It was in my first year at the dreaded boarding school and I guess I thought it would be a good character to hide behind. The piece was advertised as 'A Fantasy Based on *A Midsummer Night's Dream*', which sounds inventive but basically it was the play without Act One. I suspect the intention was just to make it shorter. As Act One is the bit where Shakespeare explains the plot, I think many in our audience were confused.

Matron hated it. Mind you, Matron hated everything about me and anything I was involved with. She was a woman who oozed disappointment with her life. She was enormously over-weight and had some problem with her eyes which meant they watered constantly. She sat in the hall each night outside the common room endlessly weeping at her lot.

I don't know why she had taken the job, unless the single room she lived in had been the clincher. She was not particu-larly suited to looking after a house full of schoolgirls as she seemed to loathe young people. Any girl caught breaking a rule was subject to her rather inventive punishments. I was always in trouble, and of an evening her favourite response was to take me to the small scullery by the back door. Here she would sit on a wooden chair reading the paper while I had to kneel upright before her on my bare knees, my cotton nightie just brushing the cold of the red tile floor as a draught swept in from outside. My back ached and my knees became sore but I would kneel staring straight at her, refusing to be broken. I remain enraged by meanness. I was not singled out for this kind of abuse. One girl was particularly frightened of the dark. Her punishment was to be shut in the common room and sit on the built-in bench by the bay window which we girls called 'The Coffin'. There she would be left alone crying with the lights off. Some people call it sadism; others might bemoan that it's the kind of upbringing you just don't see any more.

I know I enraged Matron, not just because of my American ways, but because sometimes, just to annoy her, my reaction to her bizarre punishments was to respond with intense good cheer. One evening she got me out of bed to clean the shoes of everyone in the house. I suppose there must have been about forty pairs. I like a task with a visible outcome and I've never slept well, so I set about buffing and polishing with whistling vigour and cheerfulness. I made jokes about shoe sizes and the late hour. She sent me to bed before I was even halfway through. You don't need to be a therapist to work out that this was probably the beginning of me using humour to protect myself from the world.

A big part of Matron's irritation with me was that I had nowhere to go for exeat weekends, the one weekend a term where you were allowed to go home. Once a term all the boarders were dispatched to their parents or guardians for a weekend break. Even though my English grandparents lived not far away, they remained very distant from me, so I didn't have anyone to go to and neither did two sisters from Nigeria, Funke and Funcho. Both had had a horrible time with racism in their previous school and it had made them understandably reserved. They were friendly but not my friends. The three of us were an unlikely trio and Matron, who might have had a weekend off herself if it weren't for us, was exasperated with it all. Instead of making something nice out of the time, she doubled down on her fury. What a miserable quartet we made. The weekend dragged on and by the Sunday evening when everyone returned in high spirits I thought my soul would never stop weeping.

Despite all this I wanted Matron to come to my play. It makes no sense, but I guess she was all I had. With my family in New York and my UK relatives not the least bit interested, I wanted someone to come. I guess when you are a kid anyone on your side feels nice. Following my triumphant Puck, the following year I played Malvolio in *Twelfth Night* and I asked Matron to attend again. She shook her head and declared, 'Didn't you do Shakespeare last year? That's surely enough.'

After two years at the school I was allowed to move to another boarding house. I was much happier there but then the matron in charge had a nervous breakdown. She began accusing all of us of stealing her things. I in particular was guilty, apparently, of 'running off with her umbrella'. She was eventually carted away; the boarding house was closed down and I went back to my first place and the old matron. By now I had done my O levels and it was clear there was some slight possibility I might actually go to university. This was unheard of at the school, and quite thrilling for them. In order to keep me studying I was allowed my own room. I say room; an old cupboard was converted so that it just fitted a single bed and a bedside table. The door slid into the wall but nevertheless I had to stand on the bed to close it. It was tiny, but it was mine and I loved it because Matron simply couldn't squeeze into the room.

My friend Lorna and I both ended up going to university. She to Oxford and me to Cambridge. It was such an astonishing academic triumph that the school had a half-day holiday in our honour.

When I was in my thirties, I heard that Matron had died, and all those years later all I felt was relief. I still have the report she wrote on my leaving. Traditionally the last report from a boarding house was supposed to be complimentary and kind. Mine read: 'Sandra's behaviour has been satisfactory, but she has a tendency to over-dramatize.'

Upland Road

One morning the bus is very crowded, and the only empty seat has a woman's shopping on it. I know it's not bus etiquette, but I ask her if I might sit down. This makes her annoyed. As she moves her bags she looks me straight in the face and says accusingly, 'You're Sandi Toksvig.'

'Yes, I am,' I agree, managing not to add that I have a library card to prove it.

'What are you doing on the bus?'

I smile. Perhaps this is my first new travel companion. Perhaps if I catch the same bus at the same time again, we shall be friends.

'I'm going to Oxford Circus,' I say brightly.

'Why?' she demands.

'It's where I work. At the BBC.'

Now she is getting irritated with me. 'No, why are you on the bus?'

I can't think of a new answer. 'To get to Oxford Circus . . .' I try. 'Where I work . . .'

We are not really getting anywhere. She looks around as if I might be secretly filming the whole thing. Then she harrumphs and picks up a discarded newspaper to bury herself behind. I wonder what is wrong with me being on the bus. She clearly does not think I should be here. Perhaps she is disappointed in me.

Partly to please her I get off the bus at Upland Road and stop at a café. It's called Boulangerie Jade. There is a steady stream of solitary customers, all of whom are communing with their phones. It is hard to get the young waitress's attention. This is not new. I am of an age now where people often look right through me.

The place looks very French. The tables are made of thick slabs of wood and are accompanied by gold chairs with red velvet seats which appear to be resting after an amateur production of *Cabaret*. Eight small sconces light the walls, which are a mix of shabby chic falling plaster and wallpaper covered in women in 1950s dresses with waists so narrow that the mere mention of a croissant would be the death of them. A small blackboard suggests that I can chat with the café 24/7 and gives a Twitter address. I try to think why I might decide to get up one night to do that. Who would answer at two o'clock in the morning when no one speaks to me when I'm actually there? I wonder when speaking in cafés stopped being a thing. Still, the coffee is excellent and for a while I can pretend I am in Paris.

When I was eighteen, I went to Paris with two friends from school, Julia and Elizabeth. We were Interrailing for four weeks, beginning in the French capital. Released from the genuine horror of boarding school you might think I would go giddy at the freedom. I suppose I did, but in my odd-soul way.

'We'll go shopping,' agreed Julia and Elizabeth. We were eighteen, we were girls, we were in Paris; it seemed a reasonable idea.

'I want to go and see Victor Hugo's house. In the Place des Vosges,' I said. 'Come to that.'

Julia shook her head and smiled at me. For a brief while we had shared a room at school, and she was used to my idiosyncrasies.

What a glorious afternoon I had. I loved Victor Hugo's house. I wanted to live there. It seemed perfect to me. What a place to sit and write, to invite friends over and talk about books. I stood by the table where Hugo had played cards with George Sand. I had never heard of her before but instantly I loved her too.

George Sand was the pseudonym of Amantine-Lucile-Aurore Dupin. I knew nothing about her writing then, but I loved her daring. In mid-nineteenth-century Paris she wore men's clothes and found she could go to places no woman had previously entered. The clothing itself gave her licence. She smoked in public, which was almost as scandalous as the many affairs she had. I learned about her intense friendship with the actress Marie Dorval and wondered just how intense it had been. I had no thought of lesbianism then because, incredible as it seems, I had never even read or heard the word. I only knew my own feelings for girls my own age and indeed had had my first affair with a girl at school, but I knew nothing beyond myself. I thought that Sand writing to Dorval declaring things like 'wanting you either in your dressing room or in your bed' was the most exciting thing I had ever read.

There were no women like me smiling down from my family's past. I came from an apparently heterosexual family, I appeared to have nothing but heterosexual friends and I knew absolutely nothing about any gay women from history who might stand up as role models for me. I felt utterly alone. As I watched TV or went to the movies, read any book or looked at any ad for almost anything I failed to see myself depicted. In fact, I had the terrible sensation of realising that I had landed on the earth from somewhere else utterly unknowable, with no one in my life who I could tell.

Aged eighteen I knew I wanted to find a female partner, but I had no idea how one might do such a thing. There was no gay liberation movement that I knew of. Certainly no one ever mentioned it. I had never come across a single lesbian in history or in my life. For all I knew I was the only one, bar the girl at school, and she wrote to me as soon as she left to say she was getting married to a man, a soldier. With no one on my side I grabbed hold of anything which might suggest that what I felt was a desire others too had recognised.

Place des Vosges is one of the most beautiful squares in the world, and after the excitement of the Hugo house I was thrilled to find, beneath the seventeenth-century arches along the side of the square, a small café to have my lunch. I had very little money so I ordered the *prix fixe* menu. I didn't care what I ate. I just wanted to be there. To pretend George and Marie might pop in at any moment.

At the table next to mine sat an old woman in black. Those were the days when French widows still took to sombre garb. She ate alone, but as I ordered she looked up.

'*N'êtes-vous pas boire du vin?*' she asked.

My school French was poor, but I explained that I could not afford wine. She beckoned to the waiter and ordered a *pichet* of red wine, which was brought to my table. How grown up I felt, sipping wine and trying to chat in French in the shadow of a great writer's house. The old lady had absolutely no English and we laughed at my vocabulary as I supplemented my speech with drawings on the white paper tablecloth. I was sorry when she left. I signalled to the waiter for my bill, only to find she had already paid for my meal. I raced out into the street to see if I could find her, but she was gone. I can recall every detail of that meal. I can play the scene over in my head and it still makes me smile. In all the years which have passed I have never forgotten her kindness, and to this day I keep an eye out to see if there is some young person who could do with having their bill quietly settled.

Later that trip I went by myself to Giverny, where Monet had painted. There is a museum there and in it I discovered the work of Mary Cassatt. I had been taught about Monet, Degas, Pissarro and others at school, but no one had ever mentioned that any of the impressionists had been women. Throughout the 1870s she was friends with Degas, who admired her work, but she had a tough time from the establishment, from society, even from her own American father who had declared he would rather see his daughter dead than living abroad as a 'bohemian'. A great painter I had never heard of and a female writer who needed a man's name in order to achieve success. I remember my rage, but I also recall the inspiration I found in Cassatt's courage. The fledgling feminist in me stirred on this trip to Paris.

It makes me realise that so far I have not come across a single woman commemorated in the streets I pass on the bus.

Peckham Rye / Barry Road

To 'go to Peckham' used to be a slang expression for going to dinner. People were peckish, so they went to Peckham. For cockneys, Peckham Rye was rhyming slang for a neck tie. I'm not sure what you'd say if you were going to dinner and had to wear a tie. The place is mentioned in documents as early as the fourteenth century and it was here that drovers from Kent would stop as they encouraged their livestock on the long walk to be sold at London's Smithfield Market.

Peckham Rye Park is a tribute to the Victorians. Back then London County Council bought the land because the common was getting too crowded for the commoners and the local people protested when the lord of the manor, Sir William Bowyer Smyth, tried to build houses on it. Would that anyone in charge had such foresight today.

It was here when he was eight or nine that William Blake was wandering home when he claimed to have seen a vision of 'a tree filled with angels, bright angelic wings bespangling every bough like stars'. I should love to see them. How marvellous to be touched by something other-worldly; I have longed for such a thing since I was at my first school.

I started school when I was four. We were living in Copenhagen and my mother took me on the back of her bicycle. There was no child seat, just the luggage rack. My feet swung down beside the wheel and every now and then I would dare to touch the spokes with my toes. Denmark is well geared for the bike ride my mother and I took each morning. There have been cycle lanes through the centre of every Danish town for as long as I can remember. In London everyone cycles as if it were a race but in Copenhagen there is no need for office workers to wear ill-fitting Lycra and charge through town. People wear ordinary clothes and pedal sedately.

It was the tradition in Denmark (and indeed for certain occasions still is) that children wore sailor's uniforms. For school I had a navy pleated skirt, with a white top in the summer and navy one in the winter. On my shoulders sat a detachable navy and white sailor's collar which hung square at the back and had a small silk bow at the front. My mother cycled in all weathers looking as though she carried a tiny admiral to sea.

My brother, Nick, who is two years older, went to the local Danish school but for some reason my mother decided that I should go to the French convent school, l'Institut de l'Assomption, run by the Sisters of the Assumption. I don't know why. We weren't religious. Indeed, my father was so appalled by religion that he applied legally to be excluded from the Danish state church.

We lived in a suburb named Hellerup and the school was around the corner from our house, in a large old country house painted yellow. The place had once been Rygaard, a manor farm, and it had vast grounds. The sisters of the school wore traditional nun's habits – long black dresses with white wimples which entirely covered their hair and left only a round opening for their faces. They had long wooden rosaries at their waists and the beads rustled against their heavy gowns as they walked. It was all very *Sound of Music*, with us in our miniature sailor uniforms.

There was one teacher who was not yet a nun. Miss MacDonald was a novitiate and so did not wear the full habit. She was young and beautiful with long blonde hair. She was funny, a talented artist and kind to me. Aged four, I fell instantly in love with her. The Catholic element of our education was strictly enforced, and we spent many hours in the church which adjoined the school. I remember Miss MacDonald once lying face-down on the floor in front of the altar, her arms stretched out like Jesus on the cross.

'What's she doing?' I whispered.

'Ssh,' said Mother Bernadette, who taught French. 'She has visions.'

I didn't know what that meant but it clearly impressed the other nuns. I wanted to be like Miss MacDonald, so I took to spending my break times lying face-down before the altar in the deserted church willing God to speak to me. He never did. Or before he had time to have a word someone told my mother about it and I was made to stop. Miss MacDonald didn't become a Sister of the Assumption in the end. I'd like to think she escaped that cloistered world and ran away to paint but instead she joined a silent order of Carmelites. When I said goodbye to her, I understood that she would never be allowed to speak to me again. It broke my heart.

Mère Marie-Colette, who was in overall charge, was a tough woman with little time for cossetting children. My mother has many great qualities but time-keeping is not one of them. We were often late, and one morning much later than usual. Mère Marie was furious.

'What time do you call this?' she demanded, looking down at me.

I didn't know. I was yet to own a watch.

'This happens too often,' she declared. She took me by the arm and marched me to the wide stone staircase which swept up to the nuns' quarters from the classroom corridor. It was winter, and dark in the mornings. There was no light on the staircase. She made me sit on the stone steps, halfway up, and then left me.

'Have a think about being late,' she ordered.

I sat in the dark hugging my bare knees and I thought about being late. I must have been about five and what I thought was that my arrival at school was entirely out of my control, and that really my mother ought to be sitting on the stairs and not me. I was filled with fury, a fury about any injustice which has never really left me.

When I was six I got my own back on Mère Marie. By then my mother had got a job at the school, teaching older girls about current affairs. My mother knew a lot about the news. It was, after all, my father's day-to-day business, but she was not a trained teacher. A lack of qualifications, however, was not the sort of thing that kept the nuns awake at night. One afternoon it had been raining hard and the playground was wet. The order went out that only the boys would be allowed out at break. I don't know what made me do it, but I called a strike of all the girls in the class. We made posters and wrote on the blackboard that we would do no more lessons without equal access to play-time. We were an entire troop of six-year-old girls on a mission.

Faced with our obvious passion for equality, Mère Marie burst into tears. She ran to my mother in the staff room to wail about the anarchy, but out to the wet playground eventually we went. It was an early lesson in gender protest. I was never put on the stairs in the dark again.

I don't know what William Blake was doing on Peckham Rye, for he grew up in what is now Broadwick Street in central London. Blake, the English painter, poet and printmaker, was clearly a man stuck in the P section of potential careers. Now he is considered a great artist, but in his lifetime he was largely ignored or thought to be mad. I suspect it was because he was a gloriously original thinker, and no one ever really likes that.

Having an original thought is to me the holy grail of achieve-
ment. From what we understand of the way the brain works, the
left side operates in a linear, logical way. It is the side which is
keen on order, chronology and lists. For many it is characterised
as the male area of thought. The right, however, is where the
brain dances with creativity, imagination and feelings. It is characterised as the female part. I think something has happened in
modern life where we give less and less room to imagination.
Rarely do we let the pressurised system of education release a
modern William Blake.

I should have liked to have walked with him on the Rye.
Here was an eighteenth-century man who railed against marriage without love, against senseless wars and against the abuse
of class power. Here was a man who defended women's right to
complete self-fulfilment. I think he was splendid, but I do accept
that it is also possible, of course, that he was in fact just a bit
mad. Debbie is a psychotherapist, and having lived with me for
quite some time has decided that there is a fine line between
creativity and flights of fancy which in the old days were diag-
nosed as mental instability.

Most people on the bus seem to have no interest in looking
out of the window for inspiration. They are engrossed in their
phones. People constantly checking their messages seems to
me rather like endlessly opening the front door just in case an
unexpected visitor has turned up. There is a young man stolidly
eating his way through an entire bag of sausage rolls. This is
obviously not his first encounter with such a bag for his entire
body has assumed something of the shape and colour of the roll
he is eating.

At the turn of the twentieth century there was a boy called
John Trundley who was exhibited in music halls as the Fat Boy

of Peckham. At just seven months old he weighed two stone and by age four he was up to twelve. People paid to see him, and his corpulence kept his impoverished parents out of the workhouse. There were laws about children performing on stage, but John was 'exhibited' and not acting so it was allowed. He grew up to be a watchmaker in Peckham.

I watch the large lad on the other side of the bus. Great flakes of pastry litter his chest. What is he thinking about? Does he long to be a watchmaker? A music-hall star? Or is he merely sad that the last sausage roll is in sight?

Near the Victorian gardens in the centre of the park stands a large red shed. It's now a nursery school, but it was here during the Second World War that, for reasons I can't fathom, a group of Italian prisoners of war were kept. Back then the shed was surrounded by barbed wire, not, local knowledge will tell you, to keep the POWs in, but to keep the Dulwich maidens away from the handsome Italians. In 1945 this was a place of seething sexual excitement.

Sex, who is having it, what kind they are having, is a British fascination and it has rubbed off on me sufficiently to be curious as to how people develop niche sexual practices. I once knew a fellow who had invited a woman over to his place on the clear and mutually agreeable understanding that they were going to have sex for the first time. He hadn't known her long and was startled when she arrived for their encounter with a pound of courgettes in a brown paper bag with ... how can I put this nicely? ... no desire to have the veg for supper. My first thought was that it was a rather emasculating gift and my second was to wonder how she had discovered this particular penchant. Had she once fallen accidentally into the vegetable basket and received a thrill?

No one on the bus knows I am thinking about sex. But maybe everyone on the top deck is thinking about it. Sex is not, I hasten to add, my specialist subject, but I know that some people think of it when they look at me. I'm more than happy to fight for gay rights but I dislike being characterised as 'lesbian' in instances when my sexual orientation has nothing to do with what's happening in my life. I am 'out and proud', I just don't want it to define everything about me.

Being described as 'lesbian broadcaster' when I am on air making jokes about the European Union seems a bit silly. I'm hardly going to base my comments on my sexuality. I once had a reviewer decide that a character in my play about post-traumatic stress was gay simply because I am. If we could only write about the experience of our own genitals what a tiresome world it would be.

I'm always surprised where sex turns up. In 2015, I went to see the Magna Carta, that written symbol of liberty, and ended up talking about anal sex. It was the eight-hundredth anniversary of the piece of parchment which has helped shape the world. There are four copies, and to mark the occasion the British Library decided to bring all of them together in one exhibition. Perhaps because the pieces are so delicate or perhaps because someone thought it a good publicity wheeze, only 1215 members of the public were going to be allowed to see it. There was a ballot to determine who they might be, and I applied but failed to secure a place. I was disappointed until I got an invitation in the post to see them anyway, at some press launch. Being in the public eye may have some downsides but there's good stuff too.

I went along thinking I wouldn't know anyone and bumped into all manner of lovely folk. Among them was an Australian woman who runs a charity doing commendable work for civil liberties. There was a long queue into the darkened room where the manuscripts lay so we got chatting. I have no idea how the subject came up, but we began a lively discussion about the intense pressure young women of today are under to deliver sexual practices that young men have read about on the internet.

At the very moment that we finally reached the four precious Magna Cartas the Australian woman said, 'Take my babysitter: she's seventeen and only the other day she was casually telling me about her boyfriend demanding anal sex.'

Shocked by this revelation I turned my head.

'Seriously?'

At which point a steward moved us along and I missed my moment to savour the great history presented.

What would the nuns have said?

When we moved to America in 1966 my parents decided to lend their Fiat 500 to the nuns at my convent school. Mum and Dad had owned the car for a long time, and it had done many miles. Mother Bernadette wrote us a furious note about it not long after we had arrived in New York. It seems the top nun had come for a visit from her Belgian home and three of the sisters collected her from the train station in the ageing Fiat. The entire school gathered at the top of the large circular gravel drive overlooking the lawn to welcome the Mother Superior; all the children in their sailor's outfits and the nuns resplendent in black and white. The Fiat arrived. Danish and Belgian flags were waved. At the foot of the grand stone steps up to the school, the bottom of the car gave way and all four nuns collapsed to the ground, disappearing from view. Papa laughed every time he thought about it.

The Gardens

I get off and wander just two minutes away from the main road to find a lovely quiet square, with a garden surrounded by railings to keep out those who don't belong. On a cold wintry afternoon, it does not look like a place of fun and there are signs forbidding radios and dogs and anyone without entitlement to enter. It is the sort of place that no Dane would understand. In Denmark, there is an entirely accepted but unwritten concept that everyone owns all the land communally. Britain is a place of divisions and this garden says something about social class.

What money buys you is space. You get bigger houses, bigger cars, your garden is large enough to keep you further from your neighbour and you get space to yourself in your larger seat on the plane or the train; you can be alone in a big taxi. You can pay to demand quiet and solitude. Without money you have no choice but to be thrust into the midst of everyone else's concerns. There are no quiet sections on a bus. No ring-fenced areas of peace. We are all in it together.

I find I am beginning to feel the class divide between those on the bus and the people in their cars below. An old woman gets on board very slowly and then takes even more time to make her way up the stairs to the upper deck. I get up to help her with one of her shopping bags as she reaches the top step. She smiles and wheezes. The driver waits patiently until she is seated. Buses are neglected because it is mostly women who use them and on the whole women don't make things as butch as transport policy.

It's why you can catch a bus easily into central London but not to the next village. As a generalisation, men think about commuting with purpose; women don't travel in such straight lines.

In Britain it is also the poorer person who takes the double-decker, who stands in the cold waiting for the bus. It is the poorer person who must share a seat for two with someone they don't know or perhaps care for. Margaret Thatcher, that great egalitarian, is supposed to have said, 'If a man finds himself a passenger on a bus having attained the age of twenty-six, he can count himself a failure in life.' I don't think buses deserve this. I like this communal moving forward, not confined to tracks like trains but out on the open road.

The Danes gave up the concept of class a long time ago. They got rid of titles and slimmed down the royal family and the pomp and ceremony. A Danish friend said to me recently, 'I was driving past Buckingham Palace the other day and they were changing the guard. I watched all the soldiers in the red tunics and busby hats, and I thought ... how silly!'

It made me laugh. I had thought she was going to say what a marvellous sight it was but it's typical of the Danes to find grown-ups enthralled by the fairy-tale costumes of nobility to be a bit silly. I like the royals as individuals, but it is hard to tell a child born into poverty in this country that they can be whoever they want when in fact rising to the very top can still only occur if you were born in the right bed. It is difficult to even mention these things without being vilified. I was once asked, in relation to International Women's Day, what I thought about Kate Middleton as a role model. I gave a long and fulsome answer.

'I've never met her,' I said, 'and I'm sure she's charming, but if we are choosing a role model for young women then I would probably prefer to select someone who has achieved their position through merit rather than marriage. Gaining a position by marrying well seems very Jane Austen. I expect she is delightful, but it's hard to say as, sadly, I don't know a single view she holds about anything.'

I should have known better, for this was reported as my having said, 'I don't know a single view Kate Middleton holds. It's very Jane Austen.'

This was irritating on lots of levels, the main one being that Jane Austen's work is full of women with opinions, so I came across as ill-read. That same week the brilliant author Hilary Mantel had got into trouble for daring to make some remarks herself about Ms Middleton and the tabloids went mad. With so many journalists not being friends of facts, I was headlined as having 'jumped' on the Mantel 'bandwagon' and attacked the Duchess.

Class stills matters in Britain. There is no question that it can hold people back, and it doesn't seem very grown up not to be able to discuss these things without being pilloried. Many of the royals do fine charitable work but their connection with the daily life of the population is not the same as the rest of us. I once sat next to the Duke of Kent during a formal lunch. Stuck for conversation, I ventured to say, 'I think Kent is my favourite county.'

'Yes,' he said, continuing to eat. 'I've never really been.'

It is a measure of the man that I have absolutely no idea if he was joking.

One shouldn't, however, underestimate the strange effect the family can have on the general public, and indeed myself. The first time I met a member of the royal family was when I was at university in Cambridge. Founded in 1869, Girton College was the first residential college for women in England and an important part of early feminist agitation for equal access to education. It was still an all-female establishment when I arrived, and the Queen Mother was the patron. One day she came for lunch and we were served a fine meal on exquisite china with a college crest which none of us had ever seen before.

'What a lovely lunch,' declared Her Majesty in her speech, 'and how lovely for you all to eat off such fine china every day.'

After lunch a few of us had been selected to shake the royal hand. Her Majesty had wanted to meet a range of students including 'any from abroad'. We didn't really have any of those, so I was selected to make do. Those of us who had been given the nod for a royal hello were lined up outside in the drive. We had on our black college gowns and best smiles. There was a lot of anxiety from the overwhelmed staff.

'If it begins to rain,' we were told, 'you will be informed by the Vice-Mistress.'

As we were all at one of the top universities in the world, I would have thought we could work out if it was raining by ourselves, but it was not that sort of day. I have never seen such a display of nerves, smelt such an overpowering smell of fresh paint. We stood for a very long time and I got bored. I began doing what I thought was a rather fine impersonation of the Mistress of the college being nervous when I realised to my horror that the royal party were right behind me.

'This is Sandra,' said the Mistress, 'she's from Denmark.'

I suddenly became entirely flustered with awkwardness. I put out my hand, opened my mouth and said something along the lines of 'Bjigrigledoda.'

The Queen Mother smiled and declared, 'What beautiful English you speak,' and moved on.

The class system continues to bring privilege to the few and stops equality becoming a reality. When many of the hereditary peers were removed from voting in the House of Lords, I thought it was marvellous. No one ought to determine the legislation of this country because their ancestor once did well. At the time I was working with Lord Lichfield, the photographer. He was one of those who had once had a vote in the upper chamber and now did not.

'Are you upset about losing your seat?' I asked.

'Of course I am,' he replied. 'Best parking in London.'

Peckham Rye / East Dulwich Road

The demographic changes as we leave East Dulwich, which is full of smart cafés heaving with women and baby buggies so robust you could take them on the motorway if you fancied. As the bus moves further down the route it becomes more crowded and varied. I am glad. We need difference.

Six people are all leaking different music from their headphones. I wonder if buses could be sub-divided into musical categories so that everyone who likes rap gets on the same one. A young man next to me takes out his phone. I can see his screensaver is a picture of himself entirely naked in a boxing pose. Of the many pictures I have used on my own phone, this is one which has never occurred to me. I like his boldness. He dials, then FaceTimes someone called Bonita about needing to go to Farringdon to get a ticket for his fight for his manager, who I would have thought should get his own ticket. He has a hamstring injury and had porridge for breakfast. I learn a lot about him as I sit there. I quite like this fast-track way of knowing someone, although the sight of his not-insubstantial penis may take a while to shake off.

The number of people who put the phone on speaker to chat is astonishing. The writer in me is thrilled at the detail people are happy to give away but I wonder if they realise I am taking note. Now the young man rings a young woman and I learn more about his sex life than I expected. He likes to use gym equipment in novel ways, which I suppose is one way to make the most of your membership ... or just your member.

When I was a child our local inn in the village of Filskov in Jutland, where we had a summer home, had a phone and the number was 5. That was all. You picked up the receiver, turned a handle on the phone to make a bell ring and a woman would answer. You'd ask for 'Filskov Number Five' and she would put you through. The whole village only had eleven phones. What would Alexander Graham Bell, who first patented the phone, have made of where we are now? As well as giving the world telecommunications, Bell also spent considerable time trying to breed sheep with multiple nipples. It's good to have a varied career.

Out on the Rye I can see a woman walking the world's smallest dog. So small it hardly looks worth walking. It would do well with a hamster wheel. Maybe it has a trace memory of George Wombwell's Travelling Menagerie, which in 1864 brought thirty-two vans of wild beasts including elephants, giraffes, leopards, lions, tigers and zebras to this part of town. Must have been fun. I expect there are health and safety rules about tigers these days.

It's amazing how much gossip about people survives through history. Everything I have read about George Wombwell wishes to let me know that he was short and alcoholic. There's a plaque to him in Old Compton Street in Soho where he once had a shoe shop and he's buried in Highgate, but his height and inclination to drink get the most press.

George got his tiger from Jamrach's Animal Emporium, the largest exotic pet shop in the world, which once lay north of here, on the other side of the Thames. I wrote about it in my novel *Valentine Grey* when I related the celebrated story from 1857 when a Bengal tiger got loose from the shop. A passing boy of eight or nine, who had never seen such a thing, tried to pet the creature, at which it picked him up and carried him off. Charles Jamrach, the owner, ran after the pair and prised the beast's mouth open with his bare hands. The boy was unharmed and got three hundred pounds – which is about thirty grand today, so it was probably worth the upset. The tiger was sold to George Wombwell. The rescue of the boy is commemorated by a seven-foot-high bronze statue at the north entrance to Tobacco Dock in the East End.

The bus is steaming up. I squint my eyes and look out to see if I might catch a glimpse of some spectre from the past on the Rye. There are those who think this was the site for one of Boudicca's battles. In fact, her last battle and burial place. Does she lie beneath the grass where a man is throwing a Frisbee to his friend? Did great cries of battle issue from the queen of the Iceni tribe as she led the uprising against the occupying forces of the Roman Empire? Was she poisoned? Did she die in agony? The word still whispered is about her rage at the rape of her daughters. We don't really know, but who could blame her? All we have is what the Romans recorded: she was tall and intelligent. How often height seems significant. I am short. So short that when I worked with the great jazz legend and host of *I'm Sorry I Haven't a Clue*, Humphrey Lyttelton, we never tired of showing the audience that he and I were the same height if he knelt beside me. Is my height all that will be noted when I am gone?

Mind you, it's not always noted when I'm here. I once shared the stage with Stephen Fry at the Hay Festival. We were discussing gender equality and I was commenting on low-level misogyny being everywhere. Stephen made some flippant remark about it, so I got up from my chair and moved as if to speak at the lectern. It was very high, and I couldn't be seen. I suggested maybe we might get equality when lectern-makers started thinking it's not just tall men who have things to say. The next day

Peter Florence, who runs the festival and is passionate about full inclusion, presented me with a lectern which had been made overnight and was exactly the right size. If only that's all it took.

I wonder if I could restyle myself as the Little Woman of Peckham? At the beginning of the nineteenth century there was a woman called Lucy Wanmer, who was known as the Little Woman of Peckham. She ran a school near by. She was 2 feet 6 inches tall. I think she too was 'exhibited' for a while. One of her students is said to have described her height by saying, 'When she walks, she kneels.' Being shorter than her pupils apparently didn't stop her being a disciplinarian. She died in 1821. The only image of Lucy lies in the Royal Collection and is not, as far as I can make out, on display to the public. I hope someone takes it out of a drawer occasionally. I wrote to the Royal Collection to ask if I may see her picture and they sent back not only copies of her portrait but an invitation to view them in the print room at Windsor Castle. Lucy seems to have had arms and head of a usual size but diminutive legs. In the etching from 1804 she is standing against a chair with her elbow resting at seat height.

There is public art on the corner of East Dulwich Road and Peckham Rye in the form of a carved totem pole which gradually appeared in the winter of 2013/14 under something called the 'Cleaner, Greener, Safer' scheme in Southwark. It was carved by an artist who goes by the name of mORGANICo, who says he was asked to create 'something about community, you know, people holding hands; that kind of thing'. I love it. It is stout and solid, with faces staring out apparently based on people the artist knows or has seen in the area. It is topped by wooden wings based on William Blake's own cherub designs, a man who knew angels better than the rest of us. Is it original? It seems like it, here in south-east London, but of course the totem pole is an ancient notion. We all copy and hope to improve.

A woman climbs to the top deck carrying a large cake box.

She is young and smiley. Maybe she's going to surprise someone. I move so she can sit alone with her cake and we grin at each other. I now know a bit about cakes. This past weekend I've been in the tent where we record *The Great British Bake Off*. It is our third season and you would think we would all be used to the drama by now, but a young lad has made a mess of his 'showstopper' and I can't bear to see him crying afterwards. I stand outside in the garden hugging him and wishing I were taller so I could do a better job of it. To be honest, it's not how I saw my career. I co-host the show with the comedian Noel Fielding and I don't think either of us can believe that we are still there.

Last night we returned from a day's flour fun to find the hotel where we always stay rammed with guests from a wedding party. We tried to sneak into the bar but the bride and several of her friends followed. One of them headed for Noel and in all seriousness put out her hand, curtsied and called him Mr Noel. He had to help her up. Naturally I will never let him live that down and have instructed the entire crew that no one may approach Mr Noel without a deep bend of the knee.

Noel and I working together is one of life's odder turns. I had already signed to do the show when we began searching for my dough double-act partner. There was much cloak and dagger about it all and we met secretly in someone's house in south London. Apparently there are those who rent their houses out for this kind of thing although how you even get on such a list is a mystery to me. I had worked with Noel a couple of times on the BBC panel show *QI* and loved his surreal approach to life. As ever on that show, the moment with him which I remember best was bizarre. It had to do with pooing in kettles. We had started with some serious fact or other, which in the hands of comedians had quickly descended into something more base. The lovely funny woman Holly Walsh began a diatribe about never using hotel kettles because she was convinced men shit in them. Noel listened to this for a long time before declaring, 'May I just say on behalf of all men – we do not poo in kettles.'

It is a comfort whenever I check in anywhere.

Noel turned up for the *Bake Off* audition carrying a chair entirely wrapped in brown paper. He was late and it was awkward getting it through the door.

'I've brought a chair,' he said.

'That's kind,' I said, 'most people just bring chocolates.'

It turned out he was taking the chair somewhere as part of a challenge on a show called *Taskmaster* but instead of saying that he went off into a riff about what you should and shouldn't take as gifts to other people's houses. I think we both agreed that cabbages were nice but unexpected. Within thirty seconds there was no doubt that this tall, dark-haired, rock 'n' roll goth and me, the mini-geek, were a match. It was unlikely but it was perfect. I have had a few good teams with boys over the years – Alan Coren, Jeremy Hardy, Alan Davies. I don't do sport, but I think it must be a bit like playing tennis with someone who plays like you do. You hit the ball to them knowing it will always come back.

It's hard to believe how involved we get with the bakers. A dozen people who have come from across the country to show off their skills. It is the drama of the programme which carries it. As my wife the therapist says, 'It's not really about cake.'

After the woman had curtsied to Mr Noel he sat sipping a drink. 'I'm worried about ——,' he said, naming one of this year's younger contestants. I looked at him.

'You realise you're still talking about the show?' I asked.

He nodded and looked at me. 'I'm sorry, are you speaking to me without curtsying?'

Nigel Road

The bus passes the site of a civilian Roman outpost which ruled when the city ahead was called Londinium. Further up lies the place where in Stone Age times flint was sharpened into tools in a kind of early Mesolithic industry. There is nothing to mark either moment in history. I suspect no one else on the bus cares. I wonder whether, if I stood up and said it out loud, anyone would believe me. Much of life seems made up. Actually, I doubt anyone would even look up.

I've received one of those scam emails from a woman in Uganda who says she has no arms and needs my help. I must say, she types very well given her situation. That same day, by chance, I got a letter from someone called the King of Arms, explaining that I might be entitled to my own coat of arms given that I'm an OBE – Officer of the Order of the British Empire. I mean, what are the chances of that – getting a letter from the King of Arms and an email from woman with no arms on the same day? I am considering putting them in touch with each other.

A man wearing a large UKIP badge gets on. He wants me to have a leaflet, but I decline.

I have been looking out for a flower called London Pride as I travel. I know it is small, pink and perennial. That it is a sturdy plant which grows well in those abandoned little places you find in cities, where nothing else seems to want to take root. People talked about it as a 'blanket of consolation' in the bomb sites of London in the early 1940s, a succulent symbol of resilience.

Noël Coward wrote a song about it during the Blitz. It was spring in 1941 and he was sitting on a bench at Paddington Station. The station had been bombed the night before and there was broken glass scattered on the platform from the damaged roof. Fellow Londoners were going to work, and he must have heard their feet crunch across the debris as they carried on about their business, ignoring Mr Hitler's latest efforts to stop them. Filled with pride and patriotism, Coward remembered that the German national anthem, with its stirring and mildly disturbing refrain '*Deutschland, Deutschland über alles*', had a tune borrowed from an old English folk song. He reclaimed the melody and sang about London Pride.

I like the names the little flower goes by – St Patrick's Cabbage, Whimsey, Prattling Parnell, Look Up and Kiss Me and so on. The flower itself is actually a hybrid of a plant native to the Spanish Pyrenees and one from the west of Ireland. What a pleasing melting pot of nationalities.

UKIP seem to have no idea what this wonderful country is made of. Flowers from disparate parts of Europe, German songs with English roots and, of course, St George, the patron saint of England who was actually a Greek born in Palestine who never even came to these shores.

There used to be a tile works near here where bricks were made from the local clay. I like that Peckham clay made these great suburbs. I've been reading a book called *The Pickwicks of Peckham*, which is a 'Compilation of the deeds, thoughts, adventures and aspirations of the members of the London Explorers' Club'. The bus passes Nigel Road on our left. It was here, at No. 24, Sage Cottage, that William Margrie, the skipper of the

London Explorers' Club, made his home. He founded the club in September 1930, giving it the splendid and understated motto *Arise proud Peckham and lead the world!*

Margrie himself was made the first 'Mr London', a title which has the pleasing sense of them having had a swimsuit round in the competition. Margrie believed that he was a perfect example of a new evolutionary stage in human development, which he called Peckham Man. It never ceases to amaze me how many women struggle with self-belief while the vast majority of men have no trouble with it at all. He must have been insufferable.

It is possible the world was not ready for some of Margrie's more startling notions. He conceived something he called tersid, a form of prose writing combining the concepts of terseness and lucidity which I like the sound of, but his idea of a silent orchestra that produced 'music without noise' never really took off.

Much of his time was spent encouraging members of the London Explorers' Club 'to study London in all her moods and phases'. I love this. In their first three years the LEC visited '180 places including: Croydon Aerodrome, Headquarters of the Fire Brigade, Merrie Islington which was "not as merrie as it used to be", Caledonian Market, Historic Deptford guided by the vicar of Deptford, Samuel Jones's Camberwell Beauty Mills which specialises in gummed paper, and Peek Frean's Biscuit Factory'.

Margrie was a prolific book-writer, his works including such volumes as *One Crowded Day in Dulwich. A new spring song. Showing how a man with a moderate income can enjoy a full life in a London suburb.* And who doesn't want to read *An Outline of Humour. A collection of some of the world's best jokes, etc.*

Astonishingly, both volumes are out of print. Unable to find them 'scattered' locally, I've been to the British Library to look for them. I have been devoted to the BL for more than thirty years. I began my love affair when it still resided in the old round Reading Room at the British Museum. I got my library card in the days when getting permission to work there was not easy. You had to apply and show that not only did you have good reason to want to read the library's books but also that you were of sufficiently good character not to steal them. It was not an easy interview. Joe Orton once described one of his female characters as being 'more difficult to get into than the Reading Room at the British Museum'. How I longed to enter the calming space where Karl Marx once sat writing *Das Kapital*, where Virginia Woolf produced her works of genius.

Inexplicably I passed the test. I loved showing my pass before the hours when tourists were allowed in to traipse past the mummies and naked Greeks. There is a vast glass canopy full of retail opportunity now, which links the main entrance to the old Reading Room, but when I first joined you had to walk outside to the wonderful round chamber. Everyone around me had a very specific, often niche reason to be there. Rows of wooden desks fanned out from the centre, where librarians helped in hushed tones. You found a seat next to someone perhaps deep into Etruscan coinage or merchant navy timetables from the nineteenth century. There were no computers accessing the world's books. Just heavy catalogues which you had to heave onto a sloping shelf to look for the book titles which had been pasted in on small buff cards once wrestled through a typewriter. Glorious.

In my childhood, books published in Denmark were sold with the pages still uncut. My father would sit with a letter-opener, making a swift slice through the paper before he could turn the page. Reading was a visceral thing.

I look over into people's gardens as the bus moves along. Margrie wrote,

We look into London's kitchens and backyards as well as her
front parlours. When we visit a building, we are concerned
not with dead stone, wood, and metal, but with the dramas,
romances and personalities that the wood and stone represent.
Every institution we have explored, from a cathedral to a brewery, symbolises mankind's aspirations and strivings for a better
and fuller life.

I am seeking for myself the 'dramas, romances and personalities' of London. I would have liked to be in the London
Explorers' Club, although being a woman I doubt I'd have been
welcome. It wouldn't be the first boys' club I have been excluded
from. Back in 1990 I hosted a pilot for a new TV series called
Have I Got News for You. We shot it in a room above a pub.
Angus Deayton also hosted one and after we were done the then
head of being in charge of such things said to me, 'We preferred
yours, Sandi, but everyone has agreed you can't have a woman
in charge of making fun of the news.'
    Such thoughts were openly expressed, and no one thought
anything of it.

I've been writing my annual lecture for the Women of the
World Festival at the Royal Festival Hall. Each year I pick a
theme and this time it's art. As part of my research I popped
into the National Gallery to see what books might inspire and
bought a picture book entitled *Picture This!*. Published in 2017,
it's their recommended volume to introduce kids to great art
and artists. Deb and I have read this galloping feast of great
art several times and as far as we can see there are ninety-six
paintings included, just two of which are by women. The first
is a self-portrait by Elisabeth Vigée Le Brun, which the author,
Paul Thurlby, likes because she is wearing a 'jolly straw hat'. The

second is by Judith Leyster, with the rather straightforward title *A Boy and a Girl with a Cat and an Eel*.

That's it. Two pictures by women out of ninety-six, with ninety-four of the pieces having been created by white men. This is how we introduce kids to great art and artists. Judith Leyster is an interesting choice. She was a Dutch Golden Age painter from the first half of the seventeenth century. Her work was so good that after her death all of it was attributed either to her contemporary Frans Hals or to her husband. It wasn't until 1893 that she was rediscovered. According to the National Museum of Women in the Arts in Washington DC, even though it's estimated that 51 per cent of visual artists in the world are women, their work makes up just 3 to 5 per cent of major permanent collections in the US and Europe.

On the subject of the arts and women, the Garrick Club in London has been voting about whether or not to admit the fairer sex. It's a private members' club which was founded in the heart of the West End in 1831 to support the world of theatre. Hilariously, the club's own website declares that the place was instituted by a 'group of literary gentlemen under the patronage of the King's brother, the egalitarian Duke of Sussex'. It's not often you see the words 'egalitarian' and 'Duke' next to each other. Anyway, he was not so egalitarian that he wanted to let women in. My friend and co-founder of the Women's Equality Party, Catherine Mayer, invited me to join her there for lunch. Her father belongs and he wanted to encourage the membership to do the right thing and change the rules. He is a theatrical historian and can't bear that the great Garrick library of theatre books is not freely available to females. He took Catherine and me to lunch at the club as a sort of public statement.

The rules were made clear to me when I arrived. I was allowed to eat in the dining room, but I wasn't allowed to stand on the grand staircase – that, I was told, was a men-only area. Such a statement never goes well with me, so I went and stood on the stairs for Catherine to take my picture. I was looking up to the floor above when someone tapped me on the shoulder. Ready to be soundly scolded I turned around to find I had been accosted by the former editor of the *Sun* newspaper and friend to no feminist, Kelvin MacKenzie. I had never met him before, but he was enthusiastic in his greeting.

'I want you to meet my friend,' he said, turning to a man who had reached that age where their face shrinks away from their teeth. 'This is Rupert Murdoch.' Standing on a staircase from which I was banned in a club I could not join because of my sex I somehow shook hands with two of the men who, in my view, have done more harm to sexual equality than almost anyone else in the country.

I've been looking through some old papers in my office and found a handwritten speech which I gave at school in 1969, when I was eleven. I was clearly standing for some sort of school office but I can't remember what. In the short speech I talk about the 'reforms I would like to see'. These mainly seem to centre around the differences in behaviour allowed between the junior and senior school. I state firmly that I don't 'believe in segregation' and that 'we need equality through the entire school'. How disappointed my younger self would be that I am still having to fight much the same fight.

The bus passes the Peckham Rye Baptist Tabernacle and still my childhood desire to be religious rises up in me. I have really tried to find God but my brain always objects. When I was at boarding school, we were force-fed the particular brand of Church of England celebration that primarily seems to involve being bored to death in an unheated church. Our vicar was called Canon Davey and he presided over Christ

Church, a nineteenth-century barn of place built for the masses of Guildford. Most Sundays he held sway over a gathering consisting of half a dozen old women, two matrons, our headmistress and a hundred young girls in royal blue dresses so plain and shapeless as to de-sex us entirely. For the occasion we also donned white cotton gloves and the same stupid hat I had arrived in. Apart from the old ladies, most of whom appeared to be on their last outing, we were the entire congregation. One term the head, Miss Shackleton, fell out with the Canon. I don't know over what, but it meant we didn't go to his church. For several Sundays we marched miles up to the cathedral instead, sustained only by the pleasing thought of the vicar having written a sermon which would echo against the empty pews.

Whatever the disagreement was, it was eventually sorted and by the following term normal service was resumed. I suspect Matron, with her weeping eyes and wheezing chest, had objected to the extra walking. Once a month Canon Davey would come to the school and give a talk to the older girls. We called it Davey's Disco while Miss Shackleton labelled it 'An improving evening with the vicar'. I don't know what was expected, but with the kindness of girls in gangs we just used to ask him questions about sex and see how long it took for him to declare that was 'enough for one evening'. None of it seemed to me to have very much to do with God.

Then we got a new games mistress called Miss Smith. She was young and good fun. She taught dance, loved music and a laugh. She also talked about God. A lot. She had been 'born again', which seemed an unpleasant thought. Most unusually, one Sunday I got permission to go with Miss Smith to her church. Miss Shackleton was a tough cookie, but she was always kind to me in her own way. I think she sensed my restless soul although she was too English to mention it. Miss Smith attended a large modern Baptist place down near the river. It was packed, and people seemed pleased rather than forced to be there. There was loud singing, Cliff Richard was there and sang with his guitar, the floor was opened up and someone was 'born again' right in front of us in the sort of pool children might otherwise do laps in. How everyone cheered.

My mother had instilled a fear of any kind of birth in me from an early age. I was born in Copenhagen near the Carlsberg Brewery, which is a fine Danish start. It was known as a 'walking hospital', which meant that women gave birth, had a cup of tea and then walked home with the new baby. There was no lying about for anyone. I don't think there was even a bus. My mother often told the story of how quickly I had been born ('Too fast, much too fast'), how the doctor tried to slow things down by quickly covering my mother's mouth with a rubber mask attached to pipe of gas and air, hurting her nose in the process, and how much she had cried when she got home. I very much doubted she would think me being 'born again' was a good idea but I was intrigued.

There was a lot of hugging in Miss Smith's church and I longed to be hugged. No one at school was allowed to do anything so personal. There was no touching of any kind. The Baptists had no such fears of closeness. Everyone pulled everyone in for an embrace. I loved it and so, based on hugs alone, I decided to become a Baptist and as usual with anything I do, I really tried. I never do anything by half measures. I went all out to find God. I prayed. I read the whole Bible and I prayed some more. I even started a Christian meeting in break time as I waited for a sign. I waited for a sense of comfort but there was nothing. There was never anything. Just more emptiness.

The more I read the 'Good Book' the more I thought it didn't make sense. The story of Sodom and Gomorrah particularly upset me. It's a bizarre tale on any level. According to the book of Genesis, the men of Sodom weren't behaving all that well.

This not behaving well has over many years been interpreted as them having sex together. God decided to do something about it and sent two angels to stay with a local man called Lot and his wife who, being a woman, has no name.

The angels feel there is trouble brewing and suggest Lot and the family ought to get out of there. They tell the family to run away and not look back. So Lot and Mrs Lot and their two daughters run but Lot's wife looks back and inexplicably is turned to a pillar of salt. Anyone reading this would say that Lot has not had a good day. He's lost his home, his town has been destroyed and his wife has turned into a condiment, so what does he do? He goes up into the hills, gets drunk and sleeps with his daughters. God's reaction? Not so much as a rumble of thunder. This story, which begins with a focus on the men of Sodom, has been used in homophobic attacks for decades, but I have never seen it put forward as an example of poor parenting. Years later I read that the real sin of the men of Sodom was not homosexuality but a lack of hospitality. That is what the angels were sent to deal with. It's a simple misinterpretation of the Aramaic, which ironically has caused many religious folk to be inhospitable to the gay community.

I think I had some inkling of my own sexuality even then, and all that happened was that as I read the Bible my loneliness increased. I knew I couldn't go to the church just for a hug. I could not lie to myself, pretending to believe in something. Eventually and with regret I left the happy clapping behind and went back to Canon Davey. At least there I knew what to expect. It was cold and miserable, but he was doing his best and no one was hoping for anything else.

Heaton Road

The comedian Peter Cook once said the best way for a British person to avoid someone sitting beside them on public transport is to smile winningly at them as they approach. The British loathe this kind of welcome. Some days I smile, some days I don't. It makes no difference. I have had many journeys on this bus now and I am generally ignored. I have been trying for months to get a bus driver, any bus driver, to even look at me but there is no exchange of money so there is no cheery greeting. I always say 'Hello!' loudly and without exception they all look straight ahead, having instantly spotted me as trouble.

It is raining. A young woman with long curly auburn hair sits down and shakes rain from her hair all over me. She does not even see that anyone is there. It's like sitting behind a wet dog. A Dutch man is on the phone, speaking rapidly in his native tongue. Every now and then he interrupts himself to say 'All good, all good' in English. I don't understand him otherwise. Rather pleasingly it is double Dutch.

An old man climbs the bus stairs slowly. His breathing is laboured. His breath comes in bursts like a faulty steam engine, punctuated by a cough for extra effect. I like the fact that even those with breathing difficulties want to make the journey to the top of the bus. The view is worth it. As he gets closer, I can see that, as well as his respiratory trouble, he has some kind of dreadful skin condition. Poor man. His face peels and puffs in small boils. Perhaps he has scrofula, which is a kind of tuberculosis. I shouldn't be surprised. Homelessness has gone up 60 per cent in the last eight years and TB is on the rise. I refuse to move as he slumps into a seat near by, but both the Dutchman and the wet girl hear him coming, take one look and depart downstairs with speed.

Perhaps we need to bring back the ceremony known as 'touching for the king's evil', which was popular in the Middle Ages. Both the English and the French believed scrofula – known as the king's evil – could be cured by the touch of royalty. Edward the Confessor started it, but others carried on. Henry IV of France is said to have touched as many as fifteen hundred victims at one time, and in 1640 Charles II touched many more. Mind you, the year before the crowd to be cured had been so great several people were crushed to death, which rather negates the whole thing. Nevertheless, it would be great if we could have a walk-in touching for the king's evil centre. Save the NHS a fortune.

I don't know who the Heaton of Heaton Road was. Most likely he was the same one who in the 1790s built a glorious church-like building complete with castellated tower known as Heaton's Folly on the Peckham/Nunhead border. It's gone now and the site is filled by a nondescript apartment block that hardly anyone will ever write about. There is an 1804 drawing of Heaton's Folly, showing it sheltered by trees. A bucolic scene with a small pond and several sheep. It looks religious but in fact it seems to have been built out of kindness.

In the 1790s a topographer called Daniel Lysons published a remarkable book called *The Environs of London: being a Historical Account of the Towns, Villages and Hamlets within twelve miles of that Capital*. He had time to do this because he inherited money. In his great work he wrote about Heaton's Folly and relayed the

fact that its founder wanted it built as a means of 'giving employment to a number of artificers during a severe dearth'.

Artificers? It's an odd word. An artificer was a skilled workman, and five hundred of them were employed by Heaton.
Clearly Peckham was going through a tricky time with so many
hanging about. Lysons wrote,

> Motives the most laudable, as before observed, induced the
> founder of this sequestered spot to give bread to many half-
> starved and wretched families; and, to use the phrase of our
> immortal Shakespeare, 'It is like the dew from heaven, and
> doubly blesses.'

The man behind the folly had just been trying to help. How
marvellous. Kindness is something no politician seems to talk
about any more. The UN has published a report decrying austerity and the number of people in Britain living in extreme
poverty. Philip Hammond, when Chancellor of the Exchequer,
was asked about this and replied that he thought the report was
'nonsense'. He said, 'I reject the idea that there are vast numbers
of people facing dire poverty in this country ... Look around
you, that's not what we see in this country.' Maybe I should take
him out for the day on the Number 12.

I like that Heaton wanted to use his money to make paradise
in Peckham. I look for paradise but see only a moneylender's
ready to loan money to the poor right next to a betting shop
ready to take it away again. The woman next to me has no laces
in her shoes and looks exhausted. She carries her belongings
in a faded carrier bag. I cannot tell how old she is. Somewhere
between forty and death. She shuts her eyes against the world.
The latest analysis suggests it is the women of Britain who have
borne 86 per cent of the brunt of austerity. Poor women paying
for rich men's lives.

Heaton Road was once a big part of the local effort to look after their own. There was a time when the worst off in London ended up in the workhouse and Camberwell built its first one in 1728. The inmates of the local workhouses were sent on an annual trip to the sea, and there is a wonderful story about their expedition in 1896. They set out early one July morning on a special train which had been chartered to take 650 people to the coast; ranging, according to the *South London Press*, 'from the infant to the centenarian'. Sadly, once they got to Bognor alcohol was consumed to such an extent that there were several incidents of 'disorderly conduct and indecent behaviour on secluded parts of the beach'. Excellent outing.

In June 1898, those in charge of Camberwell began a programme known as 'scattered homes', where orphans were housed in ordinary houses and sent to local schools. It was thought to give them a better chance of success in later life. Two properties were rented in Heaton Road, and twenty children were placed under the care of two foster mothers. By 1903 there were thirty-one scattered homes in the area. A friend of mine is a foster parent. The need has not changed.

A photo on Instagram is making waves. The picture depicts a man on his boat in California who is so immersed in looking at his phone that he missed a humpback whale surfacing just a few feet away.

One morning a man climbs up the steep steps of the bus speaking loudly, as if on the phone. As usual I stop to listen, only to realise he is playing both parts in the conversation. He has no phone, no headphones, no equipment of any kind, but he does have a wonderful deep baritone voice. I can't quite make out what he is saying except he is keen on telling his imaginary friend that he will be there soon. How much nicer to just make up what you want to hear.

I like the halves of conversation I hear, small snippets like miniature Alan Bennett plays. I hear a woman say to her friend as she is getting off, 'Well, we had to sell the foot spa, what with our Maureen having to give up waitressing.'

Poor Maureen! What happened? Did she lose her job? Her patience? Her foot? Had the foot spa not helped as everyone had hoped in the excitement of its purchase? Could no one else in the family benefit from swirling water? Who would buy a second-hand foot spa?

I overheard two American backpackers comparing notes about their visit to Haworth, home of the Brontë sisters.

'I liked it,' said one. 'But we didn't do the moors business 'cos it turned out it was uphill.'

The moors business? What the hell is that? And what's the problem with it being uphill? Do we now only tick off tourist sights which are on level ground?

It is early and most of the shops are still shuttered. Close by the bus stop stands the UCKG HelpCentre. It's a Christian church. They are keen to help even those who can't stop. I check their website and discover it is possible to send prayer requests.

'All requests sent remain confidential between you and those praying for you. Prayer requests are sent straight to the Bishop in charge.'

Poor man, I think. Probably a man. I can't think what to ask for, so I don't send in a request. I hear there are now nuns in the US who will pray for you if you don't have time but you do have money.

Ahead of me, a vast woman taking up two seats is on the phone.

'You might as well postpone it and do it when it's worthwhile,' she suggests. This elicits a long reply before the huge woman says, 'Bloody hell, that's past exhaustion!'

She moves slightly, and I see a small child is squashed between her and the window.

'Excuse me for using a bad word,' she continues, 'but sod it, it's got to be done.'

I don't know what has caused such an outburst, but I suspect lawyers will be involved. The tiny child appears to gasp for air.

I glance at an abandoned paper. There is an article about a friend of mine on the front page. I don't need to read it to know it is nonsense. Fabricated nonsense. Based on nothing, the paper has taken a view on someone's life. I can feel the newspaper tutting beside me.

I could've been a journalist. Maybe I should have been. It's in my blood. My brother Nick, my father, my Danish grandfather all make or made a living from writing for the papers and TV. I did work for a year as journalist. Nick and I were sharing a flat in Clapham, south London, with Nick's best friend from university, John McCarthy. John and I met at the end of my first year at Cambridge. My brother was supposed to collect me from college to take me home but, as usual, was incredibly late. When he did turn up he was wearing a cowboy hat and accompanied by his friend John, who was lively to say the least. A pub in town had drawn their attention and they were not the least bit sorry for keeping me waiting. I was irritated with them both, but while my brother can always be endearing I quickly learned that John McCarthy can out-charm anyone. I adored him from that day to this.

I was out of work and Nick got me a job writing scripts for United Press International Television News, mainly, I think, because he wanted me to pay my share of the rent. Based in the centre of town, UPITN was a news agency which provided coverage of all the international stories for ITV and also to TV channels across the world. Raw footage would come in by satellite, we'd edit it and then write a rough script to go with it. The stories we syndicated could be about anything, so you needed to keep up with pretty much every event in every country and you needed to be quick when turning it around.

Nick showed me the basics. There were two shifts of news bulletin material, one delivered just before lunch and one in the early-evening. The early-evening one also provided a package with a proper voiceover in case a smaller TV station couldn't do that themselves. After a rather casual morning's orientation I was set to work. I learned that most people speak at three words per second, so you needed to make sure that you had written the right length of script to go with the pictures. I learned other oddities of the trade – almost all countries would buy cute animal stories, and everyone bought anything about pandas. Some stories were too violent to sell to anyone except one country which bought anything, especially stories with severed body parts.

I remember the sound of the newsroom. It was always loud. Someone shouting down a phone to someone else somewhere remote, the whirr of machines in the edit suite and most of all the sound of the typewriters. I can still hear the heavy thud of each key. Each part of each word echoing and mattering. No one picked out a word thinking it could be swiftly deleted. I wonder if words are too quick now. Maybe everything is too quick. Communication is so fast that anyone who fails to respond in a day, an hour, a minute, who is off the grid, is nothing, of no importance. Take your time, think about what you want to say and you may have missed your moment.

I was only twenty-three and I learned quickly about man's inhumanity to man. The true horrors of the world passed across my desk and I never got used to it. I remember sitting in the edit suite looking at footage in slow motion of an American district attorney who had blown his head off in front of the press.

Accused of something awful, he had arrived for a news conference with an old-fashioned briefcase. He seemed calm. He put
the case on the desk in front of him, clicked it open, took out
a gun, put it in his mouth and fired. The boys in the edit suite
kept going back over the footage. They played it slowly, frame by
frame, so that you could actually see the moment the back of the
man's skull separated from his head. It was horrific, but we sold it.

The shifts were long. I loved the ones where Nick and I were
on together. We would divide up the list of what needed to be
written and then race to see who could get theirs done first. He
is a wonderful writer and there were very few days when I got to
the finish line before him. This was the early 1980s and no one
was health-conscious. As soon as the lunchtime material had
been delivered everyone from the office went to the pub. The
Crown and Sceptre was across the street. It was what used to be
known as a 'real boozer'. Now it's a gastropub but back then it
was a place for proper drinking, with nothing more sophisticated
to eat than crisps. The clientele were a mix of journalists and
straightforward criminals. The latter were mainly London lads
who were not shy about telling you what particular bending of
the law they had just got away with. Officially many of them
were cobblers by trade, as that was the skill they had been taught
in prison. One of them, Danny, was my favourite. He told stories
with masterful skill about his life. One month I realised I hadn't
seen him for a while, and I was concerned about him, so when
he did reappear I was delighted.

'Danny! Where've you been?'

Danny shook his head as if the world were out to get him.

'Oh Sand,' he said, 'I been up before the old bill.'

'Oh,' I replied, 'what was the charge?'

Danny sipped on his beer before replying, 'Murder one.'

I wasn't sure what to say, but I was young. 'Had you done
it?' I asked.

Danny shook his head and wiped the foam from his lip. 'Nah, but I was nervous 'cos I owed 'em one. Be honest, the whole time I was with 'em me arsehole was going like the clappers.'

It was an interesting sense of justice. He hadn't killed the person whose murder he was actually charged with, but he had killed someone else at another time so imprisonment to Danny would have seemed fair enough.

Everyone drank heavily at lunchtime, which made the afternoon shift louder and jollier. We dealt with serious stories of international importance while half cut and no one thought anything of it. One of the film editors was famous for sleeping on the floor behind his giant editing machine from about three. If you wanted any footage edited after that you had to do it yourself. Alcohol was never far from the newsroom and some days it was front and centre. One desk had a locked drawer in which was kept a full bottle of Scotch. This was the 'war desk'. If a major story broke then the war desk would be declared open, the drawer would be unlocked and the bottle of whisky placed in the middle of the desk for anyone to help themselves. If you walked in and saw the bottle standing there you knew you were in for a long haul. Maybe we needed the drink. We spent our days watching people getting blown up, shot and mutilated. You might think you have seen violence on the evening news, but you have no idea how much the footage has been cleaned up for public consumption.

One evening I was doing a shift in the newsroom when the actress who normally did the voiceover for the evening bulletin failed to show, so I took her place. Soon I had regular shifts both writing and presenting the news. After nearly a year of working there the boss called me into the office.

'You're doing a great job, Sandi. We'd like to offer you a permanent job.'

That same afternoon my agent phoned to say I had half a

day's work giving one line in a sketch on the Victoria Wood show. With nothing more to go on than that, I gave my notice at UPITN and never returned. I don't know why I made that choice. Guys I worked with back in those days now have their own shows on CNN or run whole TV news channels in Australia. I don't think I could bear to look at any more blood.

Back on the bus, I look ahead to the Bussey Building, an industrial structure of reinforced concrete, brick-clad with most of its decorative features on the side facing the railway tracks. George Bussey was a Victorian industrialist and entrepreneur, and the building served partly as an advertisement for his sporting goods, including the finest cricket bats made of willow from his own country estate. His bats were the secret weapon of the great cricketer W. G. Grace. Bussey set up shop in Peckham in about 1870, describing his business as 'Firearms, Ammunition and Shooting Tackle Manufacturers'. He wanted to be admired by those who passed by on the train.

It is possible that my British great-grandfather, Field Trickett, knew about Bussey as they were both in London and in the business of invention. Among Bussey's many triumphs were an early version of a clay-pigeon launcher, a device to enable golfers to practise their swing without the annoyance of retrieving their balls and a dining table which converted into a billiard table via a spring-loaded switch.

None of these things are in evidence today but instead there is a great smell of the Caribbean. In a courtyard outside the Bussey Building there is a man who occasionally sets up a large halved oil drum and grills Jamaican food. It is glorious. He always posts a menu but only ever seems to make one thing – jerk chicken, which stings the outside of my lily-livered Scandinavian mouth but is too delicious to stop eating. I sometimes get off the bus on the off chance he is there. En route I decide to pop into my favourite shop, Khans, which sells amongst a thousand other things saucepans so large your entire family could go for a swim in them. I don't want to buy anything. I just like looking around.

As I get off the bus a black-cab driver shouts out of his window, 'Nice work on *Bake Off*, Sandi!' I never cease to be amazed at the range of people who watch the show. I was giving out the National Portrait Awards last night and sat next to some high-powered American executive who only wanted to talk about *Bake Off*. Because I had never seen the show before I joined the team I didn't really know what to expect. I live divorced from the zeitgeist and had no idea the programme was as popular as it is or that there might be a market for any secret leaking from the set.

The great chef Prue Leith joined the same year as Noel and me, and we were all amazed at the anxiety that fizzed around the show. The set was inundated with executives from Channel 4 who stood behind the cameras with their arms folded, their jaws clenched in the belief that we were about to destroy their lives. The tabloids led with fabricated stories about us all fighting and someone hid in the bushes near the tent to snap and publish exciting pictures of me carrying my knitting. The production company upped the security and soon I had a lovely person in black clothes linked wirelessly to other people in black clothes following me everywhere. Going to the loo became a challenge because I never wanted to be in there too long as news of any delay in the proceedings would have been radioed to all concerned.

People always ask me if the best bit about working in the tent is that I get free cake. Truth is, I don't really like cake very much. The competitive part of the series is filmed in the grounds of a large country house called Welford Park in Berkshire. The main house dates from the mid-seventeenth century and has the most wonderful library. Early on the owner gave me permission to both read in there and light the open fire. I sit in an armchair by the fire tending to its needs and reading obscure volumes of history while Prue sits on the sofa opposite tapping away at one of her novels. Prue in particular has become like family. She has more energy than the rest of us put together and I love how she always looks ahead to the next adventure. Occasionally Paul comes in to play cards or watch Formula 1 on the TV. I suspect these private contented moments translate into our public happiness together on screen.

We also make five celebrity editions of the show and for these the tent is put up in the gardens of Pinewood Studios. It is a much more cinematic affair and we have golf buggies to take us to and from our dressing rooms. Paul, whose hobby is racing cars, is a keen golf buggy chauffeur. So keen that he manages to get the thing to take corners at a speed which I think would surprise the manufacturers. He likes nothing better than loading the four of us into one of these buggies and heading at full speed for the tent. Mandy, the floor manager, stands at the entrance patiently waiting for us and inevitably, just before we are about to arrive, Paul turns sharp left into a small wood. We disappear, speeding through the trees with Prue shrieking with laughter and Noel and me clinging on at the back. I love that. If anyone asks what my favourite bit of the show is, driving full pelt across autumn leaves in a golf buggy is probably not the answer they are expecting.

Peckham Rye Station

On the corner, where Rye Lane meets Peckham High Street, the Picture Playhouse used to stand. It was by all accounts a rather grand affair, with statues in niches holding up flaming torches. The cinema opened in 1911 under the direction of a Mr Sydney Still. It seated seven hundred and boasted 'Two Gaumont projectors, a piano and a Mustel organ'. It also had 'effects', although I have no idea what they were. Old programmes tell us that Mr Victor Geverding led the orchestra, while Miss Bertha Zander and Miss Lily Valentine tinkled on the keyboards. An orchestra! How marvellous. I long for the days of grandeur when even the cinema was a proper outing. Sadly, the picture house in all its glory lasted just six years.

I look around this part of Peckham saddened by the loss of what had been other grand entertainment in the neighbourhood – the Crown Theatre once stood down to the right, on the corner of Marmont Road and Peckham High Street. Designed in a style known as Spanish Renaissance, whatever that may be, it was an imposing place of terracotta and red brick. It opened in 1898 as a music hall venue with a bar where the walls were decorated in 'rich red flock, for the display of stags' heads, old armour, ancient halberds, &c'.

I don't know what the '&c' is all about. It was here in February 1900 that the people of Peckham could have seen Weldon Atherstone in a new and sensational patriotic drama called *Send Her Victorious: A Tale of the Transvaal* by Sutton

Vane. A spectacular piece which featured an attack by Boers on an armoured train, with real Maxim guns in action.

Theatre and Maxim guns go together in my head and not because of a great drama about the Boer War. I often talk about my Danish heritage, but my mother is English, and her grandfather was a true Londoner. He delighted in the name Field John Jackson Trickett, so named because of confusion about the form during his baptism at St Martin-in-the-Fields in Trafalgar Square. He was born in 1871 in Percy Street, which is just off Tottenham Court Road near the British Museum. It's a posh part of Fitzrovia now but I doubt it was then. He married Emily Martha Fisher and they had eight children, including my grandmother, Doris. Together Field and Emily ran the Fox pub in Lower Kingswood, Surrey. Emily knew the trade well for her parents, my great-great-grandparents, James Fisher and his wife Eliza Jane Windsor, had managed the pulling of pints at the Greyhound in Guildford.

Before he took on the Fox, Great-Grandpa Field was an engineer. His principal interest was electricity. It was the late nineteenth century and this was new-fangled stuff. Almost the only way to power anything at the time was with a gas or coal engine. Field tinkered away at electrical devices in his workshop in West Norwood in south London. By chance, Sir Hiram Maxim, an American inventor, immigrated to Britain at around that time and settled in West Norwood. He needed a workshop and went to work at my great-grandfather's. Amongst other things, Maxim created the Captive Flying Machine, an amusement ride which still thrills holidaymakers at Blackpool and was built by Field Trickett.

Sadly, Maxim also developed the Maxim gun, the first portable, fully automatic machine gun. Whenever Hiram wanted to test the thing, he thoughtfully warned his neighbours by placing announcements in the local paper. I like to think of my great-grandfather standing with his fingers in his ears while Sir Hiram blasted away.

Field died two years before I was born so I never met him, but I have recently discovered an odd connection. My first professional theatre job was as a stage electrician at the Palace Theatre in the West End, where I took my first steps in show-business by crucifying Jesus eight times a week in the musical *Jesus Christ Superstar*. I wondered what my beloved teacher Miss MacDonald, who went off to become a silent nun, would have made of it.

I got the job because Miss Shackleton, the headmistress at my boarding school, had once made the extraordinary and unexpected decision to take us all to the theatre. We went to see *Superstar*. I think she can't have read any of the reviews before we went. She must have been appalled as we watched the chorus writhing and simulating sex while Pilate whipped Jesus with his microphone cord. I loved it. I loved everything about it and the Palace remains my favourite building in London. Opened in 1891, it is the only West End theatre to stand in its own 'city block'. On a magnificent island with streets on all four sides there is this towering place of entertainment with its red and pink terracotta exterior buttressed by turrets topped by cupolas and a statue of a woman holding aloft a torch. The first time I saw it I thought it was inspirational and lost my heart to it for ever.

I lay in my narrow metal bed at school clutching the pro-gramme from the show, still transfixed by what I had seen. In the back was a black-and-white photograph of Sir Emile Littler, who had been in charge of the Palace since the 1940s. I wrote to Sir Emile. I said how much I liked his theatre and asked him for a job. Because it was a different world then, he wrote back and made an appointment for me to meet with him as soon as I had left school. Once I had completed my Oxbridge exam I took him up on his offer and, in the quiet of Greek Street, I found the stage door. Above its half-glazed door was a concrete lintel bearing the words, 'Palace Theatre Stage Door. The world's greatest artistes have passed and will pass through these doors.'

As I walked in, I felt a surge of excitement which I knew no office was ever going to provide. In a tiny cubby-hole on the right sat an ancient man called Charles. Charles was the stage-door man and he took his job as gatekeeper very seriously. It was some time before I was shown through to the lift which ran up to Sir Emile's office. It was small, with two gates making up a concertina of metal which clanged across before I headed up. Sir Emile was theatre through and through. He came from a theatrical family. His parents had once run the Royal Artillery Theatre in Woolwich. He had been an actor, a stage manager and produced over two hundred pantomimes. He married a 'principal boy' called Cora Goffin, whose legs were once insured for twenty thousand pounds. How marvellous she sounded. Cora bought her first car while she was on tour and got one of the chorus boys to teach her how to drive. Once the tour was over, she set off in her new vehicle to get home to London. She was passing through countryside when she inexplicably came to a stop. She flagged down a passing motorist who was able to impart to her the secrets of buying petrol.

Sir Emile was in his seventies by the time I met him – his hair slicked back, in a double-breasted jacket and thick-rimmed black spectacles. I didn't know I was meeting a man who had once been one of the most powerful figures in all of British theatre. Instead of being in awe I explained rather breathlessly my feelings for the theatre itself.

'Do you mind what you do?' he asked.

I shook my head. 'I just want to be in the building.'

He smiled and picked up the receiver of an old Bakelite telephone.

'Get me the Electrics Department.'

The call went through.

'I have a young lady here who I wish you to employ,' he declared.

The electrics crew room was and is a narrow corridor of a place just off the stage right or prompt corner. In the inner office sat another elderly man, Eric, who was 'The Chief'. The entire building seemed run by ancient fellows who had been there for ever. Eric sat drinking tea and I was put in the care of a slim young man called Kriss Buddle. He rolled cigarettes as he talked and eyed me up, noting my height.

'She'll need a box,' he said, and Eric nodded.

'Got one in the sub-basement.'

A narrow wooden box which had once held soft drinks was found.

'What about the lamp round?' asked Eric.

Kriss frowned for a moment, then went off to find the shaft of a broken broom and a rubber plunger. He sat quietly putting the two items together and seemed pleased with the result.

'Perfect,' said Eric. What for, I had no idea.

Next was learning how to operate the followspots – the large lights on stands, each operated by one person who could determine both the size of the light on the actors and the colour. Kriss led me up the narrow back stairs to one of the boxes in the auditorium where the lamp stood pointing down at the stage. In order to hit a specific mark it was necessary to aim the light by gripping it from behind with your right hand, holding the front with your left and placing your eye by the left side of the lamp, looking down it like a rifle sight. As Kriss had predicted, I needed to stand on the wooden box in order to reach. I stepped up and he showed me how to control the lever which opened and closed the shutter to turn the light on and off with my right hand; how to make the circle of light very small (a pin spot) or very large and how to slip the four different coloured gels at the front in and out of the light path with my left. Then he went down on stage and dimmed the auditorium lights. It took a while for my eyes to adjust to the darkness.

'Now,' called Kriss in the gloom, 'I'm going to throw a matchbox in the air, and I want you to hit it with the light when it lands.'

I got it first time. I felt as though I had come home.

I became Second Day Man in the Electrics Department. Possibly still my finest job title of all time. During the day we mended the electrics. At night my job was to arrive before anyone else and 'light up' the dark theatre. I had to tour every inch of it, making sure no light bulb had died overnight. Most of the lamps were overhead and the building was too vast to use a ladder, hence the plunger pole that Kriss had made for me. If I found a dead lamp I simply held up my pole, placed the plunger over the bulb, pushed and twisted and away it came, cupped in the rubber. I then did the reverse to replace the bulb. I was swift like a ninja light-bearer.

It was my favourite part of the work. In that hour, the theatre belonged only to me. I would slowly climb up the turrets where no one ever went but which needed to be lit anyway. In one corner as you climbed you could hear a woman singing scales. There was no woman. None of the singers were in yet but still you could hear the sound. It was probably the wind, but it was strange and consistent. Kriss knew I was intrigued by it.

One night I was in the dark theatre and I went to turn the power on for the musicians. A terrible sound of doom-laden organ music filled the empty air. Kriss had programmed it to come on and give me a fright. *Superstar* was one of the first West End musicals with electronic music.

I learned to control the main lighting board. Today everything is computerised, but in the late '70s that was unimaginable.

Superstar was a complex show and the main stage lights were worked by a converted church organ with controls operated by both hands and both feet. More than a hundred levers, known as tabs, worked the various lights and a series of pedals controlled the speed with which they illuminated or dimmed. It wasn't all showbusiness, though. One tab was there just to turn the kettle on in the crew room five minutes before the interval.

It was an odd life. The lighting organ or board was up high on a platform above the head of the deputy stage manager or DSM. I sat sideways to the stage where I had a clear view of the action and could time the fading and appearing of the lights with the music. The DSM would call into my ear through large headphones:

'Crucifixion ... Go!'

I would press a lever, magically enabling Jesus to appear on his cross from below the stage. There were several Jesuses, one of whom liked a drink. One night he liked it so much that he fell off the cross and had to be put back with a ladder. It was possibly a low spiritual moment for the audience, but it has stayed with me as a supreme moment of theatre.

Sometimes I worked the big carbon arc followspots at the top of the theatre. These were much trickier than the ones in the boxes. There was still the on/off lever, the size and colour to worry about, but in addition the light was created by sparking two rods of carbon together. I expect they're illegal now because they were hot and dangerous. The lamps produced a brilliant white light, but you had to keep 'feeding' the two carbon rods together during the show in order for them to create the necessary fire. A fire so intense it wasn't possible to look right at it. You had to glance sideways through an inch of obscured glass. The lamps were dangerously hot, so to protect ourselves we wore asbestos gloves. I anticipate a fatal lung condition any day now.

There were two operators in the carbon arc booth. It was a
separate little back room in the upper circle, the highest of the
theatre's four levels. We climbed in via a small ladder and sat in
a sort of shed shining the lights down through a wide window.
The sound of the show came in over a Tannoy while cues were
relayed through headphones. Despite this it was still possible to
chat with your fellow operator. I often worked with a gay man
called Paul. In addition to working at the theatre, Paul knitted
elaborate sweaters for a living. Somehow, he was able to knit
and keep the followspot alight and on the move. I was eighteen.
I had spent the previous four years locked up in a repressive
boarding school. I had never knowingly met a gay man before.
Paul was outrageous, and I loved him. We would shriek with
laughter until inevitably some audience member would come
and bang on the door of the box, telling us to be quiet. I learned
a lot. Those chorus members writhing and simulating sex during
Jesus' whipping? Some of them weren't simulating. It was a
growing-up time.

Eric, the Chief, had worked at the Palace all his life. He knew
every inch of the building. For historical reasons theatre electrics
departments are also in charge of plumbing. No one seemed to
have any plans of the building. What they had was Eric. A leak
would spring up in the ancient ladies' toilets in the dress circle
and Eric would tip his head slightly to one side and say, 'Hmm,
that'll be the pipe behind the wall in the rear stalls.'

Dark red panelling would be removed to reveal some conduit
no one else knew existed. Eric was that theatre and he passed
the mantle to Kriss who, nearly forty years later, has only just
retired as Chief. He is still my friend, or more like family actually. My sister Jeni has also worked followspot at the Palace, as
has my daughter Jesse. He calls us Toksvig, Toksvig Junior and
Toksvig Minor. To this day I cannot walk past the stage door
without wishing I could pop in to see if he has the kettle on. I

think about Sir Emile helping me. I don't ever remember wishing I was standing in the light instead of working it.

I was lucky to work there at all. Back in the late '70s no female was allowed to work on the electrics crew at the London Palladium. Other theatres didn't have such a strict rule, but they were unprepared for women. At the same time as *Superstar* was on at the Palace the musical *Irene* was playing at the Adelphi Theatre in the Strand, starring Jon Pertwee and the brilliant Australian Julie Anthony. The show needed someone to stand in, or 'dep' as the theatre folk say, for the followspot operator on Wednesday afternoons. I took time out from my day job and went to the theatre. It had never occurred to the designers of the Adelphi that a woman might do such a job, so the entrance to the followspot booth was up a ladder between the urinals in the gentlemen's toilets in what must have been the balcony. Five minutes before the show men were often taking a precautionary pee and I would climb up between them, trying not to look.

It was years later that I made the most amazing discovery. The Palace Theatre was one of the first theatrical venues with electric light, and the man who put the lighting in? My great-grandfather, Field Trickett.

Hanover Park

I am travelling through London's oldest borough, Southwark. It is a misnamed bus stop for there is no park. I have tried to find the history of this place, but the internet is not helpful. At home I have over a hundred books on the history of London, and I have to plough through them all until I reach a slim volume by John D. Beasley entitled *Origin of Place Names in Peckham and Nunhead*. Mr Beasley has written seventeen books about Southwark and he is keen to get it right. He includes his home address in case anyone should find fault with his book. I love his dedication.

According to Beasley, the park was named for the Hanover Chapel, which used to stand on the corner of Rye Lane and the high street. The chapel is long gone to make way for tram tracks, but it took its name from two of the sons of George III who liked to hang out there. We are European everywhere I look.

My phone pings. I have failed to answer an email within the hour and the sender is keen to know it has not disappeared into the ether. I reread the missing mail and think it is as unimportant as the first time I looked at it. In 1994 I sailed around Britain with John McCarthy, for the telly. It was a tricky trip on an old leaking boat which took three months. After eight weeks or so we visited Holy Island off the Northumbrian coast. Here a group of Buddhist monks made their life in the bitter cold. This upset fundamentalist Christians hugely and they would regularly hold prayer protests by the shoreline, trying to get God to make the orange-clad monks go away. God seemed disinclined because on the island we met the brother of the Dalai Lama, which is about as Buddhist as you can get. He was a smiley fellow, all in orange with a small matching hand-sewn bag for his mobile phone. John and I were not enjoying the trip and asked for his advice.

'Be of the moment,' he replied.

Tricky.

The traffic is bad and today there appears to be a collective wish to be somewhere else. It is infectious. A man behind me clicks a pile of coins over and over in his hand, ignoring the many people who do that British thing of trying to stare him into silence. A group of Spanish lads board and treat the bus as a private club, each one of them occupying a double seat and calling out loud jokes.

'What's wrong with you?' one of them suddenly asks me in accented English. I don't reply because there isn't enough time in the world for my answer. The young men get up and move towards me, so I move to the back of the bus and sit next to a young woman. She is listening to the musical *Dreamgirls*, which I like, but the leaked noise from her ears hisses and whines so when the Spanish club breaks up I move forward. A middle-aged man is on the phone.

'I need to get a skip, a big skip, a really big skip!' he barks. I wonder how it is that he is so burdened with rubbish.

I have a headache and am restless. I move forward again, to the very front, to get some quiet. I spy a young man reading sheet music. It is a classical piece. He has no headphones. I have high hopes of a little calm. I sit down, only to discover that he is humming the piece loudly as he pretends to play the piano on the ledge by the front window. I have nowhere else to move to, so I try to be of the moment and enjoy his quite mad concert. I can't tell if he can actually read music or is just pretending. I start miming the violin to accompany him. This doesn't faze him in the slightest. He grins at me and we keep going. Silently playing Mozart we trundle on together.

I love the shops in this stretch. A woman is laying out gold earrings in the window of the Albemarle Bond pawn shop. At Sakhi Quality Meat & Fish a man is preparing crushed ice for a fish display. He swipes the ice into shape with a smooth blade. The sign on yet another pawnbroker's calls out, 'Need Cash? We can help.'

Outside the Aylesham Centre a woman in a striped fur hat stands waiting patiently with copies of the Jehovah's Witness magazine, the *Watchtower*, to save those on their way. She smiles and tries to hand a magazine to a young woman with spectacles who is in a hurry, but she's too young to know she will need saving one day.

There is a Tube strike today so there are clearly non-bus people on the bus. They have no idea about the unwritten rule that empty seats must be filled up first. They plonk themselves down next to already seated regulars, who flinch but say nothing. I can feel the atmosphere and decide to escape into my phone. I decide to see if there is any history about the street online. All I discover is that in 2012 one person thought fit to upload an image of the bus seat fabric, that in June 2017 there were 1117 crimes within one mile of here, and that the bulk of people rent their homes in the area. Who uses this information?

A young man climbs to the top deck. Black jeans, hoody and trainers. Normal kit, but what is odd is that none of his clothing bears a single logo. It is unusual. He carries a small black rucksack, again stripped of all identity. He is maybe twenty-five years old and has a small, neat beard; he looks straight ahead and does not engage. There is no doubt that his mere presence has made the other already irritable passengers nervous. Some get up and go downstairs. At the next stop I see a woman get off to wait for the next bus. I can't decide what is happening. Is it all just chance and misinterpretation? Do people see terrorism where there is none?

There's been a fatal shooting in Copenhagen, and it has upset me more than I can say. It took place at Krudttønden, which everyone on the news keeps saying is a café but is actually an arts centre. In 2014 they put on an excellent production of my play *Bully Boy*, about the trauma of those involved with armed conflict. I got an email early in the morning saying everyone we knew was fine but nevertheless, while we waited for word, Deb and I had worried. We wondered if the person who died was someone we had met – a barman, a ticket seller. It made it more personal. The fact that in the end we didn't know the film director who lost his life didn't really matter.

There had been a discussion about free speech going on when the shooting happened. That's all he had been attend-ing. No one should have to die for an idea. Lots of artists, from the worlds of film, theatre and animation, had gathered. You begin to wonder if art can make a difference. When did murder become the new political protest? Have we run out of words?

The whole incident puts me in a dark mood. I have written a lot about conflict over the years. I wrote a whole novel about the Boer War almost by accident. I was in a church when I hap-pened upon a plaque dedicated to a bicycle regiment in that war fought in South Africa from 1899 to 1902. I'd been to that part of the world and thought a bicycle might not be the best way to get around. I idly read up on the regiment, and before you know it I had written a novel, *Valentine Grey*, about it.

As usual the Boer War – or South African War – was a conflict that claimed to be about one thing but was really about another. It represents a dark period of history when Britain violated international law and basic humanity in every way conceivable. During that time Lord Kitchener invented the concentration camp and brought warfare to a new level of barbarism. Volunteers like the 1st Surrey Rifles from Camberwell set sail thinking they were fighting for Queen and country but soon found themselves overwhelmed with exhaustion and hunger, and asked to behave in despicable ways. They were commanded to herd women and children into overcrowded and unsanitary camps while the British government told the world it was for the Boers' protection.

The British troops engaged in a 'scorched earth' policy, burning down farmhouses and slaughtering livestock, whose carcases were left to rot. To many it seemed like a white man's war but any black South Africans living on the farms were also herded up, into over sixty camps. We know all the names of the more than thirty-four thousand white women, children and men who died en route to and in the camps. They have been displayed on banners in commemoration services at the Voortrekker Monument in Pretoria, but in all my painstaking research I could not find the name of a single black person. No one really knows the exact figures, but it is estimated that about twenty thousand black South Africans died, and when I was researching my book I wanted to find some marker of their demise. Deb and I flew out to South Africa to take a look. I had read an article which claimed that such a graveyard existed in the small town of Dry Harts, so we went but found nothing but scrubland. I contacted the journalist who had written about it.

'Oh yes,' he said, 'I never actually went. I just heard about it.'

From whom, he could not recall. It is a forgotten war. We drove to the site of a large graveyard for white Africans and found ourselves in a field with high grass all around.

'It should be right here,' I declared, rechecking my map.

Just then the wind shifted and blew the grass so that it bent almost in half away from us. For a brief second we glimpsed row after row of white gravestones, long-dead sons, their names concealed and forgotten.

Even though I read a lot about the effects of violence when I was studying the Boer War, I realise it was not something I really knew much about. Near the corner of Peckham High Street and Rye Lane one day the bus comes to a halt. I see that all the traffic has stopped. The driver announces that we are to leave the bus. There is much grumbling. I am in my preferred seat at the top, on the right at the front, and have a notebook and pen out. My scarf has become entangled with my rucksack straps, so I take a moment to get off. As I descend down the stairs and out the central doors, I see a policewoman standing facing me, her arms out wide.

'Do not touch!' she calls to me.

As I step down, I nearly stand on the very thing she is trying to protect. A large carving knife lies at her feet, covered in blood. The blood is fresh and shocking in the brilliance of the dripping red. A crowd is gathering, and as I move away I see a young man holding his stomach and lurching across the road until he falls to the pavement about a hundred feet away. More police are running after him. It is a nice day. The sky is blue. I am not expecting violence, but in that instant everyone seems angry. There is shouting and mayhem. The sound of sirens begins to fill the air and more police arrive. I feel panicked and ring Deb.

'Put your head down,' she tells me. 'Look at no one and walk away down the first street you see. I'm on my way.'

I do just that but behind me there is chaos and there is nothing I can do about it. The stabbing is not terrorism, but mindless violence. The world is becoming polarised. Disagree with someone and they hate you. The Nigel Farages, Boris Johnsons and Donald Trumps of this world are allowing divisive speech to become the norm and the result spills out onto the streets. A lesbian couple have been attacked on a bus after a night out. The MP Jo Cox is dead at the hands of an extremist. Deb doesn't want me to travel alone any more. I don't want to give up the Number 12. I must refuse to be afraid.

The Academy at Peckham

I've been shooting a short drama about autism. My friend Kathy Lette's son Jules is on the autistic specrum and a very fine actor. In the film he plays a young man obsessed with capturing the essence of moments he likes in plastic boxes. I play his American therapist and have thoroughly enjoyed it. I like acting. It's like being a grown-up and still playing at shops. I've done a bit over the years, but not a lot of cinema stuff.

The only feature film I've been in was called *Paris By Night*. It was written by David Hare and starred Charlotte Rampling. I played Charlotte's assistant. I think I'd been cast to make her look taller and thinner. It was November 1987. Charlotte was to play an MEP and I got the part because my father had by then made a strange and unexpected leap from journalism to politics and actually was an MEP. David wanted someone who 'understood' being an MEP. I don't know why. Surely it was an acting job and you just had to pretend. My papa being in the European Parliament gave me no real insight. I had hardly visited him in Brussels. It didn't matter. At the audition I don't think Mr Hare was all that interested in what I actually thought about anything.

I met him at the film studios in Twickenham. I had tried to dress the part and even put on high heels. I've never liked them, so I can't say I was feeling entirely cheerful. He looked like so many of the boys I had known at Cambridge suddenly grown older. Dressed in a great crumple with sad hair. He was in a hurry, jetting off to Paris, presumably, to see what it was like at night.

'Why do you think so many tough women are coming out of Cambridge these days?' was his opening question.

Until that moment I don't think I had realised that Cambridge was unleashing harridans onto an unsuspecting world of beleaguered playwrights.

'I suppose if they are tough it's because, with five men to every woman up there, the women have to work harder to prove themselves,' I improvised.

He smirked. 'When I was there,' he said, 'it was ten men to every woman and the women just walked around grateful for the number of men around.'

The actress in the uncomfortable shoes smiled at the famous writer while the tough-minded Cambridge-graduate feminist in me stomped outside to vomit. He gave me one of Charlotte's scenes to look at and the casting agent, the delightful Mary Selway, put me out in the corridor on a plastic seat by the photocopier. She said I could have fifteen minutes. I read the speech for a minute, read it again and then couldn't think what else to do. It was short and filled with rather unexciting 'and we promise' or 'we believe' political rhetoric. Unless I was a suspected dyslexic or supposed to rewrite the thing, fifteen minutes seemed like a very long time. By the time I read it aloud I was ready to give it some force.

'Boy, I'm glad I don't live in your constituency,' laughed David.

I could have asked if he wanted it read differently, but I just wanted out, so I didn't. I left and went to see my lovely friend, the late Hilary Tindall, in a lunchtime production of *Rosalind* by J. M. Barrie at the King's Head in Islington. She was good. We chatted afterwards. The cast were paid nothing. They had hoped 'people' would come and see it. They hadn't. What a bizarre business.

I got the part in the film and quickly learned how unimportant I was. It was shot in a rather grand house in Hampstead. You could tell the owners were rich. The place was decorated with that disregard for either fashion or comfort which only the British who inherit wealth seem to manage. High ceilings, shabby furniture and a vast emotional void. Charlotte was charming but smoked Gitanes cigarettes which left a foul smell. Odd that it once was thought sexy. I spent a lot of time in summer clothes in a freezing wintry garden which had been made to appear summery with the aid of lighting and props. David mostly ignored me, apart from at one point telling me to do a 'yuppie' walk through shot. I had stood for so long my feet had sunk into some mud and I wasn't sure I could walk at all. I also wasn't clear how yuppies might move.

I took comfort from the great actor Michael Gambon, who every day seemed more interested in food than in taking direction. He was my hero. There was a scene where I had to exit a room as Michael walked towards me in the hall. He had to lean down and whisper in my ear before walking on. There was no dialogue, but David could not get what he wanted. We did it over and over, with David always crouched down in a corner as he gave direction. At last he suddenly jumped up, shouting, 'That look on your face, Michael! That's it! What are you thinking about now?'

'Lunch,' replied Michael quietly.

We did it again and this time, as Michael leant toward me he whispered the single word 'Arsehole' in my ear before walking on. I believe that's the shot they used.

I learned a lot about the insanity of fame working with Charlotte Rampling. We were pretending to drive a BMW on the Westway in London. Filming someone driving is not the easiest thing in the world. The car had been placed on what's called a low loader. It's a very low trailer with a large bubble of plastic over both the car and the trailer, which is pulled by another vehicle. Charlotte was doing the fake driving while I did pretend diary checking next to her and a small boy pretended to be a small boy in the back of the car. It was all going very well. We were travelling along the Westway pretending like mad. I was delighted to have remembered all my lines and we had nearly finished when a black cab pulled up alongside. I could quite clearly see the cab driver look across and mouth the words, 'Fuck me, it's Charlotte Rampling.' At which point he crashed into the central reservation and all you could see in the back of shot was the entire Westway coming to a dramatic halt. Needless to say, we had to do it again.

It was a truly terrible film. It was about an MEP, but it wasn't really political. Charlotte killed someone who was blackmailing her (only he wasn't), yet it wasn't a thriller. It just seemed dull. I saw it only once and then by chance. I was passing a small cinema in Tottenham Court Road and there was an afternoon showing. It was raining and I had time, so I popped in. That day only me and a man in a mac who didn't appear fussy about what film was showing seemed to have thought it was a good idea.

The bus slowly slips past the Kentish Drovers pub heading for town as so many farmers once did. There has been a pub here since at least the late eighteenth century. Now it's a Wetherspoons, which I suspect is new. It stands near the junction with Melon Road. It is hard to imagine that this area used to be famous for its fields of fruit and veg. There are records of melons being grown here in 1629, on land owned by Sir Thomas Gardiner, who sent four of them to the Court of Charles I and got some venison in exchange. There's not enough of that kind of shopping these days.

It was the bus, the horse-drawn omnibus, which brought

the working class to the area. I am travelling through the very home of the London bus. In December 1849 Thomas Tilling, a London man already in the transport business, bought a four-horsed vehicle called the *Times* and ran it four times a day from Rye Lane in Peckham to the Green Man and Still tavern on the north side of Oxford Street. Eventually he would own seven thousand horses and 250 horse buses. The transport was cheaper than trains or stage coaches and suddenly the poor could live here and still get to work.

It's hard to imagine the excitement of the inaugural motor bus, which made its first journey on Wednesday 28 September 1904. It left from Peckham at 12.30 p.m. and people gathered outside the Kentish Drovers to cheer it on its way. It took twenty minutes for the bus to get to Oxford Street. The fare from Peckham to Piccadilly was 2½d and to Oxford Street 3d. Not everything since has been an improvement. As far as I can discover, the Number 12 service was started by a competitor, the Amalgamated Omnibus Company, two and a half years later, on 11 February 1907. For 112 years people have been plying this same route through London and I love being part of that.

The Drovers was recently in the news when a young man had a glass smashed in his face for holding hands with his boyfriend. Anyone who thinks the work of equality is done should think again and be ready to battle on. Ann Widdecombe has declared that perhaps science can provide the answer to homosexuality. The Vatican has declared that gender is not fluid. We are pedalling back into the Dark Ages and the big worry is that not everyone has noticed.

It was opposite the Drovers that Matthew Flockton, the 'motion master', used to entertain with his puppets. Back in the 1790s Mr Flockton's audience 'believed the feats of a favourite dog which had been trained to fight one of his puppets, a truly marvellous affair'.

I can't picture it. Maybe it was the drink.

Drinking was a normal part of life on the road for my family, and it was common for us kids to have a little wine and water with dinner. When Papa was reporting from NASA in Houston I remember we had an evening with a large group of dignitaries. No one was paying Nick and me any attention, so we sat quietly. I sipped my wine and water, and pulled on Papa's sleeve.

'The wine's corked,' I whispered.

'Shush!' he responded.

'But Papa, the wine's—'

'Shush!' he said again, more irritated. He took a sip of his wine and then put the glass down. He reached for his knife and gently banged the side of the glass with it for silence. He stood to speak.

'Ladies and gentlemen, I wish to apologise. The wine is corked. My daughter knew this, and I failed to listen.' He turned to me, bowed his head and then looked at me, smiling. 'Sandi, I'm so sorry.'

My father was a complicated man, but he set the benchmark for my capacity for love. I adored him. Nevertheless, it was an odd upbringing.

It is mid-afternoon, mid-week, and yet there is quite a crowd sinking pints on the pavement. I have to go to work, or I might stop and join them. I think the drunkest I have ever been was in New York. I was one of the performers in the television improvisation show *Whose Line Is It Anyway?*. It consisted of traditional improvisation games which actors have used for generations. Clive Anderson was in the chair and took impromptu suggestions from the audience which the rest of us had to muck about to. I'd been part of an improvisation group, the Comedy Store Players, for some years so it all seemed very familiar. I pretty much knew everyone who appeared on the programme and became great friends with the American comic Mike McShane.

I think it's fair to say that the producer, Dan Patterson, found all of us a little trying. Ever trying to get us to behave, he banned all alcohol from the green room and was exasperated one evening when, ten minutes before the show, we all had to be extracted from the pub next door. Perhaps his most devastating experience was when the show won a BAFTA. Not one of us performers had been invited to the ceremony. I remember asking Dan about it and he replied crossly, saying, 'You people think you're the star of the show, but the show is the star.' As the show was entirely made up by comics speaking off the cuff it was hard to understand his reasoning.

To celebrate the award, we were not invited to anything grand but rather to share a bowl of peanuts and room-temperature drinks in the reception area of Hat Trick Productions, who made the show. The BAFTA trophy stood next to the main switchboard beside a plate of Twiglets looking as forlorn as the rest of us.

Later that evening I got a panicked phone call from Dan. 'Someone has stolen the BAFTA!'

I thought this was hilarious and laughed.

'This is not ... this is not funny!' he blustered. 'You may have to answer questions to the police! You may all have to answer questions to the police!'

It didn't happen, but what a marvellous series of official statements that would have been.

Despite his disgruntlement Dan took a few of us to America to recreate the show. We were flown to New York where a stretch limo waited to ferry us to the studio. This was exciting. By chance we passed through Times Square just as video of myself was being shown on the giant screen as part of the opening credits. Possibly not thinking it through, Dan had also decided to fly over the designer and carpenter who worked on the show in London. We arrived in the New York studio to find they had exactly recreated the set we used at home. This meant that for anyone watching in the UK nothing suggested that we were abroad. The only indication that we might be somewhere foreign was that the audience, mainly American university students, had absolutely no idea who any of us were. Nor did they understand any of our references or indeed find us particularly funny. It was like a bad dream doing something you're perfectly skilled at and yet failing at every turn.

In a deep depression afterwards, Mike McShane and I decided to go drinking. I can't remember where we started but I know we ended up in a smart place near Central Park. Mike is a large fellow with greater capacity than me, but even he at one point decided we ought to go home. We went out onto the street to find ourselves beside a long rank of horses and carriages waiting to take lovers around the park.

'Let's get one of those,' he slurred. 'My man!' he said to the driver of the first available carriage. 'My good friend Sandi and I need you to take us to the Mark Hotel.' The Mark was a smart establishment on the Upper East Side. It was not the sort of place people were dropped off by horse and carriage. Indeed, these particular modes of transport were not normally used in lieu of a cab at all, but Mike can be very persuasive.

How he loved it. How he roared his delight to passers-by as we clipped along. By the time we got to the Mark he was beside himself with the thrill of our adventure.

'Sandi! Sandi!' he exclaimed as he nearly fell climbing down from the carriage. 'We need a photo of us with the horse. Driver! Take a picture of me and my friend with the horse.'

This was long before camera phones, so the photo had to

be taken with Mike's proper camera. The driver duly obliged. This caused Mike to love the driver more than he could say. He hugged him, declaring, 'You're a fantastic guy! Hey, wait a minute! We need a picture of you with me and Sandi and the horse!'

Just then a resident at the hotel was arriving back from his evening out.

'You!' Mike called to him. 'Come and take a picture of me and my friends and the horse.'

It was New York. Probably nothing seems strange. The man came over and took the photo. Now Mike loved the man. 'You are a great guy. Isn't he great, Sandi? Okay, we need a picture with you as well.'

Now Mike gave the camera to the driver, who took a picture of the stranger with me, Mike and the horse.

The American version of *Whose Line* with us in it was not deemed a success. The show would go on to triumph with American comics, but we Brits were all sent home. Not in a stretch limo this time. In showbusiness, you can always tell when things have not gone well as you stand on a corner hailing your own cab to get back from a gig. A few weeks later Mike called me, crying with laughter. He had the pictures from that night developed, and I still have one in a box somewhere. It's a photo of me, Mike, a horse and Lionel Richie – who, it turned out, was the man we had hailed to take a picture.

The BAFTA was eventually returned anonymously to a London police station by a man saying he'd found it in Hackney Marshes.

It's too early now for alcohol but I do want to escape the bus, so I stop for a bite at a shop and café called Persepolis. I've had bad asthma lately and can't seem to take a full breath. The air is heavy today and the traffic fumes seem to crush my lungs. My fourteen-year-old stepdaughter has been in trouble at school for bunking off to go on the climate change marches. I think she is splendid. If I were fourteen I'd be mad at the whole world too. My generation has made such a mess of things, but I begin to have faith that the youngsters may be the salvation of us all.

A sign in the window of the café asks 'Have you any idea how many very lovely calories are lurking in our sweet display counter ready for your delectation? Pop in and drool awhile. From £9/kg.' I haven't any idea, and wonder if it costs nine pounds a kilo for the sweets or for the weight you put on.

Persepolis advertises itself as a 'Taste of Persia'. It's not a fancy place but I am transported from my life into the spices and fragrances of that great culture. It is a global corner of London. Beside Persepolis, more tastes of the world offer themselves on this corner. There is an Afro-Caribbean Food and French Grocery, a Vietnamese and Chinese Mini Market and a halal chicken shop. Across the street a poster proclaims that Jesus is the only way to greatness. The door over which it hangs is shuttered up.

To the rest of Britain, Peckham probably means *Only Fools and Horses*. The legendary sitcom was set here and the lead character, Derek Trotter, often talked about the splendour of his manor. How right he was. The Domesday Book shows there was a 'Manor of Peckham' as far back as 1086. Outside the Best Western Hotel on the corner of Lyndhurst Way there is a replica of the three-wheeled van made famous by the show. Today the hotel has a large sign advertising job vacancies. They're looking for a 'Chef, Secretary, Hotel manager, Porter, Handy man and Receptionist'. This seems to me to be pretty much everyone you need to run a hotel and I wonder how they are managing.

I've spent much of my life in hotels and wonder if it has left me with any of the necessary skills to work in one. I doubt it. My main hotel-related talent is ordering room service. That sounds terrible. As if I spent my early years lying on a bed calling down for foie gras. I did spend a lot of my childhood living in hotels, but it certainly wasn't glamorous. Mostly I remember feeling unsettled. My father was always travelling, and we went with him, so Nick and I were often far from home. (This was before Jeni was born.) Indeed, we travelled so much that I remember once, when a car rental clerk asked Dad for his permanent residence, he gave the address of the Samsonite suitcase company.

I suppose no one worried about kids the way they do now. When I say hotel, mostly it would be a motel alongside one highway or another in the US. My brother and I would look out for any neon sign advertising a swimming pool and get Dad to pull in. He would be tired from driving and didn't really care where we went. Mum? I don't remember her having a view. These roadside places were always basic at best and dinner sometimes came from a vending machine in the corridor which blinked bright lights and buzzed all night.

Nick and I would share a twin room, usually with a small table between the beds on which stood an old-fashioned telephone. My parents would go out for dinner and leave the phone receiver off the hook on the table. In theory the woman (it was always a woman) on the switchboard could listen in to make sure we were all right. It was someone literally phoning in babysitting. If they were listening they would have heard me and Nick playing the sock game.

In the late 1960s there was no endless TV available. I don't remember a TV set at all in most of the motels. We were always in a rented car so we couldn't travel with a load of toys or books. Left to our own devices in an empty, strange bedroom, we played a game with a rolled-up pair of socks. We would turn the lights out and then one of us would try to hit the other with the ball of socks. Each strike in the dark gained you a point. I won every time, but I still feel bad about it. For one of his birthdays Nick had been given a watch with a luminous dial. Wherever he tried to hide in the room I could always see him. It wasn't until he turned fifty that I finally told him the truth. All those years later he was still furious. I don't blame him. It was shameful of me.

After the sock game we would eventually lie down to sleep, except I never could in those endlessly unfamiliar places. I would lie looking at the babysitting phone wondering if anyone could hear me breathing. They did not seem to have heard the sock game, or if they had no one had said a word. Occasionally I would whisper 'Hello?' towards the resting receiver but no one ever answered. Nick would crash out and I would lie there feeling responsible for him even though he was older than me. I'd stay awake until Mum and Dad returned. I don't know why I took it upon myself to be the guardian.

It was the same when my sister was born. I was eleven when she came along. From the day she arrived my parents trusted me with her. They would go out for the evening and leave her asleep in her cot. Nick would watch TV, but I would sit on the floor beside the sleeping baby with one hand slipped through the bars of the cot and laid on her stomach to make sure she didn't stop breathing. All this being on guard has left me a poor sleeper. I feel I must protect those near me in case there is an emergency. I have a constant image of myself holding up a shield and never resting. I think I would like to put it down soon.

We pass by the Best Western and I wonder if it is as good as my favourite British hotel, on the Isle of Wight. Deb and I only stayed once but it was possibly my most memorable hotel visit. I had been persuaded to take part in a literary festival, in return for which my wife and I would have the pleasure of the island for the weekend. One of the great difficulties of touring in this country is getting a hot meal after 9 p.m. If you don't want pizza, Chinese or Indian it can be tricky. We arrived at the hotel in the afternoon and the receptionist asked if there was anything they could do to improve our stay.

'Well,' I replied, 'we're going off to an event, but we'll be back at eight thirty and it would be marvellous to have a hot meal.'

'Ah,' said the receptionist, sorry she had asked. 'The kitchen closes at eight thirty.'

I nodded. 'Okay, well, we'd be happy with anything. I mean, it could be kept warm in the oven.'

She shook her head. 'Health and safety. Can't have the oven on without the chef there. Eight thirty is the cut-off point.'

'So, if we're back at eight twenty-five we could have a meal?'

She conceded that we could, but was clearly unhappy about it.

I went off and did my event in a tent on a cliff top buffeted by an incredibly strong wind. It went rather well, although that may have been because people couldn't hear me, or they thought they were about to be thrown to the rocks below and might as well have a laugh.

I zipped through the book signing and we got back to the hotel at 8.25 to discover that the restaurant staff had set a table for us in the foyer. It was a table for two right by the revolving front door. Anyone coming or going had to walk past us. We ordered our meal. It was served by the chef wearing his zipped-up anorak; he then sat in a chair by reception with his arms folded across his chest, watching us eat. He was the picture of fury and we probably didn't help his mood by laughing all evening.

Peckham Road / Southampton Way

The bus is littered with abandoned copies of *Metro* and the *Evening Standard*. I expect not many people know that it was a woman, Elizabeth Mallet, who published the first British newspaper. On 11 March 1702 she produced the first edition of the *Daily Courant* from premises above the White Hart pub, 'against the Ditch at Fleet Bridge'. It probably wasn't a great read, consisting as it did of a single sheet of news with advertisements on the back. Mrs Mallet advertised that she intended to publish only foreign news and claimed that she would not take it upon herself to add any comments of her own, supposing other people to have 'sense enough to make reflections for themselves'. Would that someone in the news business still thought like that.

I have had the worst of the tabloid press in my time, and possibly none worse than in September 1994. My son, Ted, was six months old, his sisters, Jesse and Meg, were six and four. Delightful and a handful like any gang of kids. Peta, their birth mother, and I lived in Guildford, where I spent much of my time avoiding the roads where I had been so unhappy at school. Now it's quite the norm for lesbians to have children but back then we didn't know any other couples like us.

One evening the doorbell rang and a scruffy, overweight man declared he was from the *Daily Mirror* and did I know that the *Daily Mail* had been following me for weeks? I did not. I tend to go about the world a touch disengaged. I suspect an entire Tour de France peloton could follow me and I might not notice. The upshot was that we were to be 'outed'. Peta, who did not and does not live in the public eye, was quite rightly terrified. I too was afraid but not prepared to allow the fear to overcome us. I decided to spoil things for the *Daily Mail* by doing an article in the *Sunday Times*. In my experience, the *Mail* are bullies and you have to stand up to that when you can.

Our three wonderful children had been born by donor insemination, with all of them biologically fathered by Chris Lloyd-Pack, brother of the actor Roger Lloyd-Pack who, as it happens, played Trigger in *Only Fools and Horses*. Chris and I had been friends long before I met Peta and before he was introduced to his then wife Philippa. My pre-emptive article came out and no one we knew was the least bit surprised. Our families were all fine, our close friends too, but these were different times. There were hardly any out lesbians in the public eye. If there were any in entertainment at all then I didn't know about them. The *Daily Mail* were displeased to say the least that we had spoiled their lovely surprise. They contacted my agent to see if they might reprint the *Sunday Times* article in their own paper. We thought it would be a good way for us to control the story, so it was agreed on condition that no comment was added to the piece. The next day the paper appeared with the words 'If God had meant lesbians to have children he would have made it possible' as a strapline on the front page. It was a ridiculous sentence. Clearly we did have children, so it was possible, but logic has never been the paper's strong suit. The editor, Paul Dacre, had entirely broken his promise to publish without comment. We knew the paper had phoned almost everyone in our address book until at last they struck pay dirt with Chris's then mother-in-law. I had met her many times, she had been to my house for dinner, I thought she was part of the family, but that didn't stop her taking the moral high ground. She was the one whose insights into God's feelings about our kids had been quoted. Her considerable diatribe was printed alongside the original article. It fanned the flames of hatred and ignored the deep love at the heart of the story.

The death threats arrived swiftly. Threats today arrive via social media, which has been a boon to the deranged as they don't even have to form full sentences, but back then there was a bit more effort put into being unpleasant. These were proper letters sent by Royal Mail with a stamp and everything. They were so often written in green ink that it made you wonder what it was about that particular colour which attracted the disturbed mind.

Once my 'outrageous' private life was made public the green-ink brigade took it upon themselves to write to me with rather impressively detailed ways in which they were going to kill me and my family. They usually also declared that they were working on God's behalf, which suggested God was busy and they were picking up the slack. All of the haters shared suspect spelling skills and an inside track to the heavenly deity. The press gathered outside the house, making us an even more obvious target. We knew it wasn't safe to stay, so in the dead of night we carried the sleeping children across the garden to a back gate where a disused track led us to a waiting car. I have never been so frightened in my life. We went into hiding for two weeks with Peta's father and each night I would sit beside my sleeping kids awake with terror.

For quite a while we lived in fear, spending our days keeping our worries from the kids and letting them believe it was all a fun holiday. I knew I couldn't give up. That I had to stand up for the life I was leading. The children's school was wonderful, protecting them from intrusion by journalists, and today our babies are all grown up and amazing adults. Peta and I never really recovered from the stress of that time. Not long afterwards we sadly split. However, we are still family and remain friends. When Debbie and I got married at the Royal Festival Hall she was there. Our son, Ted, spoke at the ceremony.

'I am glad we can celebrate gay marriage today,' he said, 'but my generation is baffled about why it took so long.'

Just like my dad and my brother, my Danish grandfather, Harald Toksvig, often worked as a journalist. Farfar had a sign above his desk which read, 'No journalist should write that which he cannot say as a gentleman.' It's a sentiment ripe for a comeback.

I pass some hoardings, behind which a large red sign proclaims the name Kennedy. This was once the home of the legendary Kennedy sausage. The sausages are no longer available, but they must have been something as there is a website still singing their praises. On it a man called Alan Edwards has written such a fulsome eulogy to the Kennedy banger that even President Kennedy by comparison would have felt he had not been sufficiently remembered. There are links (which seems appropriate) to YouTube videos of actual Kennedy sausages sizzling. I love passion perhaps more than anything. I think life is nothing without it and we all strive to feel it every day for those we love and for what we do, and even if it's just for sausages it is a fine thing.

The first Kennedy's shop opened in 1877 and then spread out across London. Where my bus now stands in traffic, 86 Peckham Road, was the head office and factory. Others have posted Kennedy love on Alan's website, including the information that 'Kennedy's also had a very large house in Sandown on the Isle of Wight, with chalets in the grounds, where the staff could take their summer holidays'. How marvellous. Would that employers might always treat their staff like that.

On the other side of the road lies the Oliver Goldsmith Primary School, forever to be remembered as the school the slain ten-year-old Damilola Taylor once attended. It is named after Oliver Goldsmith, the Irish novelist, playwright and poet, which is splendid for he is an excellent example for children. Hogarth called him an 'inspired idiot', a description which is perhaps the best any of us can hope for. There is inspiration and idiocy in equal measure in this neighbourhood. Next door is Camberwell College of Art, where presumably there is inspiration, and beside it a row of elegant Georgian houses from 1790 which once housed the Camberwell House Lunatic Asylum.

The asylum opened in 1846 as the Victorians began to apply their typical bricks-and-mortar solution to a social problem. For generations there had been private 'madhouses' where the rich could lock up their less agreeable relatives but the poor roamed the streets or went to the workhouse, where they were often abused. Then the law changed and local government was required to care for the hard-up in separate establishments. Camberwell House was such a place. On the surface it seemed pleasant: twenty acres of gardens with park-like features and a place for patients to grow vegetables as part of their treatment. Tennis courts and a cricket pitch where they might regain their physical health. Such utopian notions didn't last long. Straitjackets and sedatives entered the picture and in the early twentieth century lobotomies and electroconvulsive therapy began to be experimented with.

I wonder if Oliver Goldsmith would have made TV if he had been around today. I feel he would have. He seemed to like all writing. I love making television. I like the whole range of it, from acting to game shows. The bit I don't like is when someone takes it too seriously. Perhaps one of the worst shows I ever did was *Laughlines*, back in 1990 with the indefatigable Nicholas Parsons hosting. British Satellite Broadcasting, which would grow into the vast empire that is Sky TV, was about to launch and they prepared for it by changing the face of television for ever. Gone were the repeat fees that performers had relied upon to see them through the lean times and in came 'buy outs' where, for a single sum, the broadcaster now owned your work in perpetuity.

No disrespect to the creators of the show, but *Laughlines* was not a work of genius. The game began with Nicholas reading out two lines of a poem. A hilarious panel of allegedly witty folk, plus me, came up with an instant second couplet which had, of course, been written weeks before and a member of the audience had to guess which word we would complete the verse with. The lack of substance in the format meant we were rather dependent on the punter being good value.

A marvellous woman called Sheila was introduced to the team as the ultimate contestant. Sheila was large and effusive.

'Mad, me. Quite mad,' she declared when I met her in make-up. 'But I'll do well. I've already done quite well on *The Pyramid Game*. Did you see it?'

I shook my head. I 'do' game shows but I'm not an expert. For all I knew, *The Pyramid Game* involved actual pyramids and Sheila looked too large to scale one. One of the researchers leant over to me and whispered confidentially, 'Sheila's our star contestant. We've *never* had better.'

I eyed her with renewed admiration, and she seemed to deserve it. Throughout the rehearsals Sheila sparkled, Sheila chirped, and Sheila was 'mad, just mad, me'. It was exhausting. She was more showbiz than Nicholas Parsons. Then, during the course of the day, drama began to develop. Sheila's shocking pink frock, which she had brought with her to wear on the show, had, by all accounts, been 'ruined' by the wardrobe mistress. There were loud recriminations and vague animal cries of distress which echoed down the dressing-room corridor. Now Sheila's feet began to swell. 'It's the stress, you see.'

A rumour circulated that a collection of empty whisky miniatures had been found in Sheila's overnight bag. I think someone confronted her and she fell apart in a great wobble of wailing. Sitting alone in my dressing room, I was bored to death and the tale of the whisky prompted me to wonder if there was time for a beer before the show. It was hardly work that needed my full focus. I was wandering off to the canteen when the producer stopped me. She held me by both shoulders and looked down into my eyes.

Oh God, she knows I was going to have a beer, I thought. I braced myself for a warning.

'Sandi, I have something serious to tell you,' she began. It's worse than I thought, I decided, I've been fired from a terrible show. She nodded slowly and squeezed me gently.

'Now, I am depending on you, Sandi, because I know you can cope.' Had Nicholas died? 'We're going to have to pull Sheila.' There was a long pause. Where to? I thought. Another pause. The producer gripped my arms tighter.

'Do you understand, Sandi? Sheila's off the show.'

'Right,' I said and then was silent. It seemed like a bad time to ask her about getting that beer.

By chance I was there when Sheila was told. She flung herself at her boyfriend's neck.

'It's right, of course, I know it's right,' she wailed, 'but it's so hard.'

A replacement Sheila was located and arrived fifteen minutes before the show. She was great. Relaxed, easy-going and even marginally mad as required. Sheila behaved beautifully. She pulled herself together and begged to be allowed to sit in

the audience. By now everyone felt bad, so she was allowed a
back-row seat, where she remained clutching her boyfriend's
hand as we recorded four shows back to back. All afternoon
she kept a fixed grin on her face, determined not to let the
other contestants suffer because of her breakdown. The show
was dreadful. The business with Sheila, however, would have
made great TV.

Vestry Road

Vestry – a room in a church where clergy put their vestments on, or possibly a meeting place of locals dealing with local matters. I love the people who provide the most local of government. They do the real work. The council have been trying to stop Transport for London cutting bus routes, citing the impact on the poorest and most vulnerable, who are usually those who must travel the furthest. I don't know what they can do about cuts to the arts. There are plenty of people who don't think it matters, so Deb and I have been trying in a tiny way to prove them wrong. We have been involved with helping to put drama lessons into one of the most deprived schools in the area. Anecdotally, the results are phenomenal. A young girl who had not spoken in class and was about to be statemented as having special needs has come to life through acting. The teachers are using the tools they have learned from the drama coach in other lessons. A friend of ours who is an education analyst says you can see the good it is doing but there is so much more to be done. At the end of the second year of the programme the kids were promised they could give a performance in a proper theatre. They did, but it broke our hearts when not one parent came. I don't think it had anything to do with parents not caring but everything to do with our needing to reach out even further.

Vestry Road represents the place where I finally tied the knot. Get off here and you find the register office where Deb and I officially upgraded from civil partnership to marriage. It lies in Lucas Gardens, originally the grounds of a terrace of twelve Georgian houses and later used as an extension to the Camberwell House Lunatic Asylum. It's now a small public park with winding paths and mature trees. How odd to legally marry in the same place where not long ago our homosexuality might have been treated as a mental illness.

Down beside the park lies a block of converted flats whose name suggests it once housed a piano factory. Behind it lies an unexpected place called Vanguard Court. It was here that the bodies of some of the first London omnibuses were built. Until the 1980s it was also the site of the Vanguard Luggage factory which turned out millions of suitcases. Indeed, the Vanguard attaché case was standard issue for British forces in the Second World War. Today the narrow cobbled street is still lined with low workshops. Just yards from the busy main road it is an oasis of old craft. This feels like ancient London for there are jewellers, potters, sculptors and stone masons going about their business. A sign on a half-shuttered door instructs me to 'Make tea not war' and advises that Guinness is good for you. A bust of a man's head sporting a bright red hard hat sits out amongst some plants. The place where they make 'nostalgic glass' is closed but one man has his wide garage-like doors open. He is building something vast out of wood which reaches up to the apex of the twenty or so foot ceiling.

'What are you making?' I ask.

'I am creating moral turpitude,' he declares, sanding his creation with a hand-held piece of sandpaper.

'And for whom do you create it?'

'Ant and Dec,' he mutters.

He was making sets for one of their shows.

I met Ant and Dec once at an awards ceremony and they were delightful. I admire them and suspect most people have no idea how skilled they are. I can't remember what the event was, but I know I was hosting. As usual the lectern was tall and not designed for a small woman trying to keep an evening motoring along, so I was standing behind it on a wooden box. Ant and Dec won their umpteenth award for presenting and as Ant stepped onto my small platform he broke the side of it off. Dec carried on speaking while Ant and I tried to bang the nails back in using the glass award. As they departed I turned to the audience and said, 'That's why I never let boys mess with my box.'

I've been asked to go out to be in their celebrity jungle but it's not for me. How I dislike the word celebrity, yet it seems so popular now. I don't remember anyone ever talking about fame or recognition when I first started work but now 'being a celebrity' is an ambition some strive for. I don't think I had any specific ambition. I fell into the business which is my life. A professional theatre director called Richard Digby Day saw me in a revue show at Cambridge and asked me to go and work for him after graduation. He had just become the artistic director at Nottingham Playhouse. Why not? I thought. Have a gap year after university.

I made my professional debut in the musical *The Boy Friend*.

'I can't really sing or dance,' I told Richard honestly. He shrugged and replied, 'Act as if you can.' Imelda Staunton was also in that show and we shared a dressing room. We used to sit in it waiting for the show to begin. Actors are called to the stage over a Tannoy and those who are on first are known as 'beginners'. Imelda and I were beginners. We would wait for the call and then see who dared to stay longest and walk directly from the dressing room out onto the stage at the right moment. I would never do this now. Ah, the arrogance of youth.

A glorious actress called Dilys Hamlett starred as Madame Dubonnet. She had been in the business all her life and she never spoke about fame or celebrity. Indeed, the only advice she ever gave me was, 'My dear, if you must do Shakespeare, always play kings and queens. You never carry props and you always get a seat.'

Richard kept me in work for a year in one job or another. Sometimes I had a lot to do, sometimes he was simply keeping me there to be kind. I loved just being allowed to be in the theatre and did literally sweep the stage to stay in work. On one show my sole job was to keep the lead actress company during the day so that she was sober enough to work in the evening. The Christmas show that year was Stephen Sondheim's musical A *Little Night Music*. Richard cast me as a servant, and once again I had to pretend I could sing. The show starred the legendary Evelyn Laye, who had been a West End and Broadway star and famously worked with Noël Coward. Now she was in her eighties, and her memory was not what it was.

Night Music features, amongst other parts, a young girl of about twelve. Richard had had a problem casting the child as Evelyn did not like any of them. One afternoon I was passing her and Richard at the stage door when she pointed at me and declared, 'Her! I want her!'

So, at the age of twenty-two I was cast as a twelve-year-old wearing a sailor dress and an ill-fitting wig. I had several scenes with Evelyn and part of my job was to push her in her wheelchair while whispering her lines in her ear. This should have been a fail-safe system for her imperfect memory except that she couldn't hear well either. I remember a celebrated night when she didn't catch a word I had said. It was the end of the scene and she was supposed to declaim to the audience a final dramatic line and then have me push her off. Instead she loudly said, 'Rasher of bacon!'

And then gave a great flourish of her arm while I wheeled her away. To my utter astonishment there was a wild round of applause. I learned then that it is not so much what you say on stage as how you say it.

Evelyn once spent a whole afternoon rehearsing her first entrance, which had to be downstage centre in the right light. She spent as much time worrying about the lining of her gown as the gown itself.

'How can you be so patient?' I asked Richard.

'Because it's worth it,' he replied, and it was. Whether she recalled her lines or not she was amazing. The audience loved her. She had that indefinable thing, 'star quality'. Each night she would enjoy a bottle of champagne in her room after the show. Occasionally I would be invited in. After many weeks of working I was finally allowed to call her by her nickname 'Boo' instead of Miss Laye.

'I have been thinking about your career,' she declared one evening.

'Yes, Boo?' I sipped my unaccustomed champagne and waited.

'I'm going to ring Charles B. Cochrane and have him look after you.'

It was kind, except Mr Cochrane had been dead for about thirty years.

Boo came from a different showbiz generation. When she had toured America with Noël Coward she had done so in her own train carriage featuring her name in lights on the side which lit up when they passed through stations. Boo was a star, but it was not something the rest of the company seemed to aspire to. We just wanted to do a good job. There were plenty of what were known as jobbing actors: fine craftspeople who worked all the time but whose names were unknown to the general public.

There were excellent comedians who did three months of pantomime and three months of summer season year after year with no need or apparent desire for anything in between. I don't recall a single discussion about fame backstage in the early years.

Had the modern notion of celebrity existed then I doubt I would ever have gone into the business. Being famous for its own sake is madness.

Now on reality programmes budding performers talk of little else. I met a young man recently and I asked him what he wanted to do.

'I want to be famous,' he replied.

'As what?' I asked.

He shrugged. 'Not bothered.'

I suppose not being bothered was a good thing. It left him with a wide range of options for the spotlight, from singer to serial killer. Of all the great things which go with my job – the people, the work, the places, the privilege – I think the fame part is the bit I like the least. There are nice bits, treats which happen along, but some of it is very strange.

Perhaps my disinterest in fame stems from my beloved father, who was a journalist and broadcaster. Throughout my childhood he worked for Danish television; in fact, for a while he pretty much was Danish television. In the early 1960s there was only one channel in Denmark – indeed, television was so new that the official broadcaster was, and still is, called Danish Radio. Transmission began at 7 p.m., which meant turning on the TV at 6.55 so it could warm up. The broadcast opened with Dad reading the news. There were very few filmed reports so mostly it was just him reading. For an hour. Then there would be perhaps a half-hour documentary about the Queen's silver spoon collection or suchlike and then the service would close down. My father was two-thirds of all available television.

He was probably the most famous man in the whole of Denmark. So famous that I remember going to a restaurant called Grøften in the Tivoli Gardens in Copenhagen and all the men standing up, bowing their heads and clicking their heels as my father passed by.

In 1966, when I was eight, Papa gave up reading the news and we moved to the United States. My father was to become Danish Radio's American correspondent. Actually, he was to become Danish Radio's only foreign correspondent. Having someone actually reporting from another country was a new idea and no one was sure it was going to work. It was generally agreed that if he went to New York and was based at the United Nations then he could cover the entire world.

News is so ubiquitous today that it's hard to imagine what it used to be like. My father worked with a small team – a sound engineer and a cameraman – who also imported their families from Denmark to bring the latest from the United States to the Danish public. About twice a week they would film a report about something. It was proper celluloid film in those days and the finished reel would be placed in a flat silver tin and taken out to the airport. I would often go with my dad on these trips out to JFK. We would stand near the gate where people were checking in for flights to Copenhagen. He would be puffing on his pipe while he explained to me the political importance of whatever story he had been covering. Almost inevitably some Dane in the queue would recognise Dad and he would engage them in cheerful banter before asking them if they would mind taking the film and getting it to Danish Radio. It would often take twenty-four hours from the end of filming to the receipt of the footage on the Danish editor's desk. News was never instant and I'm not sure the world was any poorer for it.

My father wore his fame lightly. He was unfailingly polite to everyone who stopped him. I never saw him display a moment of irritation, even when it was not convenient to be interrupted, and nor did I ever see him try to increase his fame on purpose. It was a measure of the man that at his funeral our local postman and the Prime Minister of Denmark were seated beside each other.

I have tried my best to follow his example and not seek publicity for its own sake. When I make something or write something of course I want to tell people about it, but then suddenly the world wants more. They want to follow you through your own front door and look in all your cupboards. More than twenty years after they caused me and my kids such pain, the *Daily Mail* have once again been doorstepping my family because apparently the public have a 'right to know' about the life of the host of *The Great British Bake Off*. Know what, I am not sure.

I head away from Vanguard Court and go past the open door of a stone mason who I can hear is busy grinding or polishing something. I should like that. Spending the day making something substantial before shutting the door and going home. There is a wonderful story about the American-Danish sculptor Gutzon Borglum, the man who carved presidents into Mount Rushmore. He was having a practice on some blocks of marble in his studio (well, you wouldn't want to make a mistake on a mountain) when a little girl came to visit. The half-finished face of one of the presidents was beginning to take shape and the little girl stared at it.

'Is that Abraham Lincoln?' she asked.

'Yes,' replied the sculptor.

The little girl looked again before enquiring, 'How did you know he was in there?'

St Giles' Church

A man in a leather jacket is speaking loud and fast into his phone. He is very cross about something and shouts. Some people treat the phone as no better than two tin cans and a piece of string. A guy across the way has two phones, which appear to be plugged into each other. Maybe the phones are starting to cut out the middle man.

At Shenley Road we passed from Peckham into Camberwell. It's a place of great history, with the Domesday Book recording it as *Ca'berwelle*, owned by Haimo the Sheriff, who sounds pleasingly like a man with a badge and a ten-gallon hat. When Haimo owned the place, in 1089, twenty-nine people were living there and it was worth fourteen quid. Camberwell is now rocking with history and packed with people.

There once was an actual well which some believed to be not only a portal to the past but a place where the offer of a coin might reveal the future. The waters were also said to contain healing properties and so people came from far and wide to drink and be cleansed by them. Some believe that it was also the home of a mermaid who was captured and put on show at the annual Camberwell Fair during the nineteenth century. According to Henry Colburn's comprehensive *Kalendar of Amusements*, Camberwell Fair ranked high in the entertainment stakes:

> There is here, and only here to be seen what you can see no where else, the lately-caught, and highly-accomplished young

Mer-maid, about whom the continental journals have written
so ably. She combs her hair in the manner practised in China,
and admires herself in a glass in the manner practised – everywhere. She has had the best instructors in every peculiarity
of education, and can argue on any given subject, from the
most popular way of preserving plums, down to the necessity
of a change of Ministers ... Being so clever and accomplished
she can't bear to be contradicted, and lately leaped out of her
tub and floored a distinguished fellow of the Royal Zoological
Society, who was pleased to be more curious and cunning than
she was pleased to think agreeable.

She eventually escaped from the fair and rumour had it that
this was made possible by the help of none other than her friend
and fellow sideshow attraction Lucy Wanmer, that great Little
Woman of Peckham. Did they both find comfort in discovering
someone who understood what being gawped at felt like? There
is something wonderful about knowing this tiny little woman
helped her friend swim away. Today she'd have had her own
television show.

I get off to look at St Giles' church. I think I ought to ana-
lyse more thoroughly my disdain for religion combined with
my attraction to places of worship. There has been a place
of Christian devotion on this site for more than a thousand
years. The present church was built in 1844 following a fire;
it has a fine spire which dominates the area. If you get up high
in London it is the church spires that help you identify where
the old villages once existed. Designed by Sir Gilbert Scott, I
had read that St Giles' contained stained glass by John Ruskin
which, because I am a geek, I wanted to see, but the church is
closed and I am disappointed. From the outside I can see no

stained-glass windows of any kind. Just crumbling stonework and a sign warning me that the building is protected by 'smart forensic water', which sounds like something made up.

I suppose the buildings have to be locked against damage now. A bright blue sign in one of the windows warns me not to break in. I am too short to reach the window so it seems unlikely but I should have liked to sit in solitude for a while. Everyone could do with stepping away from the world sometimes. Above the door there is a tiny figure representing St Giles with a deer. Like most hermits, he was an odd fellow. He lived in a cave in France about AD 700 and had a pet deer which, in the range of available pets, never occurred to me as an option. The story goes that one day, while shielding his deer from huntsmen, he was wounded in the arm by an arrow. I would have thought it was a poor hunter who couldn't see a saint in the way, but it led to Giles' career as 'patron of cripples', which is not something comfortable even to write about these days.

The name Camberwell may mean 'Well of the Britons' but it could equally derive from either 'well of the crooked' or 'cripples' well'. The actual well (in which obviously the mermaid lived) was said to still exist up until about 150 years ago. Because it was thought to be a place of healing St Giles also had the good fortune to be made patron saint of lepers.

Quite rightly no one uses the word 'cripple' any more although my friend Sharon, who is as genuine a Londoner as you can find, did say to me the other day that her mother had hurt her shoulder and was now a 'proper raspberry'. 'Raspberry?' I enquired. She shook her head at my ignorance. 'Raspberry ripple ... cripple.'

I am still on the hunt for any woman from history who has been commemorated on my bus route. The absence of women in public spaces has bothered me all my life. I don't just mean memorials. While I was at university I joined a comedy group called the Cambridge Footlights. I had acted at school and it looked like fun. There were many boys being hilarious but very few women. I met Jan Ravens, who was studying to be a teacher, and Emma Thompson, who was reading English, and the three of us began to realise that the boys were not remotely interested in letting us be funny; that if we wanted to say anything in a sketch other than 'The doctor will see you now' before departing to let them be funny we would have to write the material ourselves. Tired of waiting for a chance to raise a laugh, Emma and I decided to write our own show. We ignored Footlights and applied to the student theatre, the ADC, to produce a late-night show. We had no material at all. In fact, I seem to remember our list of sources for our sketches included Béarnaise, which we must have thought was hilarious.

We called the show *Woman's Hour*. The boys mocked and were generally unhelpful. Jan auditioned, and we cast her along with a wonderful Scots woman called Hilary Duguid. The four of us set out to be funny on our own. We wrote sketches and monologues, and I dressed up as Mae West and sang a song. The opening night, Emma turned up with a completely shaved head, for reasons I can't recall, so we rewrote the opening to accommodate her new look. She wore a shiny pink or purple jumpsuit and in the black-and-white photos from the show she looks like an extra from *Star Trek*. The show was so successful that we did that unheard-of thing for a student production – we made money and had to come back the following term for a second week. The boys were furious and no more welcoming.

Hilary sensibly went into publishing and sadly passed away not long ago. Jan is now the finest of impressionists. And Emma? I have no idea what happened to her.

*

Down Vicarage Grove I wander in search of Una Marson, who everyone ought to know about but may not. A Jamaican feminist, activist, writer, she was the first black woman to produce programmes for the BBC. Finding any women celebrated on my journey is hard. Finding women of colour is harder. Una Marson does at least get a plaque. A blue plaque sits up high on a white house at Brunswick Park, a quiet street off Vicarage Grove. It reads 'Una Marson. 1905–1965. Poet, playwright, campaigner for equality. First black woman programme maker at the BBC.'

I don't stop long to admire it. The truth is I am upset and don't know what to do about it. I got off the bus here yesterday too but that was because of an encounter which has left me shaken. Sometimes the bus is horribly crowded but just occasionally I have it pretty much to myself. Solitude is rare in London and I always enjoy its brief moments. I had been sitting alone on the top deck when a young black girl in school uniform got on. I think she was maybe fourteen or fifteen. I was reading a book about science which was describing to me a world where everything is in flux, where things are always indeterminate. I never studied science at school but I am fascinated by the notion that electrons only come into being when they collide with something else and the unexpected happens. I like that. It feels like a metaphor for life. I was quite lost in what I was reading.

The young girl sat down a few seats behind me and got out her phone. Then she put on a very loud music video. She had no headphones. There was only the two of us and the sound bounced around the bus. Like some terrible old woman I turned around and said, 'Excuse me, would you mind turning that down?' She immediately jumped to her feet and pointed at me, 'You racist!' she shouted.

I'm afraid I laughed – out of surprise or embarrassment, I'm not sure. 'What?' I said.

'You're a racist!' she yelled.

'It's just the video,' I tried. 'It was very loud. I didn't mean anything . . .'

She carried on bellowing at me, accusing me over and over of being a racist, until at last I said, 'I don't think your mother would like you shouting at me.'

There is power in mothers even when they are not present, because this halted her shouting and at the next stop she abruptly got off the bus. I decided to go after her to talk but she had gone and I stood on the pavement confused and distressed by what had happened. I couldn't get my head around it. I hadn't meant anything other than I thought the music was loud but I could see that I was an older white woman telling her to be quiet and that her experience must have meant she saw my request as somehow racially motivated. I needed to think about what her view of life was.

I walk down the street towards Camberwell Grove. It is about six in the evening and the pavements are crowded. Hard to imagine that barley once grew here and possibly even grapes. The houses on this street are stunning. There is a narrow passage which leads to the churchyard and is said to be haunted. Haunted by whom or what I do not know. Legend has it that it was here a man called George Barnwell murdered his uncle. George got a job working for his uncle, a merchant in Shoreditch. Poor George fell in love with a lady of the night called Mrs Millwood, who led him astray and eventually persuaded him to murder his uncle for the money. The story was first published around the 1650s as a ballad rather pleasingly entitled 'An excellent BALLAD of GEORGE BARNWELL, an Apprentice in the City of LONDON, who was Undone by a STRUMPET'.

Undone by a strumpet! We've all been there. As you can imagine, Mrs Millwood did lead him to sorrow and shame – and murder too. Neither George nor Mrs Millwood got away with it and ended their lives on the scaffold. Who knows if George or his uncle haunt this place.

It is thoughts not people that haunt me. At the foot of Camberwell Grove lies a large house named for Mary Datchelor, who in 1726 founded a school here. Now it is expensive flats but for many years it was the home of the Save the Children Fund. How odd that I should see this now. The week after I came out in 1994 I was supposed to host a large event at the Albert Hall for Save the Children. I had been an ambassador for the charity for some years and was looking forward to it. Then I got a call from the organiser asking me to step down. The charity rather hilariously did not want Princess Anne to meet a lesbian. I had met the Princess a few times and thought she was robust enough to have been able to cope. It was a curious message, which seemed to suggest saving the children but not the gay ones.

I see no one as I stroll along the supposed ghost passage to the lovely green garden behind the church. Here, somewhere, little Lucy Wanmer lies, as does John Primero, the first black person to be buried in Southwark. He had a couple of local firsts as in 1607 he became the first black person to be baptised in Southwark, with the ceremony taking place in St Giles'. Primero was the servant of one Sir Thomas Hunt. There have been black British since the twelfth century but in the early seventeenth century the numbers were still small. Thomas Hunt seems to have been a nice guy, leaving a great deal of money for bread for the poor when he died, although he also left money for the churchwardens to buy gloves to wear when distributing it which gives a mixed message. Did Primero suffer prejudice? No doubt. I am certain Una Marson did too.

I sit on a bench and think about hating anyone for just being themselves. I cannot know what that schoolgirl has been through. The only personal experience I have of prejudice is with homophobia. It has been such a constant thread through my life that I confess perhaps sometimes I think I detect it when I shouldn't. The hurt from the endless occasions when it has been directed at me is always just beneath the surface.

Being gay has been something I always knew about myself. If, as I suspect, there is a sliding scale of sexual orientation then I am at one end. From my earliest recollections I had absolutely no doubt about who I am but that doesn't mean that I have found it easy. I have sometimes lost work and often confidence. I have hated being defined by my sexual inclination when it is possibly the least interesting thing about me. It is not an exaggeration to say that I have on occasion felt crippled by it, so how appropriate to sit in the shadow of St Giles'. Now I am older I am happy to be who I am and hopeful that I have helped others feel less pain. I have, however, had to protect myself and my family for years, and it means I am always on my guard. No doubt the young woman on the bus had had a belly full of poor treatment in her lifetime and it's not surprising that she was angry. Clearly my comment and I reminded her of other experiences. I felt devastated that I might inadvertently have hurt her.

The only gravestone in St Giles' churchyard I can read is for a Thomas Bourne. He has a stone casket surrounded by his own iron railings. Even in death the rich get more space. I travel on the bus because I choose to, but I have other options. It's good to be reminded that everyone has a different story.

Camberwell Church Street / Camberwell Green

Buses seem to come from every direction at this interchange and it is hard to imagine this was once a rural idyll. I look down from my window and spy a young woman getting a twenty-pound note from a cash machine in the wall of a dry cleaner's next to a shop selling vegetables. Another shop sells yams and fixes mobile phones. It is a curious combination. At Cruson's fruit and veg shop an old woman is painstakingly going through all the onions netted in large red bags to find just the ones she wants. An old man in a flat cap and green buttoned overalls waits patiently to sell them to her. He looks from another era, just like the man who used to put groceries in brown paper bags for my British grandmother. I wonder if this man knows that today is the anniversary of the first banana being sold in Britain, on 10 April 1633. What is wrong with me that I retain this sort of information?

I watch the people of Camberwell going about their business. I wonder how many of their stories will get told. Will the ordinary life of this part of London be remembered? I have started taking pictures of shoe shops I see along the way. They are called things like Elite Shoes, Men's Traditional Shoes or Barrie Howard Shoes. They have window displays which seem unchanged from my childhood. Shoes for the wider fitting and an astonishing array of fluffy slippers.

It is a lovely warm evening so I stop and wander past the open windows of the Hermits Cave pub. It is one of the greatest pleasures of my journey to find endless interruption. The pub is on the corner of Grove Lane. I've never been in but it looks a no-nonsense sort of place. It has been serving the locals since 1902 but there has been beer in this place for far longer. According to the local historian Mary Boast, two women brewers were recorded in Camberwell as early as 1275.

The Hermits Cave (no apostrophe by design, apparently) is an old-fashioned watering hole with a painting of a bearded hermit swinging on the sign. He looks rather mournful as he sits staring out from the mouth of a cave, perhaps wishing he could give up seclusion and share a pint with someone. Perhaps he is St Giles. Hard to tell. I doubt he sat for either the picture or the statue above the church.

Inside one of the open windows a pair of what used to be known unkindly as 'bottle blonde' older women are having a drink. One of them calls out to me, 'Oi, you! Sandi Topstick!'

She smiles and waves. She is drinking a vast glass of red wine and her teeth are stained black with the grape. On her right arm is a relatively new bright purple cast.

'What have you done to yourself?' I ask. She slightly drunkenly raises the arm aloft and declares cheerfully, 'Not just this – gotta go up King's tomorrow for an operation!'

'Oh yes?'

'Got an annerism!' She grins as if having an aneurysm is the very thing women are hoping for these days.

I laugh. 'Is red wine the recommended preparation for this surgery?'

'Abso ... bloody ... lutely,' she affirms and takes a great swig. I love her energy and enthusiasm. She salutes me with her broken arm as her friend shakes her head and I walk on.

I do love the unexpected conversations I have with strangers and which come from being on TV. I've been on television for so long that I think lots of people feel they know me, which is lovely, and they chat to me, which is also nice, but I never cease to be amazed what some folk think is appropriate to tell me. One of the strangest encounters was at a motorway service station on the way to Bournemouth. I was taking my elder daughter, Jesse, to the university there for an open day and we stopped at the services to get coffee. As soon as we entered the place Jesse did what young people seem to be trained to do: she rushed off to a retail opportunity presuming I was following with money. As it happened, I didn't have any on me so I headed to a cash machine. I can't read well without my glasses and I had left them in the car so I was leaning in to the machine and concentrating when a little old lady barrelled up to me. She was wearing something I hadn't seen in years – a Pac-A-Mac, which makes the most marvellous early-warning rustling sound. She was very old indeed. I don't know where she was going. Perhaps she was being made to go on a coach trip to see the sea one last time. She said, 'Hello Sandi.'

'Oh hello,' I said, still trying to focus my eyes on the ATM.

'You're very funny,' she went on.

'That's very kind,' I replied, continuing to attempt my transaction.

'But that's not why I like you.'

I finished what I was doing and turned to look at her. 'No?'

'No,' she declared. 'I like you because you, like me, are not a specific shape.'

And with that she left.

I spy Sophocles Bakery and stop to get a Greek sweet treat. It was Sophocles who said, 'It was my care to make my life illustrious not by words more than by deeds.' He could not have imagined that 'Deeds not words' would become the great slogan of the suffragettes. I have been feminist for as long as I have had the ability to say such a thing. When I was about five my father came back from covering one of the early space missions. He was often away and would bring gifts purchased usually at the airport or sometimes even on the plane. He brought Nick the most marvellous kit to build your own rocket. He brought me a silver necklace. I hated it. I knew perfectly well that I could build a much better rocket than my brother and I was enraged. I still am.

It was on 6 February 1918 that the Representation of the People Act came into force in this country. It gave some women the right to vote. The general consensus in 2018 was that everyone ought to celebrate. I'd not been all that keen as it seems a slightly rubbish anniversary. The new legislation gave the vote to all men over twenty-one but women had to wait until they were thirty in order to tick a box on a piece of paper. They also had to own property or at least have had the foresight to marry a man who had some. This can hardly be hailed as universal suffrage, and no one has talked about the fact that it wasn't until 1958, the year I was born, that women were finally allowed into the second legislative chamber of this country, the House of Lords. Even when we have choice women don't seem to do much better. The Lords is now an appointed chamber yet women still only make up 25 per cent of the Upper House.

Be that as it may, the Women's Equality Party, of which I am the co-founder, wanted to mark 6 February 2018, so a giant projector was hired with the intention of projecting 'Deeds not words' onto the main body of the Houses of Parliament. We discovered that this is, for reasons I can't fathom, illegal but decided to do it anyway. On the night in question I arrived on the south side of Westminster Bridge to find a large white van parked just off the road on a wide bit of the pavement. This was the vehicle which had brought our giant projector. The unmarked van looked exactly like the sort of thing a terrorist might think useful. We had hired some projector people and they were busy trying to get our slide to focus on the Houses of Parliament. This took quite some time yet no police dashed towards us. When the motto of those great campaigners for women's rights, the Women's Social and Political Union, finally came into focus on the side of Parliament how we cheered. It looked splendid in the suffragette colours – purple, green and white.

It wasn't until about fifteen minutes later that we finally heard sirens and saw blue flashing lights. Policemen leapt from vans carrying guns.

'What's going on here then?' demanded one of them.

I stepped forward prepared – eager, even – to be the first person of the WEP to be arrested. I felt I wouldn't really have done my duty to the memory of the suffragettes if I hadn't spent at least one night in the slammer.

'Good evening officer,' I began.

'Oh, hello Sandi!' he replied before turning back to his colleagues and calling out, 'It's only Sandi. It's all right.'

I didn't get arrested. I just got quite a lot of cuddles from the boys in blue as we did selfies. Then after about ten minutes they told us we really needed to go home, so we did.

I pass Wren Road where Christopher Wren may have lived while designing St Paul's Cathedral. It is a small road and I think it unlikely. London is full of places where Wren might have rested. I have a nineteenth-century guidebook (of course I do) which tells me this is the spot where a country mansion once stood. It was so grand it appeared to have 'found its way to Camberwell by mistake'. Such finery is long gone. Now Wren Road is a place ignored and poor. The buildings are packed tightly together. A tiny house has a metal gate on both the front door and the single downstairs window. In the narrowest gap between that building and the next a tree, perhaps a fig, has taken root, its branches and leaves reaching right up to the roof line. It's marvellous.

When my parents moved to the UK they lived as usual in various hotels but eventually bought a house in Reigate in Surrey. The house was quite near where the M25 now thunders but back then the road had been planned and not finished. A great swathe of land had been cleared and small wooden crosses placed along its length like some haphazard burial ground. Then all work had stopped. I don't know why. Money? Indifference? My father and I used to walk up to a bridge which looked down on the empty dirt road. Each time we went more bushes, grass and wild flowers had taken hold. He loved to see nature fighting back.

I am upstairs on the bus as usual. A little girl is blowing on the window and using her finger to trace hearts in the cloud of her breath. I used to dream of romance when I was her age, in fact for a long time after her age too. When I was sixteen, two years after they'd sent me to the awful boarding school, my parents followed me to the UK from America. Danish Radio had decided to expand: they were going madly international and wanted to have a British foreign correspondent as well as an American one. It was such a radical idea that only one person in the world was thought competent enough to fulfil this new European task – my father.

That summer my holiday was spent with them in Brighton. We lived at the Grand Hotel, which in 1974 was anything but. It had not been done up for years and was faded, down at heel. I had an incredibly narrow single room with a strip of a window that looked out over the sea. There was a windowsill just wide enough for me to perch on sideways and I would sit for hours looking out at the people passing along the promenade. I hadn't lived with my parents for two years and felt oddly distant from them. Perhaps when you are sixteen you feel distant from everyone. I know that I thought only about one thing. I wanted to find love. I wanted to find someone who would combine all the qualities of a best friend with a passionate love. I was lonely beyond all measure and I was a teenager awash with hormones who no doubt imagined such profound feelings had never happened to anyone before.

I have been seeking my 'other half' for as long as I can remember having feelings of any kind. I have been lucky enough to find it now, but over the years my heart has broken with regularity. I fell in love at university and when that relationship ended I thought I would never recover. She was two years older than me and we had got together in her last and my first year. I called her Truman because she was president of our college and I teased her that the 'buck stopped' with her, which had been President Truman's catchphrase. In the summer after my second year at Cambridge I became extremely ill. I had a growth which was operated on and I went down to five and a half stone. The doctors advised that I take a year off but that is not my way of doing things. Instead I returned to college with medical letters sent to my tutor, Miss Duke, suggesting rest and as little stress as possible. Avoiding stress seemed unlikely. My father had had the first of three heart attacks and his health was also uncertain.

By now Truman had left Girton and was studying to be a journalist in Portsmouth. When she got a week-long break from her studies she came to Cambridge to check on me. She stayed in my room and we thought nothing of it. Lots of girls up and down the corridor had male partners who lived with them full time. But the head porter reported to the college council that he thought Truman was living with me. The first I knew of it was one morning when I got a message to see my tutor that evening. This was the late 1970s and there were no mobile phones. Any news from home was delivered by one's tutor and I was terrified something might have happened to my father. Miss Duke was mistress of Classics. She was old and lived in rooms in one of the college's Victorian towers. I was so upset about my father that I could not wait until the evening but instead ran to her rooms. I was out of breath from the climb up the tower and knocked rather frantically on her door. She opened it in a temper.

'Come back at office hours!' she barked.

'I just want to know if my father is all right,' I begged.

She knew about his health and mine but slammed the door shut. I raced to the payphone off the main entrance hall but the phone in the hall of my parents' house just rang and rang. I had no choice but to wait all afternoon, until the appointed hour. At last the moment came and Miss Duke opened the door.

'Well,' she said, 'what have you got to say for yourself?'

I had no idea what she was talking about. I was told that a formal investigation would be launched into my suspect relationship with another woman. She said it as if I had brought the plague to the college. It was made very clear that my continued presence at Girton was not welcome. The investigation began and for three long weeks I was kept in suspense as to whether or not I would be allowed to stay. The waiting and not knowing was terrible. Truman went back to her course. I didn't talk to anyone about it. Not my family, not my friends, no one. I was completely alone with my misery.

I couldn't eat and so couldn't get better. The college nurse, who had been helping to care for me and who I had become fond of, now avoided me. The only person who seemed to notice my distress was my next-door neighbour, a fellow law student, Helen, who I called Troy. Giving out nicknames was an odd, old habit. Troy was and is a devout Roman Catholic, but she never wavered in our friendship. She brought me cups of tea and made toast. We didn't talk about what was happening, but she knew perfectly well.

The person who had admitted me to the college in the first place was a law fellow called Jolowicz. One morning I was passing her in the corridor and could bide my time no longer. I was terrified and felt as though I was going to be sick but I called out anyway, 'Professor Jolowicz! I was just wondering, what's happening about the investigation?'

My heart was pounding. I did not want to be made to leave. I couldn't bear the humiliation, but I couldn't stand the waiting any longer.

She frowned as if irritated that I had stopped her at all. 'Oh yes, that. Yes ... we've decided to let you stay because of your excellent academic record.'

And with that she swept on down the corridor. Her apathy towards me was apparent. I think she'd known for ages and not bothered to tell me. If I had been of a more dramatic persuasion I think I would have collapsed on the floor there and then but instead I stood for ages, silent and shocked to my core. The lesson was clear: if you must be gay then at least be clever. After that a cloud hung over me and there were lots of people who never spoke to me again. I had gone from being a jolly, happy member of the college to someone who was shunned. It was the second time in my life I was sent to Coventry. How odd for someone who speaks for a living to have their life so punctuated by silence.

Camberwell Green

Barry Cryer phoned me today. He always calls on my birthday. 'It's your celebrity stalker here!' he declares brightly. Today he said, 'For your birthday I got you a joke which is not for public consumption!' and then went on to tell me a hilarious but unprintable tale of a mean Scotsman and a Jewish ventriloquist. The world of jokes has changed but the man remains a genius.

I keep walking to the Camberwell Green stop. The corner where I am standing is where, in the late eighteenth century, you would have found Camberwell Green farm with its stables, farmyards and barns. It was a traditional green in a small farming village whose biggest excitement for more than five hundred years was the annual fair, held each August. The fair began its life in 'God's Acre' which was the nickname for the grounds around St Giles', but as far as I can tell, the fair was kicked out and on to the Green in 1444 when the then Archbishop of Canterbury, John Stafford, took against good times in holy places. I hate to repeat old gossip but some said Stafford was born illegitimate. He was also accused by the Chancellor of Oxford University of being the 'father of bastard offspring by a nun'. This just goes to show that trolls are not a new thing. Maybe all that talk made him bad-tempered.

The fair must have been quite the event. In a description in *The Times* from 1806 there are breathless reports of it:

... the itinerant Magi, the Irish Giant, the Polish Dwarf, the wonderful Ventriloquist, and the Child of Promise. There were lions, tygers, panthers, hyenas, serpents, kangaroos, orangutans, wolverines and beavers; the ostriches, cassowaries, pelicans, storks and horned owls ...

Had you come to the fair in 1803 you might have been lucky enough to see Giovanni Belzoni, the Italian-born explorer and pioneer Egyptologist. Belzoni was 6 feet 7 inches tall and his 'personal charms soon brought him an English consort of Amazonian proportions, and the gigantic pair set about earning their living', which he did by lifting heavy things at fairs and circuses.

The woman he married was called Sarah Bane and like so many wives I think she's rather more interesting than he is. When Giovanni and Sarah went to Egypt she often found herself left to her own devices while he headed off to dig into ancient tombs. She was left in the company of local women and began documenting their lives. Her work was published in 1835 as an addendum to her husband's writings. Entitled *Mrs Belzoni's trifling account of the women of Egypt, Nubia, and Syria*, it is a rare insight into women's lives and, far from being 'trifling', represented a new kind of journalism.

I loved reading it, for I have been to Nubia in what is now Sudan. Here is one of those facts I delight in: there are twice as many pyramids in Sudan as in Egypt, but they are not packed with tourists. Back in 2007 I was in Sudan making six one-hour documentaries about the country for Al Jazeera television. Our local guide, Ahmed, was knowledgeable but had limited English. He called me 'Shendi', which is a town in Sudan. It didn't matter that we couldn't really communicate. The sights were astonishing.

What a privilege to wander where more than two thousand years ago the great Kingdom of Kush had thrived. The Nubian people had their own language and a unique alphabet which has never been cracked. Queens as well as kings once ruled over a land with an irrigation system so sophisticated it sustained thousands of people in the sometimes 50-plus degree heat. A mechanical water-moving device called a *sakia* helped to make this arid place one of successful crop production. There was metal manufacturing, textile production and international trade as far away as India and China. Elaborate pottery was made and even the trade of exotic animals from further south in Africa featured in their economy.

I and my small group of travel companions had what was left of this great enterprise entirely to ourselves. Our minibus was the sole vehicle. We climbed up one of the sides of a small pyramid and could see no one for miles, but word travels fast in the desert and before long two young lads turned up on camels and staged a race for us.

Sand began to blow everywhere. It swept across the dunes, wiping out our footprints almost instantly. It was as if we had never been. Ahmed said it meant it was raining in the south. Inside the abandoned chambers of the pyramids we saw astonishing hieroglyphs carved thousands of years ago. From 591 BC to about AD 350 this was the capital of the Kingdom of Kush. More than forty kings and queens lay buried here yet in the nineteenth century travellers thought fit to neatly carve their own names on top of the beautiful symbols. The twentieth-century visitor appears to have been too lazy even for that. Some had simply scratched poor graffiti on the surface, not even bothering to deface the place properly.

The old carvings were still very clear. I traced my finger over the Eye of Horus, the ancient Egyptian sky god who symbolised protection and good health. The boys on the camels had caught some sort of songbird, which they wanted to sell us. The bird hung upside down from a piece of string in one of the boys' hands. Its wings fluttered and its head jerked against the string. I wanted to buy it to release it but my Sudanese friend Hassan, who I was co-presenting the documentaries with, said they would just catch it again.

We hear a lot about the great Egyptian dynasties but forget about the power of the Nubian people. Tutankhamun is said to have hated the Nubians so much that he had a picture of one engraved on his sandals so that he might step on them every day. Hatred is not new.

I was so excited. I wanted to learn everything about everything. We passed a monkey in a village, tied to a tree. I asked our guide about it.

'What kind of monkey is that, Ahmed?'

'A small one.'

Hassan had been at school with Osama bin Laden. As we left the desert behind he declared, 'We should be grateful to bin Laden.'

'Why?' I asked, incredulous.

'He built this road we're on,' he replied.

I don't think he built it personally, but between 1991 and 1996 Osama bin Laden did live in Sudan, where he invested in construction and farming. I looked out at the dusty road. How odd to be grateful to him for anything.

'What was he like at school?' I asked.

Hassan shrugged. 'He wasn't good at sport.'

Osama bin Laden being a poor sport seemed unsurprising.

We were travelling before the country split north and south, looking at life in this, the largest country in Africa. One day, very late, we arrived in El-Obeid, about seven hours south of Khartoum. We were to film the Hakama women, who traditionally chant and sing songs to encourage their men as they go off to fight.

Sudan has been a place of great violence and when I was there the women were being encouraged to sing for peace rather than war. It didn't work. The country descended into terrible violence a few years later.

We reached the edge of a dry river bed and had to climb down a steep bank to cross on foot to the place where we were expected. The only water left in the river was small pools of mud where children played. We stood under a large tree while five women dressed in the most spectacular coloured outfits with great headdresses sang for us. A couple of them had travelled many miles to be here. It began to rain and, as can happen in Africa, in a moment a monsoon hit us and everyone began to run. The river bed instantly turned to mud. The rain was torrential. If we were not quick we could be swept away by the oncoming water. Hassan is a vast fellow and could not get up the slippery bank to the minibus so everyone heaved and hauled at him. In seconds we were all soaked through and filthy. We finally reached our vehicle and scrambled in. I was sitting at the back. Through the window I saw one of the women who had sung for us. Her feathered headdress hung down, plastered to her cheeks, and her peacock-blue clothes were drenched. She put out her hand to me, to get in the minibus.

'Wait!' I called to Ahmed but he shook his head and we sped away. I watched her left standing in the pouring rain. She had come to sing for us and now, shamefully, we had left her behind.

Back on the bus, I am looking down on Camberwell Green. There is an eclectic mix of the homeless on benches drinking beer and children in the far corner playing on the swings. An estate agent is advertising fancy apartments for sale facing the Green. Their website entices buyers with a picture of an upmarket cheese shop which I have yet to find. All the enclaves of

London change their character over time in an ebb and flow of arrivals and departures. Camberwell has been poor for a long time but the rich are coming back.

In the first part of the nineteenth century rich people moved in and the rich/poor divide caused trouble. Before the regular bus service a stage coach had been available from the city to the corner of Camberwell Green. Here the wealthy who lived in Dulwich got out to walk but it was said you had to be careful. There were 'ne'er-do-wells' who liked nothing better than to lighten them of their possessions on the way.

Keeping the working classes working was considered vital and the buses helped with that. Keeping them in their place was harder. Gradually, like the Archbishop of Canterbury in 1444, the Victorian middle classes fell out of love with Camberwell Fair. As part of an endless bid to mind the morals of the working classes, the fair had its last outing in 1855. Meanwhile the Obscene Publications Act was on its way which, amongst other things, was used 'to forbid the distribution of information about contraception and physiology to the working classes'. Satirical plays about politics were also targeted by this 1857 Act. Shutting down the voice of protest was important. It is a possibility we all need to remain vigilant about. Shutting down dissent is what Donald Trump tries to do now. Is this what is considered acceptable in a democracy today?

I've twice been involved in saying those things which others find reprehensible. Years ago my friend the writer and performance poet Joolz Denby was performing at an open-air venue when she responded to a heckler by telling him to fuck off. It was possibly not the most elegant rejoinder but she hadn't expected that saying it might get her arrested. As she descended from the stage a policeman appeared and charged her with breach of the peace for use of the F-word and the case went to court. Joolz had no money so I hosted a fundraiser at the Comedy Store in

London and then went along to the hearing. The judge was, as Dickens might say, 'of what is called the old school – a phrase generally meaning any school that seems never to have been young'. As the facts were presented he apologised that such language should have an airing in his court and repeated the word 'fuck' with the longest vowel sound possible.

'Fuuuuck!' he declared, his mouth wide open with the sort of disgust that might suggest he had found a turd in there. The policeman gave evidence. So did several members of the audience. In the end the only person who appeared to have been in danger of breaching the peace because of Joolz's language was the policeman who had arrested her in the first place. She was acquitted.

When I was the host of *The News Quiz*, a satirical weekly look at the news on Radio 4, we were blessed with great comic guests who could banter for Britain. We also had a wonderful team of writers who would provide between-banter jokes. One of them, Simon Littlefield, was and is a favourite writer. We prided ourselves on the fact that we had an equal number of complaints each week from every point on the political spectrum. Each accusing us of bias in favour of another.

One week the Conservatives had been busy taking a knife to child benefits and Simon wrote, 'It's the Tories who've been busy putting the N into cuts.'

I thought it was one of the funniest things I had ever read and I was delighted that the many layers of editors whom the programme is sifted through allowed it to be broadcast. The *Mail* went nuts, calling for a watershed of all radio programmes, my head on a platter and death to all funny people. (To be honest, I didn't read all of it and may be précising here.) They wrote of the outrage and distress it had caused. When the team checked the actual complaints to the BBC there was only one, which appeared to have come from a retired journalist who had once, yes indeed, worked for the *Mail*. To test true public opinion I often try the joke with live audiences. I'm afraid it has never failed to get anything but a huge laugh. Perhaps I am acquitted too.

I gave up *The News Quiz* when I founded the Women's Equality Party but I can't say I was sorry. It had become hard not to be mean on the show and I was tired of finding fault with politicians.

On the north side of the Green I pass the Planet Nollywood, formerly the Father Red Cap pub and now covered in black paint. It stands on the site of a musical hall where, on 2 December 1867, the audience could enjoy 'the great W. J. Collins, a banjoist from America, a Shakespearean sketch, Professor Davis in the renowned rope trick, and Mr Mucus Hellmore in his great delineation of Mephistopholes'. Later it was a gay bar then a party venue and is now a Nigerian restaurant and bar.

I hate the divides that still seem to exist. In 2016 I was in San Francisco to give a talk at the TEDWomen conference. After the event lots of delegates were drinking in the foyer of the hotel we'd been put up in. There were lots of inspirational women including a fabulous trio from Black Lives Matter. Deb and I couldn't help but notice that white women and women of colour were sitting in separate groups. The solution, that night, was to order a lot of champagne and pass it out on condition everyone went and sat with someone they hadn't met yet. We had a marvellous time but I obviously realise that's not always an option. I like to think we can all get on but I know that is far too simplistic a view. History matters. It leaves scars and indelible marks.

Medlar Street

The BBC show *QI*, which I host, has been commissioned for another series. The show feels like such a fixture in the television schedule, so it is odd that one has to wait each year to hear if there will be more. I am so glad. It is the finest piece of education by stealth. I think of the preparation my father did when reporting on the Apollo space missions for Danish TV. He was determined that no one should be left out of the rather complicated science so he read all of it and then worked out how he could explain it to his audience without being patronising. I try to do the same.

This year I have been trying to get to grips with time travel and entangled protons. I love our team of researchers because I phoned ahead on the day of the recording and said, 'I think we can make it clear using a banana, a knife and a biro.' No one asked me how. They just got me a banana, a knife and a biro, and explain it we did. I was so glad we actually recorded it. Those damned comedians sometimes hijack the show and we wander off up comedic avenues where no science ever rears its head. The joker in me is delighted, the student in me shakes her head. But then the unexpected happens, which is the best bit.

We were discussing how to open a whole coconut and had before us on the desks coconuts, screwdrivers, hammers and so forth. One guest was new – a wonderful stand-up called Sindhu Vee. I didn't know her work but liked her as soon as we met.

While everyone grabbed tools she simply picked up one of the coconuts, walked round to the front of the set and smashed it into two perfect halves on the concrete floor before scooping the whole thing up without spilling a drop of the liquid inside. It was one of the most impressive things I've ever seen.

QI has taught me to quibble with facts. I've been reading a book about great female criminals whose opening sentence reads, 'The Femme Fatale has been with us ever since Eve ate the apple.'

It's a good book, but I'm a pedant and the opening inaccuracy annoyed me. Eve did not eat an apple. It is one of the great myths. There is in fact no mention of an apple anywhere in the Garden of Eden. Most likely, if Eve ate anything then it was a fig, a grape or even a mushroom. For a non-believer, I've read the Bible rather thoroughly. During my American motel childhood, thanks to the Gideon Society, the Bible was the only book you could guarantee would be beside your bed each night. I know most people think Eve ate an apple, but that's probably due to a misunderstanding. The Latin word *mălum* means evil, while *mālum* means apple. You can see that there is not much in it in terms of spelling. Just a slightly different mark above the a. It may just have been someone making a bad pun, or one careless person once wrote it down wrong and off the world ran, confident it was in possession of the facts.

There are no apples growing here that I can see, but if you look carefully you can find medlars reminding us of the orchards that once stood in Camberwell. The street names give the past away. Bullace Row, where bullace plums once flourished, Melon Street and this one, Medlar. Hundreds of years ago the medlar was hugely popular, especially as it is one of the few fruits available in winter. It's not an attractive fruit and it has to be rotten before it's ripe, which feels like a metaphor for ageing. In fact, Chaucer used it for that very purpose in 'The Reeve's Tale'.

> *We olde men, I drede, so fare we:*
> *Til we be roten, kan we nat be rype*

Imported from Persia, the French call the tree *cul de chien*, or 'dog's arse'. Chaucer agreed, calling the fruit 'open-arse', while D. H. Lawrence took the time to put medlars in a poem, calling them 'autumnal excrementa':

> *What is it, in the grape turning raisin,*
> *In the medlar, in the sorb-apple,*
> *Wineskins of brown morbidity,*
> *Autumnal excrementa;*
> *What is it that reminds us of white gods?*

I've had medlar jelly. It's absolutely delicious and not at all like excrement. Medlar Street itself is no longer a flowering place of fruit. The railway runs across it and a car park has the most vicious barbed wire I've ever seen to keep strangers out. At the far end are some terraced houses. The street is one-way and used as a cut-through, but despite all this urbanisation I smile when I see four medlar trees surviving in the pavement. Does anyone pick their fruit? I promise myself that I will come back when they are in fruit. It was here, amongst the fruit trees, that the Camberwell Beauty, a butterfly with three-inch claret wings edged in blue with white spots, once fluttered. Today I don't see one. Just an empty crisp packet blowing in the wind. Up on the wall near the stop someone had carefully written, 'If it ain't racked it ain't graff'.

Good to know. I like a bit of graffiti. There is a very, very neat bit in East Dulwich which reads 'War is very naughty'.

The Number 68 is ahead of us at the Medlar Street stop and I am humming to myself. I don't worry that anyone will think me barmy. I am learning to be noisier on the bus. Naturally, it is not a modern tune but a music-hall song called 'Chalk Farm to Camberwell Green' about a young lady who went for a ride on the top of a bus with 'a fellow, a regular swell', on what is still the 68 bus route.

All on a summer's day
Up we climbed on the motor bus
And we started right away
When we got to the end of the ride
He asked me to go for a walk!
But I wasn't Camberwell Green
By a very long chalk.

I know this song because of my love for the Palace Theatre. On YouTube I found the Edwardian musical star Gertie Millar singing this very ditty in the *Bric-à-Brac* revue at the Palace back in 1915. Gertie was quite the gal and went on to marry into nobility. She passed away as the Dowager Countess of Dudley in 1952. Go girl.

An old woman gets on the bus and takes a seat beside me. She takes out a worn Bible and begins to read. I can see that she has many passages marked as favourites. I am on my way to a meeting about a new project to do with Wikipedia. I am thinking about knowledge and what does and doesn't get written down. I have decided to try to rewrite history, which sounds quite a big project when you say it out loud.

I want to correct the gender imbalance that plagues the internet. Wikipedia is the single largest online source of free information. There are approximately forty million articles in 299 different languages and there are nearly five hundred million unique visitors each month. This is all fine – except just 9 per cent of the information is about women. Women are written out of history and the reason is simple. Wikipedia is a crowdsourced online encyclopaedia. The information is edited by about 135,000 volunteers around the world, 90 per cent of whom are young, educated, white males. Women editors represent 9 per cent, and 1 per cent register as transgender. Nine per cent female editors. Nine per cent female content. Anybody spotting a pattern? Does it matter? Absolutely. Women are being left out. In October 2015 Emily Temple-Wood, one of the site's long-standing editors, told the *Atlantic* magazine that she had identified almost 4400 female scientists who met Wikipedia's inclusion standards but did not have a page. For years the physicist Donna Strickland was not deemed notable enough for an entry. She finally got her place in Wikipedia on the day she won the Nobel Prize. Surely that cannot be what it takes to be remembered? No man is held to such a standard.

I want to make a documentary about why this is happening. I want to do a theatre show about the history of the world from a female perspective and then get every member of the audience to commit to looking after one woman's history. I want to give the show away for anyone to do in colleges and schools where again their audiences might commit to protecting someone's memory. It might not rewrite history but it would be a start.

The last man who was said to know everything was Thomas Young, who died in 1829. He was a polymath, a doctor, the man who helped decipher the Rosetta Stone. He made contributions to everything from solid mechanics, whatever that may be, to musical harmony. It's a sobering thought that by the time he was my age Thomas Young had already been dead three years. So often I realise how little I know.

There was a Belgian information scientist called Paul Otlet. In 1895 he conceived the idea that it might be possible to gather together all the world's knowledge in one place where it could be classified according to his own unique system. Rather pleasingly it was thought that all this knowledge could be collated and confined to a series of index cards stored in banks of small drawers. It was probably the first systematic knowledge project, an encylopaedic survey of human understanding. Otlet called it the Mundaneum. I don't think it's a good name. It makes everything we know sound rather bland.

The project grew to a vast archive of more than twelve million three-by-five-inch index cards housed in seven-foot-high cabinets in 150 rooms. I wonder if that is what I shall need to chart the true progress of women. We have so much material at our disposal but I suspect most people on the bus are looking at the *Daily Mail* sidebar of shame or playing a game. I wonder if the idea of having all knowledge so easily available has made us intellectually lazy. I'm not the first to worry. Socrates objected to the invention of writing. He thought it would erode memory. He quoted from the wisdom of King Ammon, who said to the Egyptian god Theuth, the inventor of letters, 'this discovery of yours will create forgetfulness ... they will not use their memories; they will trust to the external written characters ... they will appear to be omniscient but will generally know nothing; they will be tiresome company, having the show of wisdom without the reality'.

We can so easily be misled into thinking we have knowledge when actually often all we have is data.

The woman beside me is reading Paul's letters to the Corinthians – the Corinthians who can't have been impressed as they never wrote back. I am reminded of another bus, another time and an elderly companion. My heart has been broken a few times. When I was twenty-three and in deep mourning for a love who had gone off with the woman who delivered the post, I went on my own to Israel. It was 1981 and not the safest place to be at the time. Israel was bombing Palestine Liberation Organization strongholds in Lebanon and the Palestinians were retaliating on Israeli targets. It was after my year as an actress at Nottingham Playhouse so perhaps the drama of flirting with death appealed to me. More likely, I think it was somehow supposed to teach my ex a lesson.

I have already freely confessed that I was an odd soul. Some youngsters might have partied in Tel Aviv or Jerusalem but I wanted to go out to the desert and visit St Catherine's Monastery at the foot of Mount Sinai. It's one of the oldest working Christian monasteries in the world. There I was again, seeking places of spiritual calm. The only way I could get there was to join a bus tour. I duly signed up for something called a Hallelujah tour, which should've been a clue to the type of people who also thought this was a good idea. I boarded an ancient silver bus. It felt as though we should all start singing something uplifting. I sat down next to a man in his sixties.

'Hi, my name is Bill,' he declared, smiling. 'I'm a bishop.'

'I'm Sandi,' I replied. 'I'm an actress.'

The entire tour group, apart from myself, consisted of a Mennonite mission from Pennsylvania. They were close to the Amish in their beliefs and did not allow any photography or alcohol. It was not exactly a fun clan to travel with. For most of the journey I sat beside an old woman called Gertrude. Gertrude wanted to go to Mount Sinai so she could climb to the top and proclaim the Ten Commandments out loud. It was an ambition that had never occurred to me. She told me that as the Book of Exodus declares it was Mount Sinai where the Ten Commandments were given to Moses by God, she wanted to echo this moment before she died.

As we passed through the desert she told me stories from the Bible as if they were the true history of the place. She was mad about St Catherine of Alexandria, to whom the monastery is dedicated. From Gertrude I learned that Catherine had been quite a girl. Whipped – or scourged, as Christians like to call it – and imprisoned for her faith, she was impressively tricky to kill. First she was imprisoned without food, but a dove fed her, which must have been annoying for the authorities. Then she was tortured on a wheel we now remember as a firework, and finally she was beheaded, after which her neck poured out milk instead of blood. It's quite a way to go.

It was a long journey to Mount Sinai in the rattling old bus. On the way we slept in the desert. It was not a luxury tour. There were no camp beds, just our sleeping bags laid out on the sand by the fire. There was no alcohol so the evenings were not exactly raucous. Bill the Bishop policed our band with a watchful eye. When I woke one morning I could feel something uncomfortable underneath me. I rolled over and discovered the completely picked clean skeleton of a small desert creature. I had rolled over and killed it in the night, and its body had been entirely consumed by the desert ants as I slept. The Sinai was not an easy place to be.

By the time we got to Mount Sinai, Gertrude, who had hardly slept, was exhausted. The climb to the top of the mountain meant getting up at four o'clock in the morning in order to avoid the heat of the day. There was no way the old lady was going to be able to make the effort so she handed me her family Bible. It had a worn black leather cover and thin tissue-like pages.

'Please,' she said, 'take this for me. Climb to the top and read the Commandments out loud.'

I did just that. It was not an easy trek and as I scrambled up I thought about Moses. He can't have known God was at the top with his list of dos and don'ts. Did he know it was going to be worth the effort? Did he know this one outing was going to have a knock-on effect through the ages? Did his sandals hurt like mine did? Had Mrs Moses sent sandwiches? I got to the top, and as the sun came up I spoke boldly and loudly to the gathered Mennonites. I channelled my inner Moses and gave the finest performance I could muster.

'I am the Lord thy God, which have brought thee out of the land of Egypt, out of the house of bondage,' I boomed against the still air. 'Thou shalt have no other gods before me.'

I paused. What did that mean? Why would God command that you shouldn't have any other gods if he were the only one? Surely that meant he recognised there were other gods? That there was god-competition? It wasn't the time to discuss it. I climbed back down having completed my gift to Gertrude. I had grown fond of her and never asked what she thought about the whole multiple-god possibility. She seemed very old to me and was probably going to die soon. I thought it wasn't the time to question her fundamental beliefs.

By the time we got back to Jerusalem I was exhausted. Amongst the many things my father taught me which have been of limited use I have the skill to find a good martini anywhere in the world. I headed to the King David Hotel and went into the bar. I was covered in a fine dust from the desert and hadn't showered for days. Nevertheless I went boldly into the five-star bar, sat on a high stool and ordered a vodka martini, straight up with a twist. As I brought the glass to my lips I looked down to the other end of the long bar. There sat Bill the Bishop, beer in hand, grinning sheepishly at me.

Years later I read that St Catherine was probably a legend (duh) based on a real woman called Hypatia. She lived in Alexandria during the Roman Empire. Born about AD 350– 370 she was a philosopher, astronomer, and the first female mathematician whose life we know anything about. She was considered a great teacher and writer on her subjects and is known to have constructed astrolabes and hydrometers. Her wisdom led to her wielding some political influence, and in March AD 415, she was murdered by a mob. Her I would have climbed a mountain for.

Leaving women out of history is not a new thing. The Bible is another great piece of communal writing. There are 3237 different people mentioned in the great book, of whom about six hundred are women. Of those women, only ninety-three speak 14,056 words – that is, roughly 1.1 per cent of the total words in the holy book. Some of the biblical women are prominent and well-known, like Jesus' mother, Mary. She utters just 191 words. Mary Magdalene says 61 words, while Sarah, the wife of Abraham, says 141. Meanwhile Eve – perhaps the Bible's best-known woman – speaks only 74 words. Maybe the whole thing with the snake left her speechless. Then she has two sons and that apparently is the beginning of the rest of us. How that works I have no idea. There is so much I don't understand.

Wyndham Road

On the other side of the road there is a launderette which has lost so many letters from its sign it now advertises itself as *under tte*. What could you be under if you were under tte? Table Tennis England? A transthoracic echocardiogram?

Near this stop is a marvellous shop called Margaret's Cakes of Distinction. Here you will find the most brilliant sugar craft in the kingdom. Her shop lies in a small parade of businesses, at the end of which is the Camberwell Islamic Centre.

Back in 1978 when I was studying law at Cambridge they offered for the first time a module on Islamic law. I signed up and was one of only three people, all women actually. I was the only non-Muslim. I liked a lot of what I learned. Shariah, the law of the Qur'an, literally means 'a path to life-giving water' or 'path to the water hole'. You have to put everything into historical context. The laws originated in an arid desert environment so a path to water would be essential for life. You find the same sort of meaning in the Jewish laws of the Torah. The word *yara* is at the root of the Hebrew word *torah*. It means to 'shoot like an arrow' but it too was used to describe rain, life-giving water. Both sets of laws are part of the Abrahamic tradition, yet too often instead of it helping us to see our commonalities it divides.

Everything I read about Islamic law indicated with great clarity the equal duty of men and women to seek education. The basic principles of Shariah – justice and equity for everyone – are laudable yet too often something happens in the interpretation.

Mind you, the Christian Church can hardly be held up as a model of forward thinking: the uproar from the right wing of the Church of England when finally a woman bishop came to the throne hardly made for edifying reading. Part of my problem with religion, almost all religion, is its male bias.

I've met the Church of England's first female bishop, Libby Lane, several times. She's a delight and so far hasn't been struck by lightning. Mind you, if she is a bishop she probably only moves on a diagonal and that might make her harder to hit.

A lot of what I know about religion comes from reading but some is from getting to know those with deep beliefs. My trip to Sudan had a profound effect on me. It involved a funny mix of crew – a Canadian cameraman, English director, South African sound recordist and our Sudanese guide, Ahmed. Ahmed was very tall and thin. He wore a long white jellabiya with an immaculate turban, and no matter how much dust swept our way he always managed to look pristine. He had deep, dark brown eyes and the look of a meerkat surveying the outside world. In the afternoons Ahmed liked to play cards and we would sit on street corners with the crew playing a complex game involving fourteen cards and fifty-one points, which we played in an odd mix of languages.

Ahmed stopped our minibus five times a day to shake out a small carpet and pray to Mecca. He once did it on a highway while other, less religious folk continued driving. Ahmed was unperturbed. He put the hazard lights on and shook out his carpet in front of the stopped bus. We sat inside with traffic screaming round us. It was hard to say whether the thought of being hit from behind was more terrifying than the idea of rolling over Ahmed at prayer as it happened.

One day he took us to visit a Sufi mosque whose stated aim was to seek *ḥaqīqah*, 'ultimate truth'. I like the idea of it. Ultimate truth must have a lot to commend it. Many men in long white jellabiyas and small white hats greeted us. They couldn't have been more welcoming. Over one shoulder they wore a brown leather strap which fastened to a belt like an old military holster from the First World War. It seemed a curiously aggressive outfit for worship.

The sheikh in charge was a sort of local superstar. He was very young and handsome. He wore a dark, tan-coloured shift over the usual white. His white turban was tied with great care and his beard and moustache had been trimmed to perfection. He smiled and had lovely eyes. Around me men and women seemed to go weak at the knees and queue up to kiss his hand. His great-great-grandfather had founded the sect. Children passed by and ducked their heads as he touched their hair.

The congregation were keen to show us around. We were taken to the kitchen. It was Friday, and on Fridays there was free lunch for everyone. Armies of ladies were overseeing huge pots bubbling on the stove. If you couldn't manage a miracle then this was surely how you sorted the feeding of the five thousand and it would be women who did it. Next we were taken to the sheikh's resting room. It looked like an airport lounge, with chairs all around the outside of the room where we sat to drink tea. Prayers began at 2.30 p.m. with all the men lined up in rows in the large downstairs hall. There were a few in Western clothing but mostly everyone was in the white belted uniform. The older men had marks on their feet and foreheads from years of praying prostrate on the floor five times a day. No one was comfortable with me, a woman, watching, so I was taken up a dark, narrow back staircase to the women's room above. It was a sort of wide balcony that ran round three sides of the main hall and was enclosed by a wooden lattice-work screen. Through the small holes we could look down on the praying men's heads.

Even though we could hear the service, we women were

somehow divorced from it. The atmosphere in our loft was entirely different from the one I had left below. A large pile of footwear lay by the door. Some of the women were relaxing on the floor reading books, others played with their children. The place was littered with abandoned handbags like some sort of school dance. I stood at the screen looking down at the men who had begun to move in slow unison. The movements were set and regimented. There was chanting and chest beating in a strict rhythm and occasionally what sounded like a single very loud exhalation of breath. The sounds that rose up to the hidden balcony were not unlike a Gregorian chant. It was an entirely male noise. One of the older women took my hand and explained in excellent English, 'We believe a person is not just a tongue. The whole person is important and we need movement in order to get closer to Allah.'

Two men with microphones alternated leading the routine like Arabic line-dance callers. They clapped their hands to signal a change of rhythm or movement and the instruction would be picked up by those closest to the mikes before moving in a wave down the line. The men in charge had no book or music and it was hard to tell if they were making it up as they went along or whether the routine was the same every time. The chanting continued and a few of the men appeared to be hyperventilating. I had a go and wasn't the least bit surprised. It was astonishingly tiring.

'Some of the men will be semi-conscious now,' continued my guide as a younger women brought round a steaming tray of deep magenta *karkadé*. It's a kind of hibiscus tea and we stood sipping its tart, cranberry flavour while below the men took care of the religion.

'How long do they do it for?' I asked.

The answer was several hours and the women seemed to settle in for the duration. They chatted, drank tea and one or two made phone calls. There seemed to be many more men in the hall than women.

'Do all the women come?' I asked.

My guide shook her head. 'Too busy,' she said, and that seems to have been true in so many religions. Buddha left his wife and young son to go and sit under a banyan tree. There he contemplated the world. I expect Mrs Buddha didn't have time.

Later we joined the sheikh for lunch. It was clear that women were not normally invited, but somehow I had been made into an honorary man. Still, I was gently shown to a separate carpet to eat a little way away from the leader. We all sat on the floor and ate the finest roast lamb I have ever tasted, along with some kind of spinach soup, large bowls of rice and bread, all eaten with our fingers. Glasses of lemonade quenched our thirst.

Outside, tray after huge round tin tray was taken out from the kitchens to feed the masses. Carpets had been laid in the streets for the men and in the courtyard for the women. There were also vast pots of water so everyone could wash their hands.

'We keep the community going,' explained the sheikh as we wandered past the giant picnic. 'In the great famine of 1984 we fed thousands.'

He took me to see his great-great-grandfather's tomb. As we entered the cool of a small domed building a man took my shoes and the sheikh removed his turban and tan shift. He put on the same leather shoulder belt as the other men and entered. At last I got a moment alone with him. Like all great leaders, he fixed me with his eyes as if he had rarely met anyone more interesting. He had spent time in London and we reminisced about places he liked. He was fond of Bromley-by-Bow in east London, which seemed surprising.

'Do you like being sheikh?' I asked.

He shook his head. 'I wouldn't wish it on anyone,' he replied. 'It is 24/7 and everyone wants a piece of me.'

He wanted to talk about the association of Islam and terrorism, which made him very unhappy. He explained that all Muslims greet each other with the words 'Peace be upon you', and wanted me to understand that at its core Islam is all about peace and love.

'All people want to get close to God somehow,' he continued. 'We have a desire to know the ancient deity.'

It felt like a private conversation. I was embarrassed that we needed to film. The director tried to get silence but the crowd of men who followed the sheikh at all times began singing. The small stone building was dominated by a large green tomb and the amazing sound of the men's voices reverberated against the grave of their sect's founder. The sheikh's right-hand man was keen for us to move on. The congregation were waiting.

'He lives in a very modest house,' whispered the assistant as we exited the building.

The sheikh laughed. 'Be careful,' he cautioned. 'You are a woman and all my friend wants is for me to get married. He says I should take four wives at once.'

'Less trouble,' muttered the assistant.

Out in the street the rest of the congregation had finished lunch and its men were now standing in a line waiting for the sheikh to exit. He walked holding a long stick with a small cleft in the end and looked very regal.

Later that afternoon we went in search of some nomads. This is not easy as nomads are never at home. It looked a romantic life on camelback but there is no education for the children and so no escape from the life if they want it. Despite their illiteracy they knew surprising things about the West. The youngest man amongst them said that if he could have anything then he wanted a driveway and a Cadillac. In pink.

On our way again I sat at the front of the bus and asked Ahmed about his faith.

'You must read the Qur'an,' he said, 'or you will be damned.'
'What if you are a nomad and can't read?' I asked.
Ahmed shrugged. 'That is your own fault.'

I think about the women drinking tea while the men beat their chests and commune with God. Maybe we could all do with a bit more tea.

I realise I often think about the weeks I spent in Sudan. I don't think it is over-dramatising to say I was traumatised when I returned. I had met FGM victims who described in graphic detail the effect of the mutilation on their lives; come across girls deliberately made disabled by their family in order for them to become better beggars; seen a level of deprivation that broke my spirit; been enraged by the aid workers I met who were so worn down they no longer seemed to care; slept in rooms owned by the World Health Organization in which rats scrambled around the bed as well as in a shipping container guarded by a man with a machine gun; and knew how unbelievably privileged I was. When I got home I found I did not want to leave the house. I was alone and afraid. Debbie, my friend of many years, was concerned about me and came over for dinner. I poured my heart out to her. It was that night we realised the strength of the feelings we had for each other.

Between Wyndham Road and Bethwin Street

I've been reading *Old and new London: a narrative of its history, its people, and its places* by Walter Thornbury and Edward Walford. Don't rush to get it out of the library. Apart from me, I doubt anyone has taken it out since it was published in 1873. According to Thornbury and Walford, Alexander Pope is more likely to have been put up at Bowyer Place than off Barry Road. Finding reliable facts is not easy.

This was once one of London's poorest areas, a place of chronic need. According to a pamphlet I have entitled 'Rare Doings at Camberwell', the streets in the 1880s were said to be 'of very bad character ... The only policemen venturing there were very foolish policemen.' Down a side street heading to Addington Square lies a tiny café called Fowlds. Only about a dozen people can get inside and I have only ever had their delicious coffee sitting outside under the awning. I'm fine with this. The Danes endlessly sit outside in all weathers. I love this café because it is merely the front for an upholstery shop that has been in business since 1926. The loo is out the back in a yard which also contains an ancient delivery van. I go to the loo even if I don't need to so I can get a quick glimpse of those in the workshop carefully re-upholstering some ancient chair.

It is a mixed crowd who frequent this place – workmen from a nearby building renovation, mothers and babies, and several people hard at work on their laptops. I am old-fashioned and carry a small notebook with a pencil tucked inside. Of all the things I do, writing is my favourite, but it's a curious activity. The playwright David Hare had a very unsettling habit of jotting down anything anyone near by said which took his fancy. It says something about me that in the time we spent together he never wrote down a word I uttered. He was not alone.

Years ago in the great round Reading Room at the British Museum there was an old woman who didn't seem to be in her right mind. She was there every day and had presumably got her pass when her mental faculties were sharper. Her clothing was extraordinary. She looked, as Dorothy Parker might have put it, as though she had dressed while fleeing a burning building. She didn't spend her time ordering books from the huge catalogues. She didn't seem to sit at all but rather walked endlessly round the room looking in the waste-paper baskets at the end of each row of desks. No one used computers then so many crumpled balls of paper representing failure of some kind or other made their way to the bins. This bag lady of the museum would carefully unfurl each ball and check its contents. If she liked what she saw she would flatten the paper further and place it carefully in a cloth bag she kept on her shoulder. I took to writing what I thought were intriguing bons mots and putting them in the bin. As a homage to the poet and novelist Stevie Smith I always wrote on yellow legal pads so you could clearly see which contributions were mine, but she never kept one of them. Everyone's a critic.

Burgess Park lies just behind Addington Square. It's a relatively new green space, having been created in the 1950s to bring some 'lungs' to a place of high-density housing. Old derelict warehouses were knocked down and the Grand Surrey Canal was filled in. It's named after Jessie Burgess, who in 1945 became Camberwell's first woman mayor. She was a champion of the park project and one of those indomitable British women who sits on every committee and does good with every breath. There are lots of commemorative and explanatory signs in the park but, as is the way of the world, I can't find one that mentions her.

The canal once carried cargo from Camberwell and Peckham to the Thames at Rotherhithe. Now you can walk on top of it. There's an old kiln in the middle of the park where in the nineteenth century barges dropped off coal and limestone to be burnt into quicklime, which was used in mortar for the building trade, as fertiliser for agriculture and as the limelight which lit Victorian theatres. Each burning took three days as about twenty-five tonnes of limestone was broken up by hand into small pieces before being incinerated at over 1000°C, making it as hot as the molten lava from a volcano. Further into the park lies Chumleigh Gardens almshouses, which in a former life housed the Friendly Female Society asylum for elderly ladies. I think I should like to end my days in such a place. Sitting with old friends.

I've been out to lunch with the actress Sheila Hancock. She is someone I've known since I was twenty, when I worked for a summer at the Victoria Palace Theatre. The musical *Annie* was playing and my much younger sister Jeni, who has the most wonderful singing voice, played one of the girls in the orphanage. The show starred Sheila as Miss Hannigan. It included a number called 'NYC' in which Little Orphan Annie wanders through the Big Apple with Daddy Warbucks. For the time, the show was very high-tech. Light-up replicas of New York landmarks like the Empire State Building trundled across the stage on a track while the actors walked on a revolving belt, thus giving the impression of striding through the city. Unfortunately technology had only advanced so far and the buildings all got their power from normal three-pin plugs. They were plugged in stage left and trundled across, and once they had reached the end of their journey stage right they needed to be unplugged before being whisked off into the wings. I was hired because I was small. My job was to ride behind the buildings across the stage, hidden from view, and then jump off to unplug them. Having delivered one skyscraper, I then had to run like mad down some wooden stairs and under the stage, then jump onto, say, the Chrysler Building before trundling across again.

One evening I was mid-run below the stage when suddenly and unexpectedly I bumped into the great Miss Hancock. I had never seen her at this moment in the show before and was startled. She was the star. I slammed on my brakes and said, 'After you, Miss Hancock.' She smiled: 'No, no, Sandi, your cue is well before mine.'

She knew my name, she knew what I did and when I did it. That understanding of the team it takes to make a show has, I hope, never left me. I don't suppose either of us could have predicted that we would one day become great friends. Sheila spoke at my wedding. She stays at my house. She is my pal but she will always be a star. Sadly no one in the place we went to for lunch seemed to know that. We were just two older women and we were ignored. I think one of the great dangers faced by women over sixty in this country is starving to death in a restaurant. We were invisible.

The bus drives past a poster for the musical *9 to 5*, which is on in the West End. It shows a great picture of my good friend Bonnie Langford. Bon and I have been friends for so many years we've lost count. I think we met in our early twenties. Years ago we toured a double act called Short and Curly in which she sang and I did jokes. Backstage we always shared a dressing room, where our different approaches to getting ready were astonishingly apparent. Bon is a true professional and would don some strange sort of plastic jogging trousers to stretch out her muscles. I don't even know where you buy such a garment. I never trained for the business so have no idea how to limber up. She would be standing with her head bowed to her leg, which was lifted to an impossible angle, while I sat in a corner reading the *New Statesman*. Every now and then she would burst into a vocal warm-up which mainly seemed to involve singing about 'many men' while I could be heard muttering something like, 'Dear God, have you seen what's happened to the Hungarian economy?' It is a testament to friendship that two such diverse souls should have been so happy in each other's company.

The bus passengers all swipe in with a card on the pad by the driver. He sits behind a Perspex screen and does not seem to notice his charges. There is no happy chit-chat like in the old days from a conductor keeping an eye. I sit alone. A man on the phone is dealing with the fact that his father is dying. He is distressed. We are all included in his distress. We are all alone.

I must ring Bon. She always makes me feel better.

Camberwell Road / Albany Road

A person is asleep at the back of the bus. They've been there for some time. They got on a while ago carrying what looked like a whole life in a series of plastic bags. I don't know if it's a man or a woman as they are so covered in layers of clothing and a hat I can't tell. Clearly this is not a journey to somewhere, it is an end in itself. There has been a 165 per cent increase in rough sleepers since the Tories came to power in 2010. I have been reading about councils clearing the homeless from their streets. Some of those on the street have managed to get tents and when the council take those they are charging up to fifty pounds for people with nothing to get them back. What have we become?

I think about Robert F. Kennedy, one-time US Attorney General and brother to the President. My father had a leather-bound limited-edition copy of a book about him which my mother has just passed on to me. Robert Kennedy said,

> Every time we turn our heads the other way when we see the
> law flouted, when we tolerate what we know to be wrong, when
> we close our eyes and ears to the corrupt because we are too
> busy, or too frightened, when we fail to speak up and speak out,
> we strike a blow against freedom and decency and justice.

Where are such politicians today? Because of him I've been looking for a particular building on the Camberwell Road. It lies on the corner of Grosvenor Terrace, just up from the Albany Road bus stop. Today it's the home of Walworth Methodist church. There's been a church there since 1813 but in the 1930s the old building was torn down and a new youth centre, called Clubland, put in its place. In 1939 Robert Kennedy, then the thirteen-year-old son of the American ambassador to London, made his first public speech here. There's a photo of him laying a commemorative stone with his name on it. The church is very present now but under a red portico a triangular 1930s light still proclaims the name Clubland.

This particular Kennedy was one of my father's heroes. Papa travelled in his footsteps and in 1968 had been following him as he took part in the presidential primary elections. On 5 June my father was waiting with the press corps in the room set aside for journalists at the Ambassador Hotel in Los Angeles. Kennedy had just scored a major victory in California. He appeared to be heading for the presidency. En route through a kitchen shortcut he stopped to shake hands with a busboy called Juan Romero and was shot dead by Sirhan Sirhan. My father called us from the hotel and wept. The moment ruined Romero's life. He got letters from people saying if Kennedy hadn't stopped to shake his hand he would never have been killed. He bore this guilt until a heart attack carried him away aged sixty-eight.

My father passed away from a heart attack aged fifty-nine. My eldest, Jesse, had just been born. He held her, and as he did so he said quite clearly, 'This is the only grandchild I will ever know.'

He died the next day not knowing Jesse would be followed by two more kids from me and four from my brother. Do you know when you are about to die?

Though it was thirty years ago my father is ever present in my life. My mother Julie, who at eighty-seven is fitter than the rest of us put together, has downsized into a lovely cottage and has been clearing out, hence giving me the Robert Kennedy book. Among the other things she has no space for is my father's *Encyclopaedia Britannica*. They are books that have travelled the world with us and they stand in a small bookcase, repositories of all the world's knowledge. Papa inherited them from his parents and they are dated 1929, the year he was born.

'Anything you need to know before 1929 is in these books,' he would say, pointing to them with the stem of his pipe. 'Anything after 1929, ask me.'

He was an extraordinary man and truly did seem to know everything, so the books took on a mythical quality of brilliance. Papa was not a great believer in traditional education. He believed that if I read the *New York Times* every day from about the age of eight and joined him on the road whenever possible then I would learn everything I needed. Ever intent on showing us the world, my brother and I were endlessly taken out of school, put in the back of the car and driven off by our parents to follow the campaign trail of American politicians or stand on the sidelines of history in the making. Accompanying us would be his small crew. It was Papa's cameraman who probably first made me a feminist. He was a large, strong man with dark Brylcreemed hair. His wife and two sons had come with him. They all became like family to us as we were so often on the road together. The cameraman liked a drink and he also liked to be in charge. If he demanded something from his wife and she didn't immediately comply, he would put his hand on the back of her neck and squeeze until she said she was sorry. I would watch him do it then I would look at the other adults and wonder why no one did anything about it. My father was a man who believed in justice but even he couldn't seem to see what was happening right in front of him. Stories like this are sadly commonplace. What keeps me going is that just occasionally there is a tale which makes everything worthwhile.

When Jesse was born, Peta and I were living in a small terraced cottage in Surrey. We had not been there long and kept to ourselves. One night we were woken by a terrible sound of screaming. There was no mistaking that someone next door was being violently beaten. The next thing we knew there was a frantic banging at our front door. I ran down and opened up to let in a terrified woman.

'My baby! My baby!' she cried.

Maybe it was because I was now a parent myself that I didn't hesitate. In full protective mode but dressed only in my pyjamas I went out into the cold night air to next door and banged on the door. A large man in a foul mood opened it.

'I've come for the baby,' I said and marched in. Fortunately the houses were small and identical so I quickly found the child, picked it up from the cot and took it home. The woman stayed with us and we called the police. This was 1988.

'I'm sure he didn't mean it,' soothed an officer while Peta insisted on taking photographs of the woman's injuries. Eventually she left her partner and took the baby, and moved away. It was more than twenty years before we knew any more.

One evening my daughter Megan, then about twenty, brought home a group of friends including a strapping lad over six feet tall. He was charming and built as though rugby had been invented for him. He was a little shy when he came over to speak to me.

'My mother says thank you,' he said.

This was the baby. The baby from that night all those years ago all grown up into a man. He became a police officer. On the day of my wedding at the Royal Festival Hall there had been reason for some anxiety about our safety. It was this same young man, the baby from all those years ago, who provided us with close protection. That is a great story.

*

Tonight I am on the bus late. I especially love this stretch of road at night. There seem to be endless barbers and hairdressers who ply their trade when it is dark out. Places like Genesis (The Beginning of Hair Trends), which is open seven days a week. In one barber's shop a man is resting his head back while another gently wipes his face with a towel. It looks calming. I wonder if they use Gillette razors. That's not as mad as it sounds. When I was eighteen I had a brief dalliance with working in a factory. I was on the assembly line doing piece work. It was all women and they quickly taught me to slow down as I worked the line.

'We work at the pace of the slowest,' the woman in charge explained. 'Don't spoil it for everyone.' It was a plastics factory in Redhill in Surrey. We assembled various things including small orange plastic robot-like men in which Gillette razors were briefly sold. My job was to put their eyes on. It was mind-numbingly boring so every hundred or so I'd make a Cyclops Gillette man.

The women were kind to each other. They were kind to me but no one was having a good time. Anyone who ever says that women like working on assembly lines because they can chat should try it first.

The sleeping person awakens and looks at me. I think it is a woman. I'm not sure what to do. I want to help but not patron-ise. I reach in my pocket and try to give her some money. She tells me to fuck off. Quite right too. I think about Theresa May's promise when she became Prime Minister – that she would lead a government fight 'against the burning injustice that, if you're born poor, you will die on average nine years earlier than others'. Not gone that well, has it?

Westmoreland Road

I don't feel well. I have a chest infection which the doctor has characterised as walking pneumonia. This seemed rather dramatic to me so I'm carrying on. When I was six weeks old my parents were posted to a remote part of what was then Rhodesia and once there I contracted some hideous fever. My mother never tires of telling me that no one could get my temperature down so the doctor put me in the fridge. Since then being put in the fridge seems to me the benchmark of how ill you are. At the moment I think I could just do with a lie down in the larder. Maybe I do believe in the adage about the show must go on.

A young woman is reading a 'celebrity' magazine. I have no idea who the person on the cover is. I am useless at knowing who the great and the good might be or seeing things you're supposed to. I have been a guest many times on *The Graham Norton Show* and they now ring before to see if I have heard of the other guests or am familiar with any of their work. I remember sitting on the sofa next to the actress Sigourney Weaver, who was talking about the film *Alien*.

'I'm awfully sorry,' I said, 'I've never seen it.'

Graham looked aghast. 'Why have you never seen it?'

I couldn't think of an answer. 'I don't know,' I tried, 'I suppose I never thought I'd end up on a sofa next to Sigourney Weaver having to defend myself.'

I think Graham is a genius. Kind and thoughtful. How far he has come from the first show I saw him do in some terrible basement at the Edinburgh Fringe many years ago. I thought he was brilliant so I took my then agent to see him. Afterwards she declared, 'He's very likeable but I have no idea what one would do with him for a career.'

Being on his show fills me with pride even if I often fail to cover myself in glory. Once I arrived at the studio reception and shared the lift with a very nice dark-haired young woman who was extremely chatty and funny. We laughed a lot. Then I saw her again in make-up. We were discussing an idea for a lesbian sitcom to be called *The Dyke van Dick Show*. I went to get changed and then was shown backstage. The set of Graham's show looks very nice, but it conceals the smallest backstage area imaginable. There are cables and struts of wood everywhere and sound engineers and floor managers block the way as the guests aim for a plastic chair where they sit with their knees under their chins waiting to go out to the red sofa and sparkle. The bright young woman was there as well. She was still chatting to me, and I was beginning to think she hadn't really understood that I couldn't really talk now. I had work to do. The show began, and Graham called my name. I bounced up the three steps to the set. He smiled, hugged me and turned to announce: 'And now our next guest ... Minnie Driver!' On came the woman I thought had been following me.

The last time I was in the show, I was on with the Hollywood legend that was Carrie Fisher. She and I were waiting to go on. Carrie was seated in the plastic chair. She looked tiny and unwell.

'I don't feel good,' she said. Graham had already gone out to warm up the audience. We were seconds away from being intro-duced and I didn't know what to do. I put my hand on her arm. 'Can I get you something?'

She shook her head and held tightly on to me. I didn't know her and was at a loss, so to my eternal shame I finally repeated the much-used phrase actors often draw upon: 'Oh well, Dr Theatre will see you through.'

'Dr Theatre' is the shot of adrenalin performers get when they step onto the stage. It can carry them through all manner of things. We went out and did the show together. Carrie was brilliant. The audience adored her, as did I. The next day she was dead. It was shocking and a sobering lesson.

I think my father gave me my work ethic. He never let anything get between him and a good story. Each summer, from when I was about eight, we would make the journey by ocean liner from New York to Southampton and back again. We travelled on the great old ladies of the sea – *QE1*, *QE2* and others – but our favourite ships belonged to the Norwegian America Line, particularly the MS *Bergensfjord*. Danish Radio paid for the annual journey home and someone in accounts had assumed that planes were more expensive than boats. As a result my father was allowed each summer to choose between transporting us economy on a plane or first class on the boat. It was a boat every time. Each trip took five days.

It was the most marvellous, if odd, life. We were not rich by any means but for two weeks each year we lived as though we were. There were no menus in first class. You just ordered what you wanted and my brother and I had baked Alaska whenever we pleased. Each night we dressed for dinner, with my father in his tux and my mother in a long dress. It felt like another era. Caviar was served nestling in the back of a swan carved from ice and waiters in white glided about giving silent service. In the day there was clay pigeon shooting on the aft deck and after supper films of horse races were run in the bar, which you could bet on beforehand. My father taught us to play bridge and each evening we made up a four amongst all the other first-class passengers who passed the time this way.

My brother and I shared a room and one morning on the *Bergensfjord* I woke up early. I had been woken by the singularly odd experience of having a heavy chair seem to walk by itself from the desk in the corner over to my bed. The first-class cabins were quite high up on the ship and I was rather startled when I looked out of the port hole to see nothing but green water. There had been a terrible hurricane, the stabilisers on the boat had snapped and now we listed severely to one side in the middle of the Atlantic.

The order went out for everyone to put on their life jackets. A rope was strung up in the ballroom to help people climb or slide from one side of the boat to another. My mother was terrified, partly because amidst the howling wind and pelting rain we could not find my father anywhere on the stricken ship. It was hours before we discovered that he was in the telegraph room, trying to get the story back to Denmark. My brother and I were too young to think we might die. Instead we spent the afternoon hauling ourselves up the ballroom floor and sliding back down to the other side. Despite the horror everyone still changed for dinner. The chef wept in the restaurant, crying, 'Steak and lobster! I am reduced to steak and lobster!'

After supper everyone played cards as usual. We played bridge on the floor, as did four elderly people in full evening dress with bright orange life jackets on top. You couldn't play on the table as the cards kept sliding off. Late but sedate, we did eventually pull into New York Harbor.

We loved that boat, so I checked out what happened to her and read the following rather sad notice:

On 17th August 1980, a fire started in the engine room whilst she was under refurbishment at Perama, Greece. She was

towed out of the docks and capsized and sank near the island of
Kynosoura, some kilometres from Perama.

Well, at least she didn't go in the cold Atlantic.

As I am under the weather I've probably chosen the wrong
day to go to Arments but my father's stoicism lives on in me.
Arments has been in the same place on Westmoreland Road
since 1914. I don't know why they chose the year a war started
to open up. The bright blue shop sign proudly boasts of its
Quality Pie, Mash & Eels. Inside, the tiled dining room with the
table booths probably hasn't changed for a while. This is old-
school London where pies are served with what's called green
liquor, a savoury parsley sauce. It's incredibly affordable and full
of returning customers. Arments is still a family business and I
love everything about it but I make the mistake of trying a portion of eels and feel horrible. I think about Henry I, youngest son
of William the Conqueror. Henry was a big fan of lampreys, an
old fish a bit like an eel. One evening he over-ate a feast of the
fishy fellows and died shortly afterwards.

I don't feel well enough to get back on the bus so I go for a
walk round the corner to Horsley Street and am saddened to see
that Flints, the theatrical chandlers, which used to be housed
behind bright blue shutters, has closed down. It appears to be
yet more posh apartments. Here was once the one-stop shop
for everything practical you might ever need to put on a show.
I used to love just wandering amongst the ropes and thick black
curtains for sale.

Last night, despite the pneumonia, I was performing at the
Palladium to celebrate Prince Charles's seventieth birthday. I
like being backstage and stood quietly enjoying the mild panic
that characterises these kinds of events. The Palladium has the

most marvellously wide stage but a tiny wing space at the sides. The place was crowded with people who needed to be there as well as entourages whose purpose was unclear. I realised I probably shouldn't have come on my own. It didn't look good, but I wasn't sure what I might have needed anyone to do.

I thought back to my days as a followspot operator and how I had longed to work here but the chief electrician had not allowed women backstage. No one thought to question his rule. Everyone was fine with it. Now it was 2018 and it didn't feel as though there had been massive progress. I was welcomed with open arms but I was also the only woman on the bill actually doing a turn. The other women on board for the event – Kylie Minogue and Cheryl (previously Cole) – were only asked to introduce somebody else or, in Cheryl's case, talk about the charity, the Prince's Trust, which we were raising funds for. They were not actually plying their trade.

I was doing some stand-up and the many producers asked if I wanted to rehearse.

'It's just me and a microphone, and I'll just be talking. If the microphone is working I think we're good to go,' I said.

They made me rehearse anyway.

I don't do stand-up very often any more, except for charity, but I have done it for a very long time: since 1979, when I performed on the very first night at the Comedy Store in London. Today stand-up is a profession which I think you can even train for, but forty years ago the idea that you might make a living from it was unheard of. There aren't all that many women who do it now and there certainly weren't very many then. It was a tough gig, partly because there was only ever one woman on the bill. I don't know why. Maybe the club managers worried that if two funny women were in the building at the same time our cycles might collide and we'd become aggressive.

Back in '79, on that first night of the Comedy Store, it was clear no one was expecting women either on stage or in the audience. It took place in a Soho topless bar called the Gargoyle which was reached through a side entrance off Dean Street. The show was performed on the top floor and you could only get there by going through the Nell Gwynne Strip Club. It was hardly a venue to make most women feel relaxed. I did a double act with Simon McBurney, who has gone on to great things with his theatre company Complicité. His then partner Emma Thompson did the sound effects for us.

In 1989 the owner of the Comedy Store, Don Ward, had what he thought was the hilarious idea of celebrating the tenth anniversary by having one night of just women comics. The male performers all stood at the bar drinking and waiting for us to fail. They were disappointed. It was a spectacular night. Hilarious. So spectacular that they never did it again.

Every time I do stand-up I think about that wonderful old comic performer Jack Douglas. In 1983, when I was twenty-five, I was cast as the Fairy Godmother in *Cinderella* at the newly opened Orchard Theatre in Dartford, Kent. I'd never been in a commercial pantomime before and had no idea how it worked. Truth be told, I didn't know much about how anything worked. Also in the cast were Wendy Richard (then famous mainly as Miss Brahms in *Are You Being Served?* as it was before she was in *EastEnders*) as Dandini and that splendid entertainer Dickie Henderson playing Buttons. I thought we would spend each day rehearsing but quickly realised the others planned to spend the day in the bar. The script I had been given seemed extremely thin and that was because the bulk of the material was decided over drinks. 'Let's do "My dad died in Baghdad!"' Dickie would declare. I had no idea what he was talking about or why his father might have passed away in Iraq. It turned out it was an ancient routine which the others all knew. They also knew about 'Busy Bee' and the ghost scene and any number of other set pieces which were a mystery to me. I soon realised I was going to have to write my own lines so set about trying vaguely to stick to the plot and, as a general rule on stage, not get in any-body else's way. Once the show was up and running I ascertained quite quickly that Dickie really liked being in his dressing room. Liked it so much that sometimes he didn't appear when he was supposed to. I'd be on stage waiting for him, for Buttons to come and be jolly with me, when all I could hear in the distance was the stage manager knocking on his door and calling out, 'Mr Henderson, it really is time!' I began developing short routines to cover these moments and often I would find Jack Douglas standing in the wings watching me.

One night he said to me, 'That's a very good joke you're doing ... It's a great set-up. It gets a laugh but you're giving the tag too soon. Much too soon. Make them wait.' The tag is the punchline. 'Do it tomorrow night,' he instructed. 'I'll wait in the wings and don't give the tag until I nod.' I liked him and trusted him. He was hilarious in the show as Baron Hardup. The next night I could see Jack waiting in the wings. I set the joke up, which got a laugh, and then looked out of the corner of my eye for Jack to give the signal. I waited and I waited. Nothing. I thought he'd forgotten. I was about to lose my nerve when finally he nodded. I gave the tag and got the biggest laugh I'd ever heard in my life. It's rare that I am out on a stage and don't look to the wings and imagine Jack Douglas standing there. Years later I tried to do the same thing for a young female comic. She told me to fuck off.

The worst night of stand-up I ever had was in Stockholm. I think it was 1988 because a film called *Punchline* had just been released starring Tom Hanks as a young comic. Someone in Sweden had seen it and decided they wanted to start a stand-up club. As I was the nearest thing they could find to a Swede who had ever tried stand-up I was asked to fly out and do twenty

minutes. At the time twenty minutes of stand-up was not a problem for me. I had what was called a very solid set. It was packed
with laughs. I arrived in Stockholm to discover that the club was
being opened on an old boat moored in the harbour.

I went out onto the stage to a small crowd who were standing waiting expectantly. I did my entire solid twenty minutes
to complete silence. There was not a sound. I was, as we say in
showbusiness, dying on my arse. I finished, and out of nowhere
the audience went nuts. They cheered and yelled and applauded
as if I'd actually been brilliant. The organiser and his wife came
up to me, beaming.

'Marvellous,' he declared. 'The funniest thing I have ever
heard,' she insisted.

'But no one laughed,' I protested.

'No,' she said, 'we didn't like to interrupt.'

The producer of the Prince Charles bash has emailed to thank
me. His fifteen-year-old twin boys were in the audience. 'They're
so impressed,' he wrote, 'that you've taken up comedy at this
stage in your career.'

East Street

I love so many of the shop names along here. In my top ten is a place called The Best Kebab, which subtitles itself as Traditional Fish Bar. A man is cleaning the window. Through it I can see racks of kebabs but no sign of fish.

A woman is speaking on her phone as if she is having to pay by the word.

'Okay? ... No way ... watch television ... you break ... now ... nice day ... '

A child somewhere behind me is kicking the back of a seat. It seems to add to the rhythm of the woman's disjointed conversation. Downstairs another child has begun screaming for its mother. The mother is there. I am sitting by the stairs and can hear her chatting to a friend. She seems to have no idea that everyone is tired and having bad thoughts about her and her offspring.

Someone else has been trying to get through to the council and finally succeeds.

'Hello? Yes, hello. I recently paid my council tax. Reference? Yes. Address? I want to check it's gone through.'

By the time this person ends their call I have every piece of information I need to impersonate them. I wonder about being someone else for a day. I worked for a while for Wandsworth Council. I was between jobs. I found temporary employment in a Portakabin above a new sewer that was being built somewhere under Spencer Park. Despite having no mathematical skills I was put in charge of something to do with accounts. Grimy-faced men would appear from under ground and ask for money in brown envelopes. At lunchtime we'd go and eat in a pub called the Roundhouse. One of the men had no formal education but an extraordinary turn of phrase. He was a sort of Alfred Doolittle. I remember him saying of someone, 'That man is so low he could climb under a snake with a top hat on and the snake would never feel a thing.'

I rather enjoyed the sewer work. I used to go home at the end of my shift and not give it another thought.

It is at the junction with Westmoreland Road that the Camberwell Road changes into the Walworth Road. It's not an upmarket place and hard to believe that the good folk of London once headed here to enjoy a proper outing. Go down Sutherland Walk to Sutherland Square and turn right onto Penrose Street and you come to the Beehive pub. Drinks have been served here for generations as this used to be a pleasure garden called the Montpelier Tea Gardens. Outdoor pleasure gardens were hugely popular in London. Hard to think of this as countryside, but in Dickens's day this was a go-to place for fresh air.

Today the pub is surrounded by blocks of identical, not very interesting flats. The hostelry is now square and grey but the original tavern was decorated with the shells of turtles from which various diners had taken their soup over the years.

I imagine sitting at brightly coloured tables in the garden and being served tea. There was a maze, a flower garden and a small wooden bridge over a stream that led to Wheeler's Fields. The garden was big enough to play cricket in, and in July 1796 the newly formed Montpelier Club are recorded as having played their first match on the Beehive Ground.

In a *Gazetteer of Montpeliers and Montpelliers in the United*

Kingdom (who hasn't read that?) I found a story of another game, which took place on 10 and 11 August 1796:

> The game, like all cricket of the period, was played for high
> stakes – in this case 1000 guineas – and the players were
> selected (by two noble lords) from the pensioners of Greenwich
> Hospital: eleven men with one leg against eleven with one
> arm. On the second day the elevens reappeared, being brought
> to the scene of the action in three Greenwich stage-coaches,
> not without flags and music. The match was played out, and
> the one-legged men beat the poor one-arms by 103.

By 1844 builders and speculators were moving into the area and the Montpelier Club were forced out of the Beehive Ground. Fortunately one of their members found out that the Duchy of Cornwall was willing to lease some land at one of its market gardens. The location? Kennington Oval. For three hundred pounds the members bought ten thousand turfs of grass from Tooting Common and by the summer of 1845 they were happily playing cricket on it.

Back out on the Walworth Road I cross over to Liverpool Grove and walk down to admire the impressive façade of St Peter's church. Built in 1825, it is a great example of the work of the architect Sir John Soane, whose museum in Lincoln's Inn Fields I love so much. I've been rather longing for a tea garden and here the lawns stretch out, lovely and calm after the pollution of the main road. At the end of the nineteenth century there used be a small zoo here, known as Monkey Park. The crypt has a coffee shop where I stop for a rest. In 1940 there was a direct bomb hit on the church and dozens of people sheltering in this very spot were killed or injured. I read somewhere that there are those who believe buildings carry a memory of sound but I can hear nothing but quiet.

The Reverend John Horsley became the rector at St Peter's in 1894 and he clearly thought the church was better put to use for the living than the dead. It was under his guidance that the crypt was cleared of coffins so he could establish a soup kitchen where free lunches were given to children. During his tenure this area was one of the most deprived in London but fortunately there was a remarkable woman who rolled up her sleeves to do something about it.

Octavia Hill is one of my heroes. Not only did she co-found the National Trust, she was a most energetic social reformer. She took this area by the scruff of the neck and transformed it. By the end of her life she was responsible for managing the housing of thousands of Londoners. Octavia's friend Dame Henrietta Barnett described her as being 'small in stature with long body and short legs. She did not dress, she only wore clothes, which were often unnecessarily unbecoming.' Sounds like my kind of gal.

This week I co-hosted BBC1's live evening programme, *The One Show*. *The One Show* is always a marvellous soup of items which seem to have fallen into a pot without anyone having a specific recipe. One minute we were talking to Gloria Estefan about her new musical, before making what can only be described as a handbrake turn into the current problems with online gambling. I love doing live shows more than anything and always salute my father. I learned everything I know about broadcasting from him.

July 1969. Nick was thirteen and I was eleven. We had driven down from New York to Cape Kennedy in Florida for the launch of Apollo 11, the rocket that would take the first men to the moon. Our pale blue Pontiac station wagon had bench seats in the rear compartment which faced out the back. I sat amongst the luggage watching Highway 95 disappear behind us. Billboards littered the route for hundreds of miles, promoting all manner of hotels and restaurants but most particularly a place in Dillon, South Carolina, called South of the Border. We were old hands at this trip, having been to many Apollo launches and party conventions in Florida, so South of the Border was our regular stop as we headed south. You couldn't miss it. It was advertised from Philadelphia onwards. Most of the signs featured a Mexican man called Pedro and terrible puns which worked best if read with a Spanish accent:

'You never sausage a place. You're always a wiener at Pedro's.
        South of the Border.'
'Time for a paws? South of the Border.'

Pedro was a frankly racist ninety-seven-foot-high statue of a Mexican in a sombrero and poncho who held beneath his bandito moustache a large sign that read 'South of the Border'. Dad followed the line of cars driving through Pedro's legs to get to the gas and food. I held strong political views from an early age and was already highly exercised about racial equality for black people. I had taken to wearing a Black Power badge at school. I think even then I knew that making fun of Mexicans wasn't a great idea either.

On 16 July 1969, at about 9.30 a.m., we were at Cape Kennedy, standing as close to the launch site as anyone was allowed – about a mile and a half away. Speakers had been set up on a metal pole and everyone pulled folding chairs from their cars to make themselves comfortable. The countdown was relayed through Tannoys as we watched the Saturn rocket shimmer in the distance. The white rocket with black horizontal stripes was attached to what looked like a giant piece of Meccano. White smoke drifted from the fuselage.

The countdown continued.

'T minus fifteen seconds. Guidance is internal,' said the announcer calmly.

'Ten, nine, eight . . . ignition sequence starts.'

Inside, at the very top of the tallest, heaviest, most powerful rocket ever made, sat three men – Neil Armstrong, Buzz Aldrin and Michael Collins on their way to the moon. It seemed incredible. It was incredible.

Massive flames burst from underneath the rocket. So massive it seemed likely the thing would explode. We had waited for hours and when the rocket finally took off it was astonishing. It remains one of the most majestic things I have ever seen. You could feel the rumble in your heart as the rocket seemed to pause briefly at the end of the countdown before finding the energy to rise slowly into a clear blue sky. The earth shook and for a moment a billow of grey smoke obscured our view.

'Lift-off! We have lift-off,' called the announcer, still calm but clearly trying to restrain himself.

'Tower cleared!'

And off it went straight up into the sky. By now everyone was up off their deckchairs, cheering. Hats were waved in the air and perfect strangers hugged one another. The huge flame beneath the rocket appeared to be chasing it rather than powering it forward. It was so slow and stately that to my childish mind it seemed the thing would never get fast enough to make it all the way to the moon. We watched and watched till our necks ached and finally it disappeared from view. My parents were busy and there is not a single photograph of any of us at this historic event.

We left the car behind and flew on to mission control in Houston, Texas. When we got there my brother and I more or less had free run of the place. No one thought about security back then the way they do now. My dad had a press pass and that was apparently enough for the entire family to wander

about the place. Dad was broadcasting live to the Danish people
and Mum was busy helping him. Papa had read every technical
specification, tried on the spacesuits, even sat in the command
module so he could more clearly describe what was happening
as it happened. It was wonderful for Denmark and it meant Nick
and I were left to our own devices.

I was a confident child and wandered about chatting to anybody. Now that we were in Texas, and ever one for wanting the
right costume for an event, I had purchased a large straw cowboy
hat which I wore with great pride. I was very small and the hat
was huge, and I must have be an odd sight amongst the endless
hordes of technical people working for NASA and the journalists writing about them. The tech people all looked pretty much
the same. Mostly men with slicked-back hair in a side parting.
They wore short-sleeved white shirts with black ties and sported
pen holders in their breast pockets filled with biros and pencils.
In the main control room there was a giant screen looking down
upon row after row of these men sitting behind computer ter-
minals. It was here that I followed the action. It was here that
I watched Neil Armstrong step out onto the moon. I knew the
importance of what we were watching as my father had been
talking about it at the dinner table for months. As I stood there
I noticed a woman standing beside me. She looked anxious.

'You all right?' I asked.

'I'm nervous,' she said. 'That's my boss who is about to step
out onto the moon.' She was Neil Armstrong's secretary. 'Don't
worry,' I said, 'I'll hold your hand.' And so it was that when Neil
Armstrong, the first man on the moon, stepped onto the lunar
surface I was holding his secretary's hand.

The motel we were staying in was like so many we had occupied
as we travelled across the United States. The rooms opened onto
a square courtyard with balconies overlooking a central swimming pool. After Apollo 11 had successfully landed on the moon

the whole of Houston turned into a massive party. The hotel had a 'splash down' party marking the re-entry of the command module into the waves of the Pacific Ocean. Armstrong, Aldrin and Collins were in quarantine but appeared none the worse for wear. They had been visited by a beaming President Nixon and all seemed right with the world. It was time to have fun.

The hotel had hired a tribute band although I can't for the life of me remember who they were paying tribute to. It was a four-piece male band with two guitarists, a drummer and a singer all dressed in pale blue tuxedos with velvet lapels, ruffled shirts, matching bow ties and long hair with accompanying moustaches. My father and his small team were sitting with the other Scandinavian journalists. They had made great headway into a bottle of whisky and kept sending me to get more ice from the machine in the lobby.

Once when I returned with the ice I saw that the entire Scandinavian contingent had made their way through the crowd to stand in front of the band.

'Play "Frühlingsrauschen"!' the Norwegian correspondent was shouting at the lead singer. The band were now taking requests, but probably not for piano pieces written by Norwegian composers in 1896. I have no idea why anyone thought this piece would be suitable but now the Danes and the Swedes took up the cry for 'Frühlingsrauschen' or 'Rustle of Spring'. The band, intent on playing hits from the 1960s, ignored them.

Rage soared in the breasts of the Norsemen and they began to plot. I sat at the table drinking a non-alcoholic cocktail called a Shirley Temple.

'We have to do something!' declared the Swedish cameraman.

'They can't get away with this,' affirmed my father.

I don't think I really knew everyone was drunk. It seemed a rather normal end to the day to me.

'You could turn the power off,' someone suggested and the plan was agreed. The entire delegation set off to find the electrical source that was powering the electric guitars. I followed them as they traced the cable back to a large cupboard behind the changing rooms. With great glee the men danced in a small circle before pulling out a massive plug. The band slid to a stop as though the air had been taken out of them. Not content with stopping the noise my father and his team now turned out all the lights as well. For reasons I can't fathom about drunken adults this seemed to be the cue for everyone to jump fully clothed into the pool.

The next morning it was impossible to go for a swim as the entire surface of the water was littered with beer cans, ashtrays and one very fat man from French television who was asleep in the middle of the pool on a lilo. Man had gone to the moon but he had also gone to pieces. A team of Hispanic women were trying to bring some order back to the place. I learned then that magnificent moments in history can be disappointing. There is a great book about women's history by Rosalind Miles called *Who Cooked the Last Supper?* I expect there were women who cleaned up after that too.

In London the East Street Market is in full flow. Charlie Chaplin was born here but it has no doubt changed since his day. He might not have recognised the many African and Caribbean goodies for sale now but there are also some marvellous shops which must have been there for years. One has a display of slippers individually wrapped in cling film. A handwritten sign on a piece of card reads 'Ladies + Gents Slipper's. The Ideal Gift.' I feel my age when I realise I too consider slippers a very fine gift indeed. I gave a pair to my friend Kate Mosse, the novelist, which I believe she still wears when writing.

Down at the end of the market, at 153a East Street, there is a blue plaque to Dr Charles Vickery Drysdale. Dr Drysdale was a founder of the Family Planning Association and the plaque proudly proclaims that it was here in 1921 that he opened his first birth control clinic. There is no plaque for his mother, Alice Vickery, who I find much more interesting. Alice too was a doctor but she was also a suffragette and the first British woman to qualify as a chemist. She and Charles's father met in 1869 when Alice began her medical studies at the short-lived Ladies' Medical College in Fitzroy Square. They were together for decades but never married as they both considered the institution to be nothing more than legalised prostitution.

I wonder what debates Alice and I might have had, for I so love being married. Deb and I were civilly partnered in 2007 and did the 'upgrade' to legally wed in 2014. Being married to her is one of the most joyous parts of my life. It means everything to me. I suspect, however, if I had been a straight woman back in the late nineteenth century I too might have railed against marriage. It's odd to find myself so ardent a supporter. I think it's probably because of a guy I met when I first started work at Nottingham Playhouse. As is often the way with actors, we used to finish each night in the theatre bar. The barman was an openly gay white-haired man in his fifties called John. John was the life and soul of the place and he and I would often chat. I wasn't yet out to any of my colleagues or even my family and I think I liked talking to John because it made me feel better. He told me a story which lit a fire in me that has never gone out.

John had a partner called Stephen. They were together for twenty years but in all that time Stephen's family never spoke to him. They had thrown him from the nest when he came out, so for two decades John had been all the family he had. Then Stephen became ill and, in hospital, he went into a coma. John knew the end was close and he fretted. He knew how hurt Stephen had always been by his separation from his mother and father, his siblings. John wanted peace for his lover so he called

Stephen's family and told them what was happening. They rushed to the hospital and immediately took over, but not in a way John could have predicted. They had John removed from the ward and forbade further access. This was before gay marriage or civil partnership. Despite their many years together John had no rights whatsoever where Stephen was concerned. The love of his life passed away and was buried without John even attending the funeral. When I knew John his sorrow at not even knowing where Stephen was buried was mind-numbing.

I have spent much of my life fighting for same-sex couples to have their relationships recognised and respected. It pleases me beyond all measure to call Debbie my wife and for her to do the same but I don't think it was until the moment we took our vows that I realised I hadn't just been fighting for the Johns and Stephens of this world but for myself too.

Larcom Street

Larcom Street. Thomas Larcom? Undersecretary to the Lord-Lieutenant of Ireland. Is that enough to get a street named after you? On the corner of Larcom Street is a wonderful health shop called G Baldwin and Co. which proudly proclaims it has been selling natural products since 1844. I've started taking my own coffee on the bus and salute them with it as we pass for it is full of natural health. I call it coffee with medicine. Black coffee with strong spices added, a blend of my own concoction in a rather fine thermal mug given to me by my son-in-law, Adam. He is my Jesse's partner and we are all under a strict Jesse edict to protect the environment. She is quite rightly hot on recycling and reusing so I am commanded wherever possible not to buy takeaway coffee in disposable cups.

I do what I can but I know it is not enough. Someone has spat out a large wad of chewing gum on to the floor. It has been trodden in and now makes a shape like a splat of paint. I sit staring at it. Gum arabic is a natural gum made of hardened sap taken from two species of the acacia tree. It's edible and mostly used in the food industry as a kind of glue or binder. You find it in chewing gum but also in every soft drink, M & Ms, gumdrops, jelly beans, cake icing, marshmallows and even edible glitter. But there's a whole lot of other uses such as brewing, printing, paint production, glue, cosmetics, shoe polish, watercolour paint and the lickable adhesive on stamps, envelopes and cigarette papers. It is both amazing and terrible stuff.

Gum arabic has been causing wars and keeping people enslaved for centuries. Its origins date back to four thousand years ago: the Egyptian artisans appreciated its sticky qualities, using it both as a binder for papyri pigments and as a thickener in cosmetics and for mummification.

Gum arabic – Sudan again. Hundreds of thousands of Sudanese are dependent on gum arabic for their livelihoods. The country is the world's largest single producer of the stuff and the production of it is heavily controlled by the government. When the US threatened Sudan with sanctions over their connection to the Janjaweed militia group, they simply retaliated by threatening to stop providing gum arabic, which would have been the death of Coca-Cola. It worked. Soft drinks trump human rights every time.

I went to a gum arabic factory. Much of the work had been mechanised but not the initial labour. When gum first arrives it is shaken out onto the floor in large nuggets of amber about the size of a pear. In a closed room women – only women – beat the nuggets with huge wooden sticks. The ends of the sticks look burnt but it is actually the wear from the women's hands. There was a continuous thwacking sound as they raised the heavy sticks over their heads and brought them down to crush the gum into smaller particles. Each woman had her own work area which was divided by rolled hessian sacks. The women were shy but smiled at us. One was so beautiful she could have been a model while another looked old and tired with no bottom middle teeth.

She gave me her stick to have a go and the women laughed when I could barely raise it above my head. The backbone of the economy was reliant on the backbone of these women.

'Why don't you mechanise this?' I asked the manager.

He shrugged, uninterested. 'It doesn't taste as good if the women don't break it.'

It was the women of Sudan who got me through that trip. No

matter where we went there was always a woman somewhere making and selling coffee in the open air. She would be hunched over an open fire with a pot made from an old instant coffee tin. 'Coffee with medicine', everyone called it – strong black stuff with a huge infusion of ginger. I drank some every day. The men all told me not to, that it wasn't safe, but I watched the women boil the water and take great care with their preparations. We were there for five weeks and I was the only one of the team who never got sick. All these years later and I still make coffee with medicine and think of those women.

I pass a plaque to Charles Babbage, father of the computer, who was born in 1791 in a house that once stood on the corner of Larcom Street. I am pleased to remember that Ada Lovelace, the woman who told old Charlie how to make his machine actually work, has a blue plaque in St James's Square.

On the corner of Wansey Street and the Walworth Road stands the old Walworth Town Hall. Completed in 1866, its fine gothic walls have been obscured by boarding since a fire in 2013. A sign tells me it once housed not only the 'Surveyor of Sewers' but also the 'Inspector of Nuisances'. There's a job to aspire to.

I wish I could tell my friend Jeremy Hardy about it. He would have loved to be an inspector of nuisances. I have been to speak at his funeral, which was held at a small church in Dorset. For reasons I can't recall Deb was organising the buffet and struggled to relay to the local caterers the need for some vegan sandwiches. 'So they'll have the cheese, then?' she kept being told. Bloody Londoners, they must have thought. I can't get my head around the fact that Jeremy is dead. He was at my side on *The News Quiz* for so long. Part genius, part schoolboy, he always dared to deal with stories that the rest of us felt faint about. I remember when some Austrian man had been found to be keeping his children locked in a basement none of us wanted to include it in the show. Jeremy, however, had no such fears. Off he went on a rant about

Austrian childcare, referring to the von Trapped children and declaring that such a terrible thing would never be allowed to happen in the UK because of planning permission. It was genius. I don't think it was ever broadcast but those of us who were in the room when he spoke were lucky to have been there.

I think back to a recording of the quiz where Simon Hoggart was in the chair, and Alan Coren, Linda Smith, Jeremy and I were on the panel. I am the only one left. All those brilliant people are lost to us by some kind of cancer or other. I don't know what to make of it except to know I cannot fill the vacant spaces.

A man wearing a chequered cap gets on the bus with a dog on a filthy lead. It is instantly clear that the fellow is a character. He speaks to everyone without stopping.

'He's been playing with his friends!' he announces to the half-empty top deck as he points at the dog. 'He's got two friends who are huskies!'

The dog, we learn, is called Rusty. The man found him tied to a stake. He has checked his teeth and thinks the dog is eight or nine.

He sits down beside me. 'My philosophy is to get to and from the park as quickly as possible. It's clean and straightforward.'

It is. So I agree.

After a while the man gets up and leaves.

Papa told me that when his father took the train he always concluded the journey by tapping on the window of the steam engine's driver and thanking him most profusely.

'Thank you, driver!' the man calls cheerfully. It makes me smile.

The driver says nothing.

*

My father passed away after giving one after-dinner speech too many. He was in the Lake District, he was exhausted and his heart gave out. Last night I gave a speech to fifteen hundred in the Great Room at the Dorchester Hotel. I thought of Papa as I waited to go on. Maybe time to stop soon and live a little more.

Heygate Street

I can't see words without reading them. I know that sounds ridiculous. It's what they are for, but I mean labels and instructions and all manner of useless blurbs. This morning I read my cereal packet, which told me that if I savoured the present then life would be delicious.

It bothered me to think of looking to muesli for a philosophy of life. But I wonder how many people do savour the present. An old man behind me is sucking on his false teeth. Is he savouring them or is it just a piece of toast stuck there since breakfast?

A woman sits down beside me on a not very full bus, which I've learned is poor etiquette. She should've chosen one of the empty double seats and not joined me. She has an old-fashioned PVC sports bag from which she extracts a Thermos and begins eating soup. It seems an odd choice for a bus. She not only slurps from her flask but has brought a spoon to get out the bigger bits. Mushroom soup. It reminds me of the time I saved somebody from drowning in their soup at the Savoy.

It was years ago and I was attending the Women of the Year Lunch, an event I would go on to host for many years, and indeed become its president. That particular lunch, however, I was young and didn't really know anybody. To be honest, I wasn't really sure why I'd been invited. There were about four hundred women, 399 of whom were among the great and the good of this country and then there was me.

It wasn't the sort of event where you could bring a plus one, and as soon as I arrived I realised I should have worn a hat. I scanned the large board with the seating plan. The room had been laid with round tables of eight. In telling this story I don't want to be mean by naming anybody, so I'll try to be discreet. Chit-chat is not my strong suit and I felt anxious about possible small talk at the lunch. On the other side of the table from me was a world-famous javelin thrower. Sport has never been a strong point either. Apart from sharpening the bread sticks and seeing who could chuck them the furthest, I couldn't really think what we might talk about. On my left was the daughter of one of the world's most successful tycoons. From Australia. It will give you some idea of how long ago this was when I tell you that she was smoking. I turned to her and learned quite quickly that it's possible to be too rich for small talk. I gave up and finally looked to my right. Here was seated a very elderly woman. She was one of the world's most prolific novelists. She was an exceptionally successful woman but now really very old indeed. Despite the fact that the lunch had not yet started I could see she had already had enough and was beginning to nod off. Her eyes closed and her chin slowly slumped forward. Then her whole head began bobbing back and forth like one of those small plastic birds one used to be able to buy which dipped rhythmically into water.

The staff at the Savoy, who are excellent, chose this moment to serve the soup, and they were quick. They shot round our table with steaming bowls of something fishy and managed to slip a plate of broth in front of the old woman just as her head gave a final bounce and was about to hit the tablecloth. Without thinking I thrust my hand between the hot soup and the woman's face. She seemed to like this for she now rested the full weight of her head in my open palm. It wasn't pleasant. I could feel her teeth clicking in and out of my life line. I didn't know what to do. If I lowered my hand I would burn my knuckles but if

I pushed back I might give the old dear whiplash. I could see the javelin thrower looking at me thinking I was trying to steal the woman's croutons. In the end I did manage to push gently back and apart from some artificial fruit flying off her hat she seemed fine. She slept for the rest of lunch. A few weeks later I read that she died. I felt bad. I can't remember what she died of but I'm pretty sure it was better than going in her soup.

The woman beside me continues to slurp contentedly. I am glad she is enjoying her meal.

Many years ago I was filming in Mozambique. The civil war there had been over for only about six months and it was not entirely safe.

An impromptu street market had popped up and what little food there was had been laid out on old hessian sacks from aid deliveries. There was almost no money in the economy yet the market was busy. At one end a woman was selling bulbs of garlic for ten cents.

'Why would you spend that if you have no money?' I asked my guide, Wadzi, a Zimbabwean doing development work in Mozambique.

Wadzi turned to me. 'Sandi,' she admonished, 'the people are poor, not dead. Everyone still wants food to taste nice.'

She also advised, 'Walk where you see cow pats.'

'Why?'

'Because if a cow had time to excuse itself then there's probably no landmine buried.'

Round the back of the Elephant today, actual art is taking place. Two men in hoodies are spray-painting a shipping container. One of them is standing on a blue bin turned on its side. He has a can of green spray paint but I can't make out what he is painting.

'What's it going to be?' I ask.

He gets down off his bin and both men explain their vision for a Nordic scene of snow-covered fir trees. He points to the top of the container where trees in the distance have already been completed. I now know that the sign 'If it ain't racked it ain't graff' which I saw at Medlar Street means that if the paint has not been stolen then it is not real graffiti. I think the sentiment written out in full like that would have been even funnier but I restrain myself and don't ask the artists how they came by their materials.

'It looks great. I'll come back when it's finished,' I say and they grin. Everyone likes a nice review.

Mostly I come to this part of town to visit Ecuador or Colombia, for this is the heart of London's Latin American community. There are about 150 Latin American businesses in the area and a surprisingly large expat community. According to Latin Elephant, a charity that brings them together, nearly 9 per cent of people in Southwark hail from Latin America. The people and the businesses came here in the 1990s when no one else wanted to. Now there are cafés, restaurants, hair-dressers, fashion shops and some businesses which make money where they can. One place under the arches seems a curious combination of international shipping and underwear for pregnant women.

Further along the arches another shop has also taken to combining unexpected enterprises. La Vida Loca Ltd is a coffee bar where you can also get your hair done and your jewellery repaired whilst engaging their money transfer services and renting a video in Spanish. '*La vida loca*' means 'the crazy life'. I think it's something many of us believe we want. I pass a girl in a T-shirt that declares that she is 'Living the Dream'. I wonder if she is. I wonder if we are any of us brave enough for *la vida loca* or whether, like the shop, it is actually just La Vida Loca Ltd.

A forty-three-storey apartment building called the Strata dominates the skyline. Behind it lies Maldonado Walk. Until 2014 this was an alleyway known as Eagle Yard but it was renamed following a campaign led by a local councillor with Ecuadorian heritage. The walk is now named after an early eighteenth-century scientist, Pedro Vicente Maldonado. Born in Ecuador, he was a physicist, mathematician, astronomer, topographer and geographer who, despite only living to be forty-three, held many marvellous jobs in his time. He was Horseman of the Golden Key, Gentleman of the Camera, Lieutenant of the Magistrate and Governor of the Emerald Province. He was so well thought of that in 1748 he was invited to London to speak to the Royal Society but the trip did not go well as he died unexpectedly during his visit. He's buried at St James's church, Piccadilly, so has a permanent home in the city. I am glad for him but baffled that it is easier for an ancient man from Ecuador to be memorialised in London's streets than for any woman.

I've been asked to climb Mount Kilimanjaro for charity but I don't think I have it in me. My last great African adventure, I canoed the length of the Zambezi which was one of my more frightening experiences. I have done a lot of what can only be termed tricky travel. That one I can blame on my father. One day when we were living in New York he came home with a wooden canoe. It was a most unusual craft. Built of mahogany, it could be split into two complete halves for transport and then swiftly made whole again using two brass handles, three hooks and a rubber seal. Wide-bottomed with rounded ends, it was large enough for two people. We had a small above-ground swimming pool in the back garden and I have a photo of my father sitting in the canoe and sipping whisky while floating in the pool.

He had bought it from a second-hand shop and I suspect my dad had been drinking before the purchase as well as after.

'This canoe,' he declared to us all with his usual *joie de vivre*, 'is the very vessel which Dr Livingstone used to chart the Zambezi!'

Well, it was wooden and it looked old so we all believed him. It became known as the bean pod and for years, from one posting to another, Livingstone's canoe came with us. It was during a casual conversation with a BBC producer that I was asked if there were any journeys I would like to undertake. He was making a series of documentaries to be entitled *Great Journeys of the World*. I don't know why I didn't suggest something relaxing but instead I replied, 'I'd like to take Livingstone's canoe back down the Zambezi.'

Television production was a bit more relaxed in those days. He thought it was a marvellous idea so off we set. Seventeen hundred miles. Four countries. It's a long way in a canoe. I'm sure not many people realise or care that Livingstone died on the banks of the Zambezi when his haemorrhoids burst. It gives you an idea of how long the trip took that we occupied many a watery hour trying to work out exactly where. Along the way there were a fair number of terrifying encounters with creatures who wanted to kill us and a memorable day flying with an off-his-head-on-drugs helicopter pilot who very nearly finished the job. It was only after I had gone all that way that I discovered the canoe I had taken so many miles had never had the pleasure of Livingstone's bottom. It had been built in Britain at the old Spitfire factory in the late 1940s. How it had then got to America is a mystery. Someone somewhere was telling fibs about the whole thing. How Papa would have laughed.

Elephant & Castle Station

I've been riding a tandem with Björn from ABBA which, of the many odd sentences about my life, is one of the more unexpected. I met Björn a few years ago when I asked him to come and conduct the WOW orchestra. WOW stands for Women of the World and it's an annual festival at the Royal Festival Hall. Started by Jude Kelly, it's been going for nearly ten years and I've been with it from the beginning. Jude asked me to come up with a show to bring a weekend of feminism to a close and I began something called *Mirth Control*. We gather an all-female orchestra who play forgotten pieces by great women composers interspersed with a themed lecture on history from me. One year we did Scandinavia as a theme and even though it wasn't written by a woman it seemed sad not to have our orchestra play 'Waterloo' by ABBA. I got a message to Björn and, Swedish feminist that he is, he surprised the audience by coming on stage at the end.

A few years later I got a message that he wanted me to fly out to Stockholm to see a show he was doing. Deb and I went to see what was kind of a mad but brilliant evening. A Greek taverna seating about five hundred people had been built in an amusement park in the city. The diners gathered for their meal only to find they were also in the middle of a show about the waiting staff and those who ran the restaurant. This went on all the way through the dinner and concluded with the entire gathering dancing on the tables to ABBA tunes. It was surreal watching it with Björn at our table.

'I want you to do this for me in London,' declared Björn over the music. As I can't sing a note I presumed he meant write it, which I did, and we have been preparing for the opening night. The London restaurant is being built out at the O2. It's vast and looks just like ... well, a Greek taverna. We have found the cast and Björn and I are making some adverts to start selling the tickets. We filmed us riding the bike out at the O2 as just one way we suggested you might get there. It was fun. Björn is a delight, a clever man, passionate about everything he does, but as I sat behind him, pedalling like mad, I did think it was a curious way to spend an afternoon.

Pretty much every job I have ever had has turned up unexpectedly. In fact the only one I ever applied for in my working life was a kids' TV show called *No. 73*. It was a live programme on Saturday mornings back when there were just three channels to choose from. The most popular channel was BBC1, BBC2 was for anyone who had read a book and then there was ITV, which my grandmother dismissed as cheap and tawdry. *73* was on ITV. I saw the ad in the back of the *Stage* newspaper. It read, 'Would you like to have breakfast with a gorilla?' I thought perhaps I would so I applied. The ad requested a letter with contact details and a photo of the applicant. Those were the days when actors looking for work sent off glossy black-and-white pictures of themselves known as 'eight by tens' because of their large size. I didn't have any showbiz photos of myself so I toddled off to Victoria Station to get some passport photos. The booth had one of those stools which sat on a screw thread so that it could be wound up or down to suit the height of the sitter. Obviously I needed to get it as high as possible but the wretched thing was broken. All I could do was stretch my neck up towards the camera and in the end I sent a black-and-white photo-booth picture showing only the top half of my head. I think the producers thought I was trying to be funny because I got the job.

There is a new roundabout system at Elephant and Castle which confuses everyone. It was ever thus. There's been a junction here since at least the seventeenth century. Then it was horse shit everyone stepped in, now it is fast-food wrappers. At first sight there is nothing to draw you to the Elephant but the London Explorers' Club, quite rightly, felt it was an under-rated location, as it is the geographical centre of London.

The myth about the name Elephant and Castle is that it was some Londoners' poor attempt to hail the Spanish Catherine of Aragon when she came to town to marry Henry VIII. She was a daughter of Castille or *Infanta de Castilla* and the story is that the locals anglicised that foreign phrase as Elephant and Castle. It's a good tale, but most likely the name came from a black-smith's shop which once stood at the junction. The symbol of an elephant with a howdah on its back matches the coat of arms of the Cutlers' Company, who used to make knives and weapons – presumably with ivory handles, hence the elephant. Eventually it seems the blacksmith worked out he could make more money selling beer and turned his place into a tavern. By then everyone knew the name so he just kept it.

Now busy being gentrified, this part of London was once home to violent gangs who happily plied the trades of book-making, extortion, kidnapping, beatings and the occasional murder in the 1920s and '30s. There were many English gangs around at the time – the Birmingham Boys, the Cortesi broth-ers of Saffron Hill, the Camden Town gang, the Finsbury Boys and the Elephant and Castle Mob. The leaders of these criminal enterprises had great names like Darby Sabini, the

McCausland brothers and Dodger Mullins. For twenty years the McDonald brothers, Wag and Wal, ruled the roost over the Elephant boys.

I've been reading *London Labour and the London Poor*, which was written in the 1840s by the Victorian journalist Henry Mayhew. What I like about Mayhew is that he was a pedant and knew that the devil is in the detail. He wrote about how the poor lived and earned a crust so minutely that, years after, you feel you can walk the streets with him. Among the more hideous jobs he details was that of the pure finders. These were mainly women who walked about collecting dog shit in buckets, which was then sold to the tanners, who processed leather. Mayhew listed the street people of London and the pure finders were pretty low down. They came after all manner of people selling useful things in the open air.

Mayhew wrote about the '"hard-ups", as they are called, who collect the refuse pieces of smoked cigars from the gutters, and having dried them, sell them as tobacco to the very poor; the dredgermen or coal-finders; the mud-larks, the bone-grubbers; and the sewer-hunters'.

A pink elephant statue looks down on us all from the shopping centre. I had a tricky encounter with an elephant on *No. 73*. Actually I had a lot of tricky encounters in the six years I worked on the show. I was attacked by an emu, had to finish a show on my own because the comedian Spike Milligan decided to go home early, and managed to make it halfway to the Isle of Wight in a hovercraft made out of an old wardrobe. (We had to be rescued.) The elephant, however, stays with me as a low moment. The show was an hour and three-quarters of live broadcasting. It was set in a house called No. 73 where I supposedly lived as the landlady, Ethel. The story was a mix of sitcom and magazine show, and each week we had an animal item of some kind. Our resident vet was a marvellous man called David Taylor. One week I asked him what creature we would be dealing with and he announced, 'This week we are going to have an elephant and a mouse in the back garden so we can discuss their basic physiological differences.'

I thought you'd have to be a pretty stupid child not to spot the basic differences by yourself, but fair enough. On the morning of the broadcast I was racing about as usual, chatting to the other characters and generally running the place when the moment arrived for David's item. I ran into the back yard and there was the aforementioned elephant waiting with David, who held a small mouse in his hand. I had asked David before the show if the two creatures would get on.

'Oh don't worry,' he had replied, 'elephants are vegetarian.'

Well, not this one. David was busy explaining the basic points when the elephant, clearly bored with the discussion, reached out his trunk, picked up the mouse and placed the poor animal right in his mouth. It was horrifying. We were broadcasting live in front of millions of children. At this point David did what you would hope any vet might do. He reached first into the elephant's mouth and then deep down into its throat and retrieved a frankly rather shaken mouse. He turned to me and declared, 'Oh look, they're playing!'

Playing the part of Ethel was my first proper job on TV and it has haunted me. Almost every week some grown-up stranger or other calls me by that name. I was once driving late at night across a remote piece of country. There were no street lights and I noticed that, ahead on the quiet lane, there appeared to be someone lying in the road. I stopped the car and ran to see if they were all right. A man had been in a car accident and thrown clear of his vehicle onto the road. He was in terrible pain, moaning as I rushed over. I looked down at him.

'Are you all right?' I cried.

He looked up at me as if I had arrived from outer space. 'Fuck me,' he declared, 'it's Ethel!'

The bus skims past the Metropolitan Tabernacle where religious hatred of the LGBTQ+ community has found a home since 1970. The man in charge at the Tabernacle, Dr Masters, sports a footballer's comb-over last popular in the 1970s. Neither his hair nor his prejudices have had an update. You can see hours of his pontification on the internet. Being that cross must be exhausting. He looks as though he could do with a laugh. I feel one ought to try to understand one's enemy so take time to watch him sermonise online about 'the abomination of same-sex relationships', a story about two goats and the 'message of uncircumcised fruit', which was possibly the bit I understood least.

Yesterday I had lunch with with an old friend at the House of Lords. She is a baroness, which sounds wonderfully like a character from opera. I'd been instructed to bring all manner of ID but in the end no one asked for it; my pal had forgotten to put me on the security list but the police just waved me in anyway. I told them I had a penknife in my pocket and that seemed fine too. More and more I realise what a great sleeper terrorist I would make. Going into the Lords is a bit like entering the cloakroom at boarding school. There are racks of gold hooks where each peer has his or her own peg with their name on to hang their coat. It hardly seems the place of considered government. I pop to the ladies' and learn how cross the male peers were when it was suggested that the women needed a loo at all. This is the citadel that the Women's Equality Party would like to storm but the chances seem slim to none. So far, just being allowed to be excused in the place has been a girl-power triumph. At half-past two the House begins its deliberations for the afternoon but there is hardly anyone there. Those who have turned up have left their bags by the door like children abandoning their books for PE.

'Haven't they got things to do?' I ask.

My ennobled friend looks resigned and sighs. 'There's no governing going on. I think the whole country is being run by civil servants. Still, it seems to be working.'

You can feel the paralysis in the place. An entire legislature frozen in its tracks, waiting till we leave Europe. I think about the homeless woman sleeping on the bus and I could weep. I look at my friend. I know she has tried to invigorate the ancient system but it is moribund.

The actual building of Parliament looks very grand but beneath the gold leaf the place is crumbling. Riddled with asbestos, it is soon to be closed down for refurbishment. I have been fantasising what might happen if all the parliamentarians moved into a round chamber. If, instead of sitting opposite each other shouting, they sat side by side, listening. I ask about this.

'Oh no,' she says wearily, 'we are moving but the layout will be exactly the same.'

'Why?' I ask. 'Surely what this country needs is less of that politics where you just disagree with someone because they're sitting opposite you. Wouldn't it be better if there were shades of opinion and less black-and-white thinking? Surely the very shape of the chamber encourages disagreement instead of compromise.'

The baroness smiles. I know she agrees but she has been there long enough also to know that I am a merely a dreamer. There are six thousand pieces of art in the building which will need to be rehoused during the renovations. My friend has been trying to get them sent out round the country for everyone to enjoy. Apparently all the powers that be just shake their heads at her.

*

I've been reading about the Tree of Ténéré. This solitary acacia used to stand in the Sahara and was a landmark on caravan routes in north-east Niger. A symbol of hardiness, it was considered the most isolated tree on earth, the only one for 250 miles. It had been there for generations. Just one tree and a lot of desert all around it. Literally nothing else anywhere near by. In 1973 a drunken Libyan male truck driver hit the tree and knocked it over.

I do not know how men have ended up ruling the world.

London College of Communication

I'm in my favourite seat, at the front on the right-hand side. Across the aisle on the left sits a young man. He is wearing tracksuit bottoms and sits with his hand down his trousers. He is not masturbating . . . as far as I can tell. I've been a bus regular for some time now and it's not unusual to see a boy in a tracksuit holding on to his penis. I don't know why. Penises are not my speciality. Do they wobble about too much on public transport and have to be held in place? I move away from him because . . . Oh, I don't know. Maybe I don't want to share the bell he will press to get off. He looks at me as I go. Maybe he worries that I am a witch.

In medieval times there was great anxiety over the belief that witches liked to steal penises and keep them as pets. I think they'd make bad pets because they seem a troublesome organ. Boys have such an unreliable relationship with their penises it's hard to imagine why they are so pleased with them. I think of Napoleon. Nearly two hundred years after his death people are still talking about the fate of his penis. If you search for 'Napoleon's Peninsula Wars', before you have finished typing the word 'peninsula' acres of stuff comes up about the proud Emperor's most private part. Apparently it was only an inch and a half long, and we know this because the poor appendage has been endlessly bought and sold.

According to legend the doctor who did his autopsy, for reasons best known to himself, cut the penis off and gave it to the priest who had conducted Bonaparte's last rites. That holy man, Abbé Ange Paul Vignali, kept it in his family (well, I guess you would) until at last it was sold in 1924 (listed as a 'mummified tendon') to a rare book dealer in the United States. In 1927 it was displayed at the Museum of French Art in New York, where it was variously described as a 'shriveled eel' and 'a maltreated strip of buckskin shoelace'. Fifty years later it was sold for three thousand dollars to a urologist called John J. Latimer. The Latimer family still have it. They keep it in a small leather case in their basement. You can see a video of it online. The case is tucked at the back of a low shelf, under some plumbing pipes. Perhaps the world would be a better place if more penises were kept with the Christmas decorations and only brought out for special occasions.

I once saw a penis on the Tube, which is not what you want on your way home. I prefer the bus to the Tube because I am intensely claustrophobic. I don't like the idea of being under ground but sometimes I give the Tube a go. I do it because of a telling-off a friend of mine gave me.

'If you feel bad under ground that is because you are thinking about yourself,' she admonished. 'If instead of worrying about your own issues you spent all your time under ground seeing if someone else needs your help then you wouldn't have time to worry about yourself.'

So I do my best, but it's possible I am over-keen in being helpful. I'm pretty sure I have assisted a few women with buggies down stairs they didn't want to descend. I was on the Tube because I had been to visit a friend who lived near an Underground station and I didn't know the local buses. She's vegetarian and had made mushroom risotto. It was the day the adult actress Stormy Daniels had compared Donald Trump's penis to a mushroom and we had spent a happy half-hour going through the ingredients for our evening meal trying to imagine which particular fungus was most like Donald's. I suppose it meant penises were on my mind.

I headed home. It was late and there was only me and a young man in the rattling carriage. He was in his mid-twenties and seated at the other end from me. It was the District Line and as we passed under the Houses of Parliament I was wondering if it were true that this part of the tracks was laid on layers of tree bark so that the rumbling trains would not disturb the men in power above.

Suddenly the young man called out, 'Oi! What do you think of that then?' and pointed to his lap. Thinking about tree bark, I had not been paying attention.

'Sorry?' I said.

He smiled broadly. 'That! What do you think of that!' He pointed enthusiastically to his lap again. He was quite a long way down the carriage and I couldn't see what he was pointing at. Perhaps he was a tourist and proud of some purchases recently made. Mindful of my duty to assist those with me under ground, I got up from my seat and made my way through the swaying carriage.

I can't see all that well without my glasses so as I got closer I began looking for them. I always forget which pocket I've put them in so I paused in front of my fellow passenger patting myself down, searching for my spectacles. At last I found them. My young man was beginning to get slightly irritated. Now I could see clearly that he was pointing to his penis, which lay tragically exposed from his jeans. It was pale and looked surprised to be in the light. Like a baby mole on a first outing. I must be the worst person in the world for a flasher to either upset or impress. I had had no idea what he was talking about, don't find penises remotely interesting and then had been unable to see this proud member anyway. I laughed out loud at my own ineptitude for this encounter. Once I had started laughing I couldn't stop. I collapsed on the seat opposite helpless with mirth. Tears ran down my face as the train pulled into the next station. Mortified, the young man got up and ran off. I suppose it's a sign of how British I now am that as he ran I yelled after him 'I am so sorry!'

If you are wary of penises then it's worth knowing the story of what happened in 1938 at 429 The Strand. I suspect that if you look right on the Number 12 as you come up to Trafalgar Square you can just see the great grey edifice which is Zimbabwe House. It was built in 1908 as the headquarters of the British Medical Association and adorned with eighteen marvellous statues of extremely fit naked young men. These were carved by the sometimes controversial artist Jacob Epstein and quite took Edwardian breath away. Each nude was eight feet high and the ones displaying themselves full frontal were endowed to scale. In 1938 the building was bought by the then Rhodesian High Commission, who did what we all do when we buy a new home – gave it a jolly good clean. Much of London is held together with grime and this washing down is thought to have loosened one of the stone penises, which fell from its carved-loin home and killed a passer-by. Shortly afterwards all the statues were emasculated for health and safety reasons. I do wonder about the person who was charged with telling the family of the poor deceased that he had been felled by a carved phallus.

Today I don't want to think about boys, their parts and their disproportionate influence on history. The bus turns left on to St George's Road and I get off to walk up to Elliot's Row, the former home of a woman known as Alice Diamond, one of the Forty Elephants or Forty Thieves, an all-female crime gang who specialised in shoplifting. They too were based in Elephant and Castle, but as with much of women's history, we don't have much detail. The women were shoplifting queens and we know for certain the gang was operating in 1873, as they got a write-up in the papers. There is some thought, however, that they actually began their business back in the late eighteenth century. Mostly they targeted posh shops in the West End but sometimes they'd have a day out at the seaside and nick stuff there. They would 'put on the posh' for their work, wearing specially adapted clothing with secret pockets in their coats, skirts, bloomers and hats to hide the loot. Back then shop staff were too prudish to check what any woman had under her coat.

Posing as housemaids using false references was also a great way to ransack the homes of the wealthy and an affair with a married man was a happy route to profitable blackmail. It seems to have been a family business. Mothers passed their skills to daughters. Certainly it was successful. Many an Elephant kept her more idle husband in beer money. During the early twentieth century they were led by Alice, who lived on the top floor of the Hayles Buildings on Elliot's Row.

Today there is a 'pocket park' on the corner, a tiny green space with a bench and a slide reminding everyone that families live here. The street is now a blue cycle route where many men badly packaged in Lycra whizz past. A man on a racing bike shouts and nearly knocks me over as I cross the road. I don't know why everyone who cycles in London today is always in such a hurry. Too fast to stop for any pedestrian. Copenhagen is full of cyclists but they wear jeans or corduroys and pedal gently as if enjoying the ride.

I look up to the top floor of the Hayles Buildings, which probably look the same as when Alice lived there. Did Alice count her loot here? There is, of course, no plaque for her. I think there should be. Who doesn't want to celebrate the Queen of the Forty Thieves, who wore diamond rings as knuckle dusters? And maybe some memorial to Alice's closest friend, Maggie Hughes.

Maggie was not quite five feet tall and a terrible drunk with a temper. She had tattoos on both arms and drove a Ford V8 car, an Al Capone-style vehicle with running boards. Maggie's car was famous. It had a periscope on the roof so she could spot police before they saw her.

Alice went to prison for beating up a member of her entourage. The woman had broken the gang's code by marrying a man who didn't come from Southwark. By the time the queen of the streets was released the world had moved on: there was a new leader called Lilian Rose Kendall, the Bobbed-Haired Bandit, who specialised in getaways too fast even for Alice. There is a black-and-white photograph of Lillian resplendent with bobbed hair, a kiss curl falling across her forehead and cupid's bow lips pursed with a barely concealed smile. She stares at the camera as if butter wouldn't melt.

I'm not a fan of crime but I don't blame the women. Born into the profound poverty of the area they had few choices. There was almost no work unless you could stomach prostitution, so a life of thieving seemed both preferable and profitable. Often it was that or suicide, which was rife. No one could have predicted that the introduction of gas ovens would provide women not just with better cooking facilities but also an easy exit from their lives.

A down pipe is leaking on the top floor of the Hayles Buildings. Water cascades down several storeys of brickwork. It would probably be a cheap fix but I suspect nothing will be done until there is long-term and expensive damage. It feels like a metaphor for how the whole area is treated. I like it round here and walk on to West Square where, despite it being November, the roses are still blooming. It is an elegant oasis of homes from about 1800 built around a small square of mulberry trees. This green space is open to the public.

I am weird enough to walk on down Orient Street in search of what I believe to be the last horse scratching post in London. I find it. It looks just like a large piece of metal; nevertheless, I take a photo. Back in the square and past No. 19, the birthplace and childhood home of John Newlands, the nineteenth-century chemist who helped foist the periodic table on us all. He was at first ridiculed for his discoveries and others got the credit he deserved. 'Twas ever thus.

Numbers 32, 22 and 23 of the square were all homes for destitute girls run in the 1870s by Charlotte Sharman, who cared for over two hundred girls. These were the very children whose harrowing lives Dickens was determined to portray. Charlie Chaplin's earliest memories were of living here with his parents and his brother Sydney at No. 39. He didn't stay long. His alcoholic father left and Charlie's mother, Hannah, struggled to make a living. Age seven, Charlie was separated from the family and sent to the Central London District School for paupers. His mother was committed to an asylum and at times Charlie lived on the streets to avoid the harsh life in the workhouse. Today the water tower of one of those workhouses looms overhead, now converted into luxury flats with great views of the city. History goes round and round in circles. The one-time leader of the Elephant and Castle Mob, Wag McDonald, finally gave up controlling these streets and moved to Los Angeles. There he became a bodyguard to the most famous movie star in the world, a boy from his hood, Charlie Chaplin.

Down a side street you can still see the Victorian gas street lamps, now devoid of light. From here the dome of the Imperial War Museum stands out. I've filmed there but I can't remember what about. War, presumably. After so many decades on TV there's not much I haven't covered one way or another. When I was sailing around Britain with John McCarthy he and I were filmed painting the outside of a lighthouse. We were suspended by ropes as we slapped on white paint.

'I bet this is the first time you've done this,' said John cheerfully.

'Actually, it's the second,' I realised. 'I painted a lighthouse when I was on kids' TV.'

Back on to St George's Road. Across the street a nun in white robes with blue trim like Mother Teresa is shaking out a door mat. Her outfit reminds me of our tea towels. She's like an apparition from another era as the traffic of London zooms past. Above her the Virgin Mary rests on top of a small portico labelled 'Ave Maria'. The cream building is dilapidated. Paint peels from the walls around a small blue sign declaring 'Gift of Love'. I look up and see that every window seems to have a wardrobe in front of it. Maybe the sisters are not very outward-looking.

In the very first place I lived alone the view was blocked by a cooker. It was a tiny attic room in Kentish Town where for nine pounds a week I resided along with many others with varying attitudes to cleanliness in the shared bathroom. For another fifty pence I could have had my own loo but it seemed an extravagance. Rats scuttled along behind the skirting boards at night and the single gas burner for my meals gave off a continuous stream of potentially lethal fumes. I don't recall ever looking out beyond the cooker to see what view it blocked.

One night I came home to find the landlady scrubbing blood off the front step.

'Been a murder,' she said, 'but it's all right. Wasn't one of ours.'

There's a comfort. I wonder what Alice Diamond would have made of it.

St George's Road / Imperial War Museum

There have been two more mass shootings in America. At least one appears to be a hate crime by a white supremacist. The language of present politics is driving this agenda. In Russia, opposition parties are arrested, and here good sense is no longer on the table. I feel what the Germans call *Weltschmerz*, or world pain. The planet has been taken over by testosterone-fuelled madness. I despair, and this is a good place for it. Here is where bedlam ruled. The war museum is the former site of the Bethlehem Hospital, the oldest existing psychiatric institution in the world. I realise what a lot of opportunity for historic mental instability there is on this route.

The hospital was founded as the Priory of the New Order of St Mary of Bethlehem in the mid-thirteenth century. It was originally in the City but maybe it upset traders because in 1815 it was moved here. The conditions were terrible and the contraction of Bethlehem as 'Bedlam' came to signify uproar. In the eighteenth century this home for the bewildered and distressed was on the London tourist trail. Along with visiting the Tower of London and pleasure gardens, newcomers to town could enjoy the spectacle of what was billed as a sort of freak show. By 1770 this form of 'entertainment' began to be curtailed but ironically the lack of exposure to the public turned out to be bad for the patients. With less public scrutiny some of the worst patient abuse occurred.

Finding entertainment in this quarter of London was not something new. Before the hospital the area was famous for a tavern called the Dog and Duck. In the seventeenth century the tavern stood in St George's Fields, which were mainly swamp. It was a good place to get robbed so seeing a light on in the tavern must have been welcome. The eighteenth-century English playwright and poet Hannah More set some of her work in the infamous Dog and Duck Fields. It's wonderful that a woman made a living from writing back then but I can't say she and I would have got on.

Writing to Horace Walpole in 1793 she said of Mary Wollstonecraft's early feminist writing, 'I have been much pestered to read the "Rights of Women" but am invincibly resolved not to do it ... so many women are fond of government ... because they are not fit for it. To be unstable and capricious is but too characteristic of our sex.'

By the 1930s the good people of Lambeth had had enough of Bedlam and the hospital moved to the Surrey suburbs. In its place, the Imperial War Museum opened. From one kind of madness to another. The museum entrance is protected by two massive naval guns which saw service in the Second World War. I'm not sure anyone was thinking it through because they point directly at the Tibetan peace garden that lies in front of the museum. It was opened in 1999 by the Dalai Lama and has a stone pillar with messages of peace from the Lama himself in Tibetan, English, Chinese and Hindi. I wonder if his brother came with him.

The peace garden looks out to St George's Catholic Cathedral, which stands across the street. It was on this site in 1768 that a great public demonstration was held to protest the imprisonment of an MP called John Wilkes. Wilkes had the then rather mad idea that the people themselves should choose who represented them in Parliament instead of the King. Wilkes wrote many an article criticising the King, George III. Eventually the powers that be found a reason to lock him up and he was sent to the King's Bench Prison near St George's Fields. For two weeks people gathered near by to protest.

Eventually there was a crowd of about fifteen thousand chanting 'Wilkes and Liberty', 'No Liberty, No King', and 'Damn the King! Damn the Government! Damn the Justices!' Soldiers were sent to protect some Justices of the Peace up from Surrey. The crowd, especially a man in a red coat, goaded them. The soldiers gave chase and the man ran off into a barn. Racing after him the soldiers shot dead a man in a red coat, only to discover it was the wrong man. They had killed a farmhand called William Allen. The Riot Act was read to the rest of the protestors and half a dozen or more were shot dead in what became known as the Massacre of St George's Fields. Take a detour to Newington churchyard and you can find a memorial to poor William. Wrong man, wrong place.

Wilkes ended up Lord Mayor of London and fêted by his fellows. Knowing when you are on the right side of history doesn't always make standing up for what you believe in easy. The peace garden lies in Geraldine Mary Harmsworth Park, which has been there since 1934. It is a place filled with irony. The park was a present to the 'splendid struggling mothers of Southwark' from Harold Harmsworth, 1st Viscount Rothermere, and named after his dearly departed mother. So far so good and so sweet until you recall that Harold Harmsworth was the founder of the *Daily Mail* and a happy supporter of the Nazi Party. Harold also founded the *Daily Mirror* and used both publications to try to persuade Britain that 'Adolph the Great' was actually a very nice guy. His papers were also the only ones to support the British Union of Fascists. Indeed, on 15 January 1934 the *Daily Mail* published an editorial which Harold wrote himself, entitled 'Hurrah for the Blackshirts', in which Oswald Mosley was praised for his 'sound, common-sense, Conservative doctrine'. So fulsome was the papers' support that the *Mail* even planned a beauty contest to find Britain's 'prettiest fascist', but sadly the contest never quite got off the ground.

I am the daughter, granddaughter and sister of journalists. I am passionate about the profession but I believe some of the tabloids stain the soul of this country. When I had the furore with Save the Children, I think the people at the charity who made the decision assumed I would be quiet and go away but I had come too far for that. I phoned a contact at the *Guardian* and did an interview about it. The reaction from the staff at Save the Children was fantastic. So many of them were appalled. Ian McKellen called me and asked if I would appear at a different concert for a different charity. This one was for Stonewall, the gay rights organisation. I was terrified. I had never done an openly gay anything.

That night the Royal Albert Hall was full. More than five thousand people crammed in. I knew that about a hundred members of staff from Save the Children were in the audience. I stood backstage and even back there the noise was deafening. I wanted to run, but as I tried to get my breath I felt someone's arms reach from behind me and pull me into a firm hug. It was Ian. He didn't say a word. He just stood holding me until I was announced, then he gently let go and pushed me onto the stage. It was the single kindest professional moment of my life. I stepped onto the stage to the loudest ovation I have ever heard.

'Well,' I managed when the noise finally died down, 'I must come out more often.'

Yesterday I was hosting an awards ceremony at the Great Room in the Grosvenor House Hotel. It is a grand room and fifteen hundred people in bib and tucker were being served the finest of food. I've played this room many, many times and know it well. As I waited to go on I sat in my usual place, a corridor stacked with old chairs just outside the entrance to the kitchen. It is a miserable and far from glamorous location. An older woman wearing the shapeless grey jacket and white gloves of all the servers passed by me. I smiled and she stopped.

'Are you having a good day?' I asked.

She shook her head. 'Some young girl just told me off,' she said. 'And you know what? I am too old for this shit.'

We had a hug. We agreed. We are both too old for this shit. Some days it's just hard to find the fight inside yourself. I am so tired of fighting. I look at the lovely park that Harold Harmsworth named for his mother. Mothers often get blamed if their children turn out poorly. I do hope Geraldine thought her son was an arse.

Years later I met Princess Anne again. She was funny, bright and charming and never once seemed shocked.

Lambeth North Station

A head of us another bus has had a run-in with someone pulling a camping trailer. There are a lot of people shouting in the street. It appears a holiday is ruined and some people will be late for work. No one dealing with it has a plan other than shouting, so I settle down to wait. Inexplicably, my parents once decided to buy a camping trailer. I think my father had had some odd notion that we all ought to commune a bit more with nature. He booked us into a little place in upstate New York called Pine Acres where Papa, who was a dreamer, probably thought we'd do whittling while singing by the campfire. We headed north from the city with our new mobile home bumping along behind our long Pontiac estate car.

Dad parked our extremely compact trailer in a nice little glade and got out to smoke his pipe as he considered the important matter of collecting kindling. Just then another, but much, much bigger, trailer pulled up beside us. I had never seen a recreational vehicle so large. A husband and wife got out. It was clear from the outset that these were professional campers. The man immediately got a roll of plastic out and began enclosing their trailer with a little white picket fence. The woman was hot on his heels with a Hoover, with which she began to vacuum up all the leaves. I'm not sure it was the weekend Papa had in mind. My brother and I discovered they served pizza at the local pool and didn't reappear until it was time to go home. We never went camping again. My parents sold the trailer.

*

Some people on the bus are beginning to involve themselves in how we should get past the problem ahead. I'm not saying a word. I've decided I ought to keep quiet more. I think my instinct is always to try to solve a problem. Deb says I would make a terrible therapist as I would endlessly be trying to find the right hobby for someone lonely and depressed to get them out of the house more. She says I don't need to keep trying to sort things for everyone; that sometimes it would be nice if I could just sit. She has a point. Trying to help out at a simple family barbecue led to me writing a musical to open a long-lost theatre.

When I started out in showbusiness there were one or two theatres where everyone wanted to work. Among them was the Leicester Haymarket. Indeed, for a long while it was the regional home of musical theatre. Then it closed down and was stripped of everything, including its seats. There was just a shell where a theatre had once been but, bless the planning laws of this country, no one was allowed to knock it down. None of this was anything to do with me but I was sitting under the apple tree in our garden when I got chatting to my middle daughter's boyfriend's brother.

'What are you up to?' I said, the way you do at these things.

'I'm helping to reopen the Haymarket in Leicester,' he replied.

I was thrilled. Theatres never reopen. It's unheard of.

'What show are you going to do?'

'*Treasure Island*,' he said. 'But I can't find a version I like.'

I had had a beer or two. 'Oh, don't worry,' I said, 'I'll write you one.'

Within weeks I was locked in my office at the bottom of the garden with my sister Jeni, talking about the 'Call to Adventure' and trying to work out the minimum number of actors we could get away with to tell such a story. There was no money and no time.

I quickly discovered that lots of people say 'Oh, I love *Treasure Island!*' but hardly anyone has actually read it. I'm afraid I found it a rather dull book and there didn't seem quite enough in it to make a whole show but Jeni, who writes musicals for a living, is a genius at plot. Soon my office wall was covered in Post-it notes, with different colours for scenes and musical numbers. We had the best two weeks of working I can ever remember. Jen bought some plastic doubloons and if one of us had a good idea the other paid for the thought. Childish but it kept us going.

Then Jen and her friend David Perkins wrote the songs while I toiled away at the script. From my ill-judged offer in the garden to opening night there was only a few months. We did it and it was wonderful to see the Haymarket back in the business it was meant for. The songs were brilliant, the script, having had no development time, needed work, but we reopened a theatre and that will always feel good.

Yesterday I went to meet Michelle Terry, the artistic director at the Globe Theatre on Bankside. I love the Globe not because it is a reconstruction of Shakespeare's theatre but because it is a working theatre in the borough I live in. I liked Michelle immediately but made the mistake of saying I thought she needed a proper Christmas show. Now I seem to be writing that too . . . and being in it. No idea how to tell Mrs T.

As we cross over into Lambeth a woman on her phone is complaining loudly about her daughter, who seems be in all manner of trouble with the law.

'She won't listen! She never listens,' the woman keeps repeating. 'I've said to her, "You need to listen when I tell you things," but oh no! It's like she can't hear me. Doesn't listen.'

The woman goes on in the same vein without drawing breath. The person on the other end doesn't seem to speak. I suspect all the daughter can do is listen. So far none of my children have been in trouble with the law but until now I hadn't thought of it as such a plus in my parenting.

Lambeth is first recorded in 1062 as Lambehitha ('landing place for lambs'). It was here that farmers brought their sheep to market. It reminds me of a joke Barry Cryer told me. He once told me that a good joke is like a small play and gave this example:

> A ventriloquist gets stranded in the Australian outback. He walks until he meets a farmer but the farmer is uninterested in the man's plight. He is busy and doesn't want to help.
>
> 'Don't worry,' says the ventriloquist, 'I'll chat with your horse.'
>
> He turns to the horse and says, 'How's things?'
>
> The horse replies, 'Not bad.'
>
> The farmer shakes his head and declares, 'You chat all you like to my horse but those sheep are bloody liars.'

There is almost a country air here as the traffic islands outside Morley College are heady with lavender. It was planted there by the Guerrilla Gardening movement, founded by another Lambeth local, Richard Reynolds. Since 2004 they have been transforming neglected urban spaces and selling bags of London lavender to fund their project. Power to the people.

A young lad next to me is having trouble opening the plastic wrapper on his sandwich. I offer him the small scissors in my penknife. I don't know what startles him the most, that someone spoke to him or that an older woman handed him a knife. I always carry three things wherever I go – a penknife, a clean handkerchief and some money folded into a silver money clip. The knife is small. It has a neat but surprisingly sharp blade, a tiny screwdriver-cum-file, a miniature pair of scissors, tweezers and a toothpick. It is the best of Switzerland in a tidy form. I have several knives in different colourful designs and am never dressed without one. My wife thinks that I am really a ten-year-old boy in a sixty-year-old woman's body. Much as my family teases me, not a day goes by that one of them isn't heard to request my knife, my hankie or my money.

I am not the only woman with a knife. Emma Cons, the founder of Morley College, was also never without a penknife in case some small job needed her attention. I love Morley. It is an adult education college and a beacon of the notion that none of us should ever stop learning. It was Emma's idea yet it carries the name of Samuel Morley. Samuel was a good guy: anti-slavery, a model employer and a philanthropist who provided the money to found the college back in 1889. Because he had dosh his name is the one that is remembered.

Emma Cons was a Londoner through and through. Born in St Pancras, she trained as an artist and joined the Ladies' Co-operative Art Guild. She tried to get work but to help make ends meet she worked as a rent-collector for Octavia Hill. Perhaps it was going door to door collecting rent that inspired her desire to change the city. Women have been multi-skilling long before anyone thought it was worth mentioning and Emma did it in spades. She was a passionate social reformer, a believer in the provision of education to the poor and a theatre manager. It's quite a combo.

The college grew out of Emma's work at the Old Vic theatre, which lies five minutes' walk away. In 1880 she took over what had been a rather rowdy music hall and renamed it the Royal Victoria Coffee and Music Hall. She believed it was time to bring Shakespeare and opera to the working classes. No alcohol was served and science lectures were given for the improvement of local minds. The lectures proved hugely popular and drew the attention of Samuel Morley, who gave her the money to expand them into a more substantial college.

Emma must have been a force to be reckoned with because in 1889 she was appointed as the first female alderman on London County Council, where she joined the first elected women members Jane Cobden (elected for Bow and Bromley) and Lady Sandhurst (elected for Brixton). Lady Sandhurst's election was challenged in the courts, her seat eventually given to the man who had come second, and she was fined five pounds for every vote she had taken during her time on the council. Anti-suffragists also brought a court case against Cobden and Cons which ruled that while they could legally be members of the council they could not vote.

Undeterred, Emma carried on doing good work. She helped found among other things the first horticultural college for women, a model housing association, a hostel for working girls in Drury Lane and a number of crèches and clinics for women, as well as spending one holiday in Cyprus trying to help refugees. In 1908, Emma Cons became the first woman ever to speak at the Institute of Directors. I know all that but I still don't know enough about her. I know that she never married and that she died at the home of her friend Ethel Everest, the daughter of another man with something named after him. What were she and Ethel to each other? Friends? More? I can't find anything about Ethel at all. I did discover that, as well as the penknife, Emma also carried a ball of string, which is a marvellous idea. My wife is going to be appalled.

Lower Marsh

I never cease to be surprised at what I do for a living. I'm still not sure I have the right attitude to a showbiz life. The first time I met the comedian Linda Smith, the funniest person I ever worked with, I was sitting reading in a café near the Bloomsbury theatre where Radio 4's *The News Quiz* was recorded. It was my first time guesting on the show and Linda and I had never met. I was eating a yoghurt when she came in and sat beside me.

'You Sandi?' she asked. I nodded. She pointed to my yoghurt before adding, 'I knew you'd be rock 'n' roll.'

Lower Marsh is one of my favourite streets in London. It runs along beside Waterloo Station. There is a market here but it is a recent development. Up until the early 1800s a lot of North Lambeth was a place people only wanted to pass by. It was marshland which someone, possibly a reliable Roman, built a raised road over. Now it's bustling with stalls.

I stop in a café where two earnest women in business suits are sitting in the window talking very loudly about 'PPA funding' and what sounds like a complaint about an 'Emily adviser'. I don't want to listen but I have no choice. The conversation is at high volume. Although I can hear every word I have no idea what they might do for a living. One of them is very worried about her 'division' and she talks in endless acronyms about her need 'to get people round a table'. The other one is keener to talk about 'my team and your team' and things on 'the program-matic side' but they both agree that the 'Malala workshop about markets' is the way forward. Dear God.

I think life generally ought to be conducted at a lower volume, although sometimes mine is that way unwittingly. I remember Mark Damazer, the then controller of Radio 4, ringing me to offer me the job of host on *The News Quiz*. I love the show and by then had been a guest on it for more than a dozen years. The previous host, Simon Hoggart, had left and it never occurred to me that anyone might think I should replace him, so the call came as something of a surprise.

I was parking my car in Hallam Street, beside Broadcasting House, and the driver of a car behind me was getting really irritated. I shouldn't have answered the phone but I did because I thought it might be one of the kids. Once I realised it was the head honcho at Radio 4 I didn't feel I could just hang up. I put the car in reverse at the precise moment that he asked me if I wanted to take over the show.

All I really wanted was for him to get off the phone and for the man behind me to stop beeping. 'Uh, lovely, Mark,' I said. 'Thanks very much. Bye.' He probably wondered why I wasn't more effusive or even excited.

After it was announced that I would be taking the chair there was a lot of talk about the terrifying idea of having a woman in charge. In fact it was pretty much all anyone talked about. My first show as host went out on a Friday night, repeated on the Saturday morning. The following Monday I got a phone call from the producer.

'Good news!' he said cheerfully. 'No complaints!'

Wow. Well done me.

When I got the job of co-hosting *The Great British Bake Off* I was equally distracted. I don't watch a lot of television and hadn't really taken on board the success of the show. When I was first asked if I was interested in taking over from Mel and Sue I phoned my daughter Jesse to ask her if she had heard of this programme.

'What is wrong with you, Mum?' she wailed. 'Everyone's heard of it!'

When the producer from Channel 4 phoned to say I had got the job I was sitting in the quiet carriage of a train. I had forgotten to turn my phone off. I take the instruction to be quiet very seriously and I was mortified. I answered the phone.

'Hello?' I whispered.

'You're the new host of *The Great British Bake Off*!' said a voice excitedly.

'That's so kind,' I said as quietly as possible. 'I have to go now.' And I hung up.

I stroll down to admire the outside of the Old Vic, of which I am inordinately fond. It's safe to say the demographic around here has changed since Emma Cons's day. In 2007 I did panto here, playing the narrator in *Cinderella*. There was an obligatory cooking scene in which a child was hauled up from the audience to help prepare a meal. One evening a small boy of about eight took his place on stage as Buttons and I began the preparations.

'What would you put in cooking to make it taste nice?' I asked, awaiting the reply of salt or perhaps pepper, but without a moment's hesitation the boy replied, '*Herbes de Provence*.'

Kevin Spacey was running the theatre when I was there. I only met him once. I made a couple of ad-lib jokes about him during a matinée and ran straight into him in the wings where he was skulking in a baseball cap. He barely said hello.

I realise how many reprehensible men I've worked with. So many famous fellows from the 1970s/80s have gone to prison.

Many of them I worked with. People like Fred Talbot, who everyone remembers as the ITV weather man who jumped about in Liverpool docks on a floating map, but for me he was the science guy on *No. 73*. I feel weird about it because the truth is I had no idea how vile they were. I worked many times with Fred, with Gary Glitter and once or twice with Stuart Hall. All I knew was that I thought they were all creepy. I didn't like them or their attitudes but I think I presumed it was because I wasn't heterosexual. They made sexist or crude remarks and everyone just laughed. I felt what I have felt so often, that I was an outsider.

I am sorry that the media seem to have focused on appalling behaviour as a BBC problem. It was and sometimes still is a general problem. Women were treated badly. Many men in the industry thought their position of fame or power gave them the right to treat the females they came across as they pleased. Not long before Harvey Weinstein's fall from grace I sat next to him while being interviewed for Chris Evans's radio show. He was physically gross yet inexplicably smug. The night before I had been to a party in London. A friend in publishing was retiring and I wanted to wish her well. I met a young woman in her early twenties and asked her what she was doing.

'I do Harvey Weinstein's sex diary,' she replied.

I thought I misheard. 'I'm sorry? What?'

It turned out she was an intern in Weinstein's office. Part of her job was to filter out the prettiest actresses coming up for audition and put them in a separate diary for Harvey's personal attention. The young woman's mother, a senior figure in show-business, stood listening.

'Are you okay with this?' I asked her.

She shrugged. 'It's the business. She might as well get used to it.'

I've been clearing out our old vinyl records and came across an LP by Rolf Harris signed to me with much love. I have no idea what to do with it.

Back on the bus and up Westminster Bridge Road. When I first started travelling on the bus I thought I would meet lots of people. Now I am glad that I don't. For a brief while on each journey I am not someone 'off the telly', I am not a political activist or a woman from whom anything at all is expected. I am not funny or clever or opinionated or anything. I simply sit and lose myself in the city.

The Lincoln Tower rises up on my left. Created out of red and white Kentish ragstone, the spire soars up as a sort of stone Stars and Stripes. I like to think it survived the Blitz as some kind of tribute to the American contribution in the war for it is a curious architectural rendition of the US flag. This was the church where William Wilberforce and his associates based themselves for their battle to end slavery in the British Empire. As a thank-you to the people of Lambeth, Abraham Lincoln's family helped pay for this curious landmark. It was opened on 4 July 1876, the centenary of the Declaration of Independence.

I miss America. I spent the best part of my growing-up there and am always comfortable going 'home'. I especially love that it's wonderful, quirky and full of life. I once took part in an annual competition in Calaveras, a county in the northern part of California. It's a beautiful place resplendent with acres of giant redwood trees. It looks lovely, although it is actually the number one spot for suicide in the United States.

I was there to film something else but as we checked into a motel we saw a large illuminated sign at the entrance was welcoming people to the Calaveras County Frog-Jumping

Competition. I'd never even heard of frog-jumping competitions but once it was in my head nothing would stop me trying to participate.

'It's because of the Mark Twain story,' explained the receptionist. 'You know, "The Celebrated Jumping Frog of Calaveras County".'

I didn't know at all. I was just amazed that people kept saying the words 'frog-jumping' and 'Calaveras County' in the same sentence. I was desperate to have a go. The only flaw in my plan was that I didn't have a frog, which I suspected was key to participation. I went along anyway and made friends with the organisers.

'I'm from London and I'd like to take part in the competition.'

They nodded as if anyone might fly several thousand miles for the purpose.

'Not a problem,' said the nice woman who had taken me under her wing. 'Just stick your hand in the bucket.'

A large blue plastic oil drum filled with water was alive with the sound of frogs. It was less of a bucket and more of a barrel. I don't know if you've ever put your hand in a barrel of frogs but they dislike it as much as you do. I don't think I had really thought about what kind of frog I would end up with. But I'm pretty sure I was expecting a European one. Maybe even something kissable.

The creature I pulled out of the barrel was the sort of frog you might encounter after a nuclear accident. It was a giant. I held him under his ... well, I don't know what you call them ... armpits. His upper body completely filled my hand as his legs stretched out from my grasp down towards the ground for more than a foot. His legs were longer than mine. Good job he was doing the jumping.

'Lucky day,' said my new friend. 'That's a good one.'

She explained the rules. The small stage had a large black

spot on it. All 'jockeys' had to place their frog on the spot, let go on command and then the frog had three jumps to get as far away from you as possible. The frog who jumped the furthest was going to be the winner. The current record was set in 1986 by Rosie the Ribiter and her jockey Lee Giudici. Rosie managed 21 feet, 5¾ inches, which equates to 7.16 feet per jump. It was something to aim for.

I've stood at the side of many stages waiting to go on, but nothing was quite like this. The contestant before me put his frog down but instead of just standing there he immediately got down on all fours and began to bark like a dog. The frog nearly jumped out of its skin. Apparently, frogs are afraid of dogs so this was a popular technique. The more ferocious the bark the further the frog would travel. Despite my long theatrical career, when it was my turn I couldn't bring myself to bark on stage. I put my giant fellow down and waited for the whistle. The whistle went and my fellow continued to just wait.

'Go on then,' I said encouragingly. He sat contentedly on the spot and didn't move. Eventually he shifted about an inch from my foot before settling down again. My career as a professional frog-jumper was not looking promising.

'Well,' I said afterwards, 'I suppose if your frog doesn't do well in the jumping you can at least eat it.' Jokes in America can be tricky. The woman shook her head and wagged her finger at me.

'I don't think you know, Sandi, that we have laws about that kind of thing. If a frog dies during a frog-jumping competition it's illegal to eat it.'

'Wow,' I replied, 'that's quite a specific law. What if the frog hasn't been in a competition?'

The woman shrugged. 'Well, then enjoy!'

St Thomas' Hospital / County Hall

I pass the Florence Nightingale Museum at St Thomas' Hospital and sigh. Florence Nightingale always makes me sigh, and then I am cross with myself. The feminist in me is too strong just to accept what I am told. Great woman and all that but she is also the archetype of how women have to be reinvented to be palatable. Every year, on or near Florence's birthday, 12 May, there is a ceremony to commemorate her. Quite right too, for it also celebrates the glorious professions of nursing, midwifery and healthcare work. Celebrants gather in Westminster Abbey where a member of the Florence Nightingale Foundation carries a lamp and passes it to a student nurse to celebrate the symbolic handing on of knowledge. It is a homage to the 'lady with the lamp', except no one ever called Florence that apart from a journalist from *The Times*.

The Crimean War, which began in 1853, like all armed conflict, had nothing to commend it. The loss of life was immense. In total 1,650,000 soldiers from Britain, France, Sardinia, Turkey and Russia fought in the conflict, of whom nine hundred thousand died, mainly of disease.

The Times went looking for a story with at least some optimism in it and they fell upon the good works of Florence Nightingale. 'She is a "ministering angel",' wrote the journalist. 'When all the medical officers have retired for the night and silence and darkness have settled down upon those miles of prostrate sick, she may be observed alone, with a little lamp in her hand, making her solitary rounds.' Thus the legend was born. But the truth is much better.

Florence Nightingale was a woman with a mission who cared only about saving as many men as possible. She was uninterested in rank. When Florence arrived with her self-trained volunteer nurses at the Selimiye Barracks in Scutari she was appalled at the poor conditions she discovered there. Men were dying in droves.

Florence immediately instituted simple hygiene practices such as hand washing and set about reducing the death rate: it would drop from 42 per cent of the patients to 2 per cent. Nothing was going to stop her. When she was denied access to a store room of medicine she took a hammer and smashed the lock off. The men did not call her the Lady with the Lamp. To them she was 'The Lady with the Hammer', and how much better that sounds. Pass the new nurses a hammer. The way the NHS is going they'll need to build wards rather than just turn the lights on.

In the grounds of St Thomas' there's now a statue to the Jamaican-born Mary Seacole, who also did service, providing rest and recuperation for soldiers behind the British lines. I'm delighted she is there but that's not how everyone felt. Hard to believe, but her memorial caused trouble. Ardent Nightingale fans said it would damage Florence's memory to have someone who wasn't a real nurse being allowed a statue. Ridiculous. Let's celebrate any woman who puts her head above the parapet.

I go past St Thomas' and remember a time when I went there for help and received none. It was 1981. It was the year when the American tennis player Billie Jean King became the first professional woman in her sport to come out but no one in my circle talked about being gay, except perhaps to laugh at camp comedians. As far as I knew there were no out lesbians in British public

life. Even Liberace denied that he was gay. I had never told a
soul. When Truman, my girlfriend from university, left me after
nearly four years together, I was devastated. It wasn't just that
I loved her. As I didn't know a single other gay person, I could
not imagine how I might ever find someone else. I felt destined
to be unloved for ever. I was twenty-three. I could not function.
I had lost the only person with whom I could be myself. I was
utterly alone and devastated. I couldn't think or speak or eat.
I was already on British television presenting *No. 73* and had
to carry on being unbearably cheerful at work while my insides
were shattered. I looked ahead to a life I did not want to live.

I tried travelling to Israel but it didn't help. I knew I was in
terrible pain and not functioning, but there was no internet to
seek help through. I had read somewhere that there were psy-
chiatrists at Tavistock Square in London so I went up to town
on the train and in the pouring rain walked round and round the
square looking for their brass doorplates. I found no one.

In the end my mother could see I was unwell. She locked us
in the bathroom for privacy and I told her. She was shocked,
and decided I needed to see our local doctor. Our GP was a
woman the age of my grandmother. In fact she was also my
grandmother's doctor. She had known me all my life, from our
holidays to Britain and then from when we moved to the UK.
She was unmarried, and when I think back on it she had lived
with the female receptionist for as long as I could remember but
no one ever said anything. She put me on Ativan, a strong and
addictive drug which made the world blur at the edges. Once
the world was fuzzy I was sent to see a psychiatrist at St Thomas'
Hospital. I don't remember his name, which is a shame because
I should like to track him down and give him a piece of my more
mature mind.

What I really needed was some reassurance. Instead I had a
nasty encounter with a man devoid of empathy. I was shown into

his office. It was a time when medical men still wore white coats to indicate authority. I sat opposite his desk and it was clear he had no time for me. He had my notes and barely looked at me.

'So, you're having a breakdown?' he muttered. No one had said so but it was possible. If it was written down then maybe I was, but it was a funny way to tell me. On reflection I think I was having a rather straightforward collapse because I thought being gay meant always being alone.

'Think you're crazy, do you?' he continued.

'Uh ... well ... I ... ' I didn't really have an answer to this. I wasn't crazy, just in unbearable pain. Lost and frightened.

He got up and walked to the window. 'I had a woman patient of mine grab a knife and try to kill me today. What do you think about that? Does that sound crazy?'

I thought perhaps it did.

He spun round. 'Yes! *That* is crazy!' He jabbed a finger at me. 'You are wasting my time with this nonsense.'

Without further discussion he filled in a prescription for five different kinds of pills. Three to keep me upbeat in the day and two to knock me out at night. It was enough medication to kill myself, which on reflection was possibly not the best gift for someone who already felt their life was over. The pills came with a leaflet written in bold which warned that I might have, amongst other things, a brain haemorrhage if I ate something ordinary like eggs while taking the advised course. I didn't even need to overdose in order to die. I could just eat a full English.

That day at a newsstand I picked up a copy of the London listings magazine *Time Out* while waiting for the train. I was furtive and didn't buy it because I thought everybody would know why I wanted such a magazine. I wanted to see if there were any gay listings. I flicked through it while checking that no one in the shop was watching. There was only one entry for Gay Women – a 'discussion group' held once a week at the Gay's the

Word bookshop in Bloomsbury. The following week, zombied on pills, I went to a meeting and met Peta, who was to become the mother of my three fabulous kids and my lifelong friend. I will always be indebted to her for bringing them into the world, but also for the fact that a week after we met she took all my pills and flushed them down the toilet. I didn't need medication. I just needed to know my life was going to be all right. My now wife Debbie is a therapist, and over and over she has witnessed that the best cure for distress is love.

All the while I was 'coming out', my mother's great anxiety was telling her own parent, my grandmother, the news. Apparently, she took ages, warning my grandmother that she had 'serious information about Sandi'. When at last she revealed that I was a lesbian my grandmother waved her hand dismissively, saying, 'Oh, we had those in our day! I thought you were going to say she was ill.'

Just before Westminster Bridge, by St Thomas', stands a lion made of Coade stone, an artificial ceramic called Lithodipyra, which was invented by Mrs Eleanor Coade and was famously waterproof. There used to be a factory near by that made the stuff. It is at this stop that the first view of the Thames is available on the Number 12. Probably my favourite place I've ever lived was up river at Wandsworth, where I spent five years on a houseboat. The boat was small and I couldn't find a desk to fit. So I made my own. It folded up into the wall and the materials cost me about five pounds. It's still the best desk I ever had. My little writing nook looked out over the water towards Putney Bridge. How I loved life on the river. The power of the daily tides, the passing of boats. On match days you could hear the roar of the crowd from the football stadium at Craven Cottage: a deep, male sound rolling up the river.

Whenever I looked up from my home-made desk there was always some creature going about its business. Often it was a cormorant diving down into the waters in search of food. No matter how busy I was it was impossible not to wait the twenty or thirty seconds it took for the bird to reappear, sometimes triumphant with a flapping white fish clamped in its beak. When not fishing the cormorant is an ugly bird, but on the hunt it is magnificent. I guess we all have our moments.

There was much feminism in the air where we were moored. Putney Bridge stood as a testament to powerful men. It only exists because the Prime Minister, Sir Robert Walpole, got cross with a ferryman and decided to put him out of a job by having a bridge built. The Prince of Wales too 'was often inconvenienced by the ferry when returning from hunting in Richmond Park' and helped move things along. The bridge itself is a rare sight anywhere in the world in that it has a church at either end. Despite this spiritual embrace it is and always has been a popular suicide spot. We would regularly see police boats racing towards the crossing to stop some poor unfortunate casting themselves into the deep. It was from this bridge that, in October 1795, Mary Wollstonecraft threw herself into the Thames. It was her second suicide attempt that year. Her heart was broken.

I love this story even though I lack sufficient details. All I know is that Mary was rescued by a 'passing boatman' called Mr May. He took her home and in his house his wife persuaded Mary of 'the rightness of living'. Given the time she met Mrs May I suspect it is highly likely that both the boatman and his wife were illiterate. Mary was a brilliant writer. She was well travelled, while Mrs May probably only really knew that stretch of water. So what did Mary and Mrs May talk about? What could anyone say to persuade you of the rightness of living?

*

Both times I've been close to arrest have had to do with the Thames. Some years ago I was asked to open the new Foyle's bookshop on the South Bank, underneath the Royal Festival Hall. Christopher Foyle had thought it would be a marvellous idea to arrive by speedboat at the pier right by the parade of shops. In order to make the best impression we set off from the same pier half an hour before the press were due to arrive, so that we might look as though we had come from somewhere up river. Waiting for the appointed moment we hung about outside the Houses of Parliament, only to find the river police arriving with great speed and blue lights.

'What are you doing here?' they demanded.

'Opening a bookshop,' I replied before realising, like most of my life, it made no sense whatsoever.

As the bus crosses Westminster Bridge I can see that it is high tide. It used to be thought that there was a ford here. There were stories of the Romans wading across in front of St Thomas'. They can't all have waded because in 1909 the remains of a Roman boat was found, but there was a man called Rufus Noel-Buxton, who was rather obsessed with the idea of Romans wading. On 25 March 1952 he walked into the Thames at low tide. Lord Noel-Buxton was 6 foot 3 and ended up in water up to his neck. In true British fashion he clung on to his theory and blamed rain in the Cotswolds.

Westminster Station /
Parliament Square

We glide into Parliament Square, which in 1926 became the UK's first official roundabout. It's not what most people think about when they reach this part of London. This site is arguably the birthplace of British democracy as it was here the Great Council, the forerunner of the House of Lords, used to meet. I'm not sure about that being democracy. It is also, of course, the location of the first elected representatives summoned by Simon de Montfort in 1265, which is better. I've been inside the Houses of Parliament and am not sure much of what happens is really about representing the populace at all. It is beautiful, I'll give it that.

I've spoken in Westminster Hall, which overlooks the square. It was built about 1097, in the reign of William II, third son of William the Conqueror. He was known as Rufus because of his red hair and I think he was only king because no one else was available. His oldest brother, Robert Curthose (a marvellous name derived from having short legs and having to have his leggings altered), was made Duke of Normandy, which meant he must have been busy, and the next brother, Richard, was killed in a hunting accident.

Rufus never married or had children. He may have been a homosexual but we'll never know as the history of gay people is nearly impossible to track. According to his critics, he was addicted to every kind of vice, particularly 'lust and especially sodomy'. Hard to know if it was true. It's the sort of accusation that used to be levelled against anyone who wasn't liked. Orderic Vitalis in his *Historia Ecclesiastica* (come on, who hasn't read it?) complained that at the court of William, 'the effeminate predominated everywhere, and revealed without restraint, while filthy catamites, fit only to perish in the flames, shamelessly abounded themselves to the foulest practices of Sodom'.

The *Anglo-Saxon Chronicle* has nothing good to say about Rufus either, but on the plus side he did start the building of both Westminster Hall and Durham Cathedral. Rufus died in an 'accident' which may have been murder. Everyone rushed off to crown a new king, leaving a Mr Purkis to take the body of the slain leader to Winchester Cathedral. He did so in his coal cart and the body of the King was quickly buried at the foot of a tower which later fell down. What did he tell Mrs Purkis when he got home?

Mrs Purkis: How was your day, dear?

Mr Purkis: Well . . .

I like Mr Purkis, just as I am fond of Mr and Mrs May from Putney. These are the glorious unsung characters of history.

Outside Parliament stands a statue of Oliver Cromwell. I've looked into his dead face. His death mask is kept, for reasons unknown, at the Prime Minister's country home, Chequers. We'd been invited as a family to Sunday lunch with Gordon and Sarah Brown. Sarah showed us round. In a small room she opened a drawer and there was the dead Cromwell staring up at us from inside. It's not what you expect before lunch. My son

Ted was with us. He was about sixteen at the time. It was a large lunch party which included the businessman Alan Sugar. After the meal Sir Alan cornered my boy, practically jabbing a finger into his chest as he demanded, 'What are you going to be when you grow up?'

Ted looked straight at him and replied, 'I'm going to go into business.'

'Good lad, good lad,' said Sir Alan, clapping him on the back.

As we left I whispered to Ted, 'Why did you say that? I thought you wanted to be an actor.'

'I do,' said my boy, winking at me. 'Good performance, eh?'

So proud.

Westminster Abbey is to my left. It makes me think of hearts, two being eaten and one being mended. William Buckland became Dean of Westminster in 1845. He is possibly the only person to have eaten the heart of a king. William was keen on zoophagy, the practice of eating animals or animal matter, but his love went well beyond going out for a burger. Buckland lived his life determined to sample the entire animal kingdom. Having chomped his way through moles, panthers, mice and bluebottle flies, he continued to be in search of strange things to consume.

Since about the thirteenth century, the French, for reasons best known to themselves, were keen on separating the bowels, heart and other internal organs from the body of a dead monarch. The hearts would be embalmed before being placed in some kind of elaborate container and buried apart from the rest. King Louis XIV wanted his heart next to his father in l'Église Saint-Paul-Saint-Louis and indeed for seventy-seven years after his death there it lay in a small chest bedecked with angels.

History moves on and the French Revolution led to chopping

the heads off current kings and disposing of the hearts of old ones. You couldn't make this bit up, but at the time painters made a shade of paint called called Mummy Brown by grinding up Egyptian mummies. I don't know who thought of it, but by the sixteenth century there was quite a trade in old human flesh and although it sounds barmy, Mummy Brown was a proper favourite with the Pre-Raphaelite painters.

A landscape painter called Alexander Pau seems to have got hold of Louis XIV's heart (I lack detail here) and there is some talk that a landscape view by Pau of Caen is rich with royal blood. Pau it seems did not use up the whole heart – there's only so much brown a painting requires – and the remaining portion of Louis's ticker, about the size of a walnut by now, may have ended up as a curio belonging to the Harcourts of Nuneham House in Oxfordshire. Here it was shown off one evening over port by the Archbishop of York, Edward Venables-Vernon-Harcourt, and William Buckland was there. The heart went round the table and when it reached the venerable Dean he is supposed to have said, 'I have eaten many strange things, but I have never eaten the heart of a king before.'

And with that, he ate it.

I don't know if it's true but it ought to be.

The great writer Thomas Hardy is buried in Westminster Abbey, apart from his heart. In theory his wife buried his heart in St Michael's churchyard at Stinsford in Dorset, but actually his cat ate it. What are the chances of one great ecclesiastical building housing two stories about the eating of famous hearts? It seems Mrs Hardy didn't want to give her husband to the nation so she had the family doctor remove his heart for a more local burial the next day. I suppose it's hard to know what to do with a heart overnight. The doctor put it in a biscuit tin in the larder. Cats are cunning and the Hardy feline managed to get the lid off and feast on his dead master's organ.

My own heart finally found happiness in the Abbey. I had one of my first dates with my wife there. I think she should have known what a nerd she was stepping out with when I arranged to meet her inside. It's not everyone's idea of a hot date. On the north side of the high altar, in the small chapel of St John the Baptist, there is a half-hidden memorial to Lady Catherine Jones (1672–14 April 1740) and her long-time 'friend' Mary Kendall (8 November 1677–4 March 1710), so that 'even their ashes, after death, might not be divided'.

I thought it was romantic and Deb must have too because within three weeks of our first going out she asked me to marry her. Result.

Today I got off the bus to have lunch with all the judges at the Supreme Court. I met Brian Kerr backstage at the Liberty Awards for human rights, which I was hosting.

'What do you do?' I asked the handsome older gentleman.

'I'm a Supreme Court judge,' he said.

'Is it fun?' I enquired.

'Sometimes,' he said. 'Come for lunch and find out.'

So I did. The Supreme Court lies to one side of Parliament Square and I suspect not many people know that anyone can go in. In fact, if you're in the hood, the coffee at the café inside is excellent. Obviously it's the sort of place where naughty people might want to cause trouble so there is security at the entrance. Two men in ill-fitting uniforms were operating a large scanner through which all bags had to pass. As I waited my turn a rather commanding woman came in carrying a bag of dog poo. She was smartly dressed in a tweed skirt and the sort of padded jacket one should only wear while lunging horses. She had a loud, clipped voice that suggested she lived somewhere ancestral where you had to speak over the draughts.

'I say, have you got a bin?' she demanded. The security guard was not at all sure how to deal with this.

'It's the Supreme Court,' he replied carefully.

'Well, that may be,' she responded, 'but that doesn't mean you don't have a bin.' It was a fair point but still no one moved. She was becoming irritated.

'Look here, I'm with my friend who is blind and can't see to pick up the mess her guide dog has just made. You can't expect me to leave it on the green so it's in this bag, but I am not carrying it around all day.'

I turned to the bewildered guard. 'You do have a ladies', don't you?' Here the security fellow was on firmer ground. Yes, they did have a ladies'. And so it was that my bag went through the scanner at the Supreme Court along with a small plastic bag of dog shit which I duly disposed of in the sanitary towel bin in the ladies'.

Lunch was lovely. Brian brought in home-made ice cream in a Tupperware.

Horse Guards Parade

We go past Downing Street. I know odd things about it. The last civilian to live at No. 10 was a Mr Chicken, which is oddly pleasing. I spoke there once for a charity. Samantha Cameron was then the first lady or whatever we call it. She came up to me afterwards and said most kindly, 'You speak very well. You should think about doing it for a living.'

I've been to Brussels to address the European Parliament at a special forum on women's issues. I emphasised the need to engage women in the great European project before nationalism raised its head in other countries and they too headed for the exit. Mairead McGuinness, the First Vice-President of the European Parliament, nodded.

'This has been great,' she said brightly. 'Maybe we should even do this twice a year.'

I was enraged. 'Dealing with women's issues is not an add-on. It should run like a thread through everything you do!' I protested. She nodded again and went on to her next meeting.

None of the British political parties truly take an interest in the women of this country. Despairing of the endless battle for equality, in 2015 Catherine Mayer and I founded the Women's Equality Party. Fully costed and pragmatic, the implementation of our policies would make the UK a better place for everyone – women, men and children – but we have learned hard lessons.

I already knew it, but it has reinforced the message that money equals power. We have no big businesses or unions to back us and without a solid financial base we will always struggle. We hope one day no longer to be necessary. We actively try to get the other parties to steal our policies and to some extent that is working. Our very appearance on the scene has led to change.

When our leader Sophie Walker appeared on stage at the hustings to be Mayor of London she spoke last. Not one of the other seven candidates had mentioned the women of the city in any capacity whatsoever. Afterwards Sadiq Khan, now the mayor, came up to me and declared, 'I like your policies. Good vote-winners. I'm going to steal them.' Pity he didn't enact them as well.

Disappointingly, the Labour Party has been the least welcoming to us. Indeed, we have had straightforward aggravation from Labour supporters when we campaign. It doesn't surprise me. Years ago, I was working with a well-known member of the Labour Party's National Executive Committee. The party was showing no sign of campaigning for the repeal of Section 28, a notorious piece of legislation which had a terrible impact on the LGBT community. I remember appealing to him to help bring about change. He shook his head and said, 'You don't understand, Sandi. The Labour Party is a bunch of white middle-aged men. They don't give a fuck about gay people.'

I'm not sure they give a fuck about women either.

I look up Whitehall and think of the noise we made when the January 2017 Women's March brought London to a standstill. Buses and taxis were immobilised in a sea of pink pussy hats and placards. Twenty thousand had been expected and more than a hundred thousand turned up. It was good-humoured and kind. There were men too, maybe a fifth of the crowd, but mostly it was women looking out for each other, and all around was that tell-tale sound of a female gathering – laughter. So many smiles and so much laughter. Deb and I went with her daughter and my sister.

Finding the WEP contingent for the march was not hard. On the corner of Brook Street, they were easily the largest group gathering. The artist Grayson Perry was there, smiling and waving his placard. Catherine Mayer wore a cowboy hat. She and I had had the idea for a new women's party at the same time and decided to join forces despite the fact that neither of us had any idea how to do such a thing. Now there were Women's Equality Party placards and T-shirts everywhere.

'Look what we did!' she yelled. We grinned at each other and in that moment everything we had been through was worthwhile. The magnificent Chris Paouros, who is now a fierce force on the WEP steering committee, took command of the troops, yelling out instructions. As I stood there, I heard a noise and looked up, thinking it was a helicopter. The sound grew and came towards me in a great wave and I suddenly realised it was the people. The noise of the jubilant cheers rolling across the crowd was deafening.

Jesse is a brilliant professional photographer and she was taking pictures for the party. Catherine and I took a selfie for ourselves. All around us were great placards. 'We Shall Over Comb' was probably my favourite, although I loved the fur hat topped with a toy tiger holding a small sign declaring 'My pussy bites back'.

WEP's Chief of Staff, Hannah Peaker, kept checking her watch. The march had been due to depart at noon but it was already half past and there was no sign of movement.

'We'll have to go,' she said.

I was due to host the final rally at Trafalgar Square and there was a sound check on stage at one o'clock. Hannah led the way holding my hand but the crowd was so dense it was almost impossible to move. Taxis and minicabs were stranded in a sea of people trying to get to the American Embassy in Grosvenor Square. It took more than half an hour to extricate ourselves from the start of the march as we battled against the tide. When we looked back we could see that every street was full of protestors. Peaceful, kind, gentle women standing up against misogyny. The sky was bright blue. A perfect day for protest.

It seems the police had not expected so many to turn up and, rather like Brexit, no proper plan had been made. No streets had been closed to deal with the mass movement. Some distance from the square we grabbed a cab and the driver shook his head.

'They haven't told us anything about the route. We don't even know where to avoid.'

At Trafalgar Square there were already hundreds gathering. Up under the portico of the National Gallery I could see half a dozen police in high-vis jackets but otherwise I had seen no police at all.

The stage was tiny and far too low but an American stage manager called Jerry was on the case and soon I was standing on a box looking out. The backstage consisted of a tiny white tent where a small gas fire, with only one of its three panels alight, was doing its best to provide a suggestion of heat in the freezing cold. One of the co-organisers trotted about in gold lamé shoes, seeming to be all bustle and no business.

I had spent the evening before prepping all my notes to introduce the twenty or so speakers who were slated to appear. It didn't take long for any organisation to fall apart. Speakers were still stuck in the march or couldn't be contacted as mobile phone service became patchy. Ted turned up and between us we began ripping my notes into small sections as speakers appeared in random order. Beside us Stella Creasy, who had not been on my list at all, gave an interview to ITN in which she claimed credit for the Labour Party in the day's activities. It was an astonishing statement. Only the Greens and WEP had officially endorsed the march. The other parties, and most especially Labour, had not. There were individuals from the various parties – the Labour MP Yvette Cooper, who spoke movingly about her murdered colleague Jo Cox, and Sarah Olney, who had so brilliantly beaten the smug Zac Goldsmith to become MP for the Lib Dems in Richmond Park – but they spoke for themselves and not their parties. No one from the Tories, of course, despite that infamous picture of Theresa May wearing a T-shirt which declared 'This is what a feminist looks like'.

I have spoken quite a few times at rallies in Trafalgar Square but I had never seen anything like this. For three-quarters of an hour I was on the stage introducing speakers and then leaping off to be given handwritten notes about tweets – the right-wing oddball Katie Hopkins called everyone who turned out 'pathetic', which felt heartening. Ted and Hannah kept scribbling new running orders for each section as I ran back and forth to speak from my box. We heard news that Oxford Street was blocked with marchers trying to find a way through and that some people had still not left Grosvenor Square. I gave a shout out to my doctor daughter Megan, who was on shift in A&E, and asked for a cheer for our beloved NHS. The crowd roared.

'The police are saying we will have to close at three. There's been an incident.'

I was standing with Yvette Cooper and we looked at each other. Since Jo Cox's murder no one in the public eye feels safe.

It turned out that the 'incident' was that we women had caused London to grind to a halt. We had brought the great city to a standstill. The square needed to be emptied to clear the surrounding streets.

'I need some words to finish with,' I told Ted and Hannah as someone brought Stella Creasy, Sarah Olney, Kate Allen, the director of Amnesty International, and some woman from the British Pregnancy Advisory Service all on together, where they stood like well-meaning mutes.

A choir were hustled on to sing Labi Siffre's 'Something Inside So Strong' but hardly any of them were miked. Now a poet had turned up with a ten-year-old girl and the actress Juliet Rylance. I sent the crowd off with words Hannah suggested: 'You joined the March, now join the Movement – and if I have my way, join the Women's Equality Party.' I came off and rather ridiculously burst into tears. My shoulders ached and I felt I had been carrying a great weight.

'You're hungry,' said Deb, who can be very practical for a therapist. Juliet Rylance came to the rescue. She looked marvellous, dressed in a green coat with a hat straight from the 1970s, as if she had walked in from the set of *The Avengers*. She had a rather fine matching bag and produced a smoked salmon sandwich which we shared, sitting on plastic chairs in front of the spluttering gas fire.

The next day the papers were full of the triumph the march had been. Did it make a difference? Were all our voices heard? Maybe not by everyone, but we're far from done yet.

As Whitehall comes to an end at Trafalgar Square the bus passes the Silver Cross pub. It is said to be the last legal brothel in London. Allegedly Charles I granted the premises a 'licence for ladies' that has never been revoked. The ghost of a murdered prostitute is said to prop up the bar. It was Cromwell who closed down the brothels, the drinking houses, bear pits and cock pits which once abounded. He can't have been much fun. It was around the same time that several alleys in London called Gropecunt Lane had their names changed.

I need a wee and so I pop into the Cross for a soft drink. Public loos are getting scarce. Perhaps we need to go back to the ancient profession of privy provision. Before the Victorians realised we all need to relieve ourselves somewhere, I'm told there were men and women who wore large black capes and carried a bucket. You'd look for one, give them a farthing (a lot of money at the time) and they'd surround you with the cape while you sat on the bucket and did your business.

I once stayed in a brothel. Not on purpose, you understand. It was when I was eighteen and doing Interrailing round Europe with my school friends. We were fresh out of boarding school and knew nothing about anything. We had had the sort of education which fitted us for no more than being finished off somewhere in Switzerland. At the railway station in Rome a man had approached asking if we were looking for somewhere to stay. It was late. Well, late to us. It was at least nine o'clock at night. We were delighted by his kindness and thrilled when he wrote an address down for us. Wearing those old-fashioned backpacks with great heavy metal frames we seemed to walk for miles. The handwriting was poor and we were unsure of the address but eventually we arrived at an apartment building and headed for the number we had been given.

The dark wooden door was covered in naked gold cupids. I thought of our English teacher at school who had squirmed with awkwardness when explaining that the word 'pity' in art meant naked.

'Why?' I asked.

'Because,' she replied firmly, 'it is a pity they do not have clothes on.'

A small elderly woman dressed entirely in black answered the door. She spoke no English, and other than things like 'tutti-frutti' we had no Italian. I mimed that we wished to stay. She shook her head. I mimed pleading. She shook her head again and tried to shoo us away. It was dark now and one of us started crying. I think it might have been me. The woman looked at us and sighed. At last she threw her hands in the air, spoke a great deal of Italian and led us inside. There were many rooms off a long corridor and we were shown a large chamber dominated by a circular bed covered in red velvet. Beside it stood a shower with no obvious door. She departed with yet more incomprehensible instructions. We were nice clean girls and all desperate for a shower but there appeared to be no water. I went in search of the woman. She was sitting in a small office with a much younger woman who was painting her nails.

'*Aqua?*' I managed as my right hand imitated water falling on my head.

'*Domani,*' she declared.

Tomorrow. I thought that meant tomorrow.

We went to bed but we couldn't sleep. There was plenty of room for three in the round bed but the apartment was surprisingly busy. For an old lady the owner seemed to have an endless stream of friends who visited. People knocked on the front door all night, and then at about four o'clock the shower came on and sprayed the entire bed. In the morning the woman gave us a breakfast of bread rolls and coffee. She refused our money but wrote a single Italian word down for us to take with us. She pointed to the word and shook her finger at us. 'No!' she declared in clear English. We didn't need to look it up. The word was bordello. I doubt we thanked her properly. She had no need to take us in and had clearly given us one of her best rooms. That bed-wetting shower was probably a premium accessory.

I wonder if these were the matters which occupied Charles I while he was in charge. Did he concern himself with what services might be available when he granted licences for sex? The man himself, sitting on quite a small horse, stares down Whitehall towards Banqueting House, the very spot where on 30 January 1649 he stepped out onto the scaffold to his execution. In fact, it is the very heart of the capital, for all distances from London are measured from here. Thus, I know that I am 1118 miles from the brothel in Rome.

We pass Admiralty Arch, where milk used to be sold. For over two centuries grazing was let out in St James's to the milk-women who sold their wares at the end of the Park. They paid half a crown a week, and after 1772 three shillings a week, for the right to feed cattle in the Park. The last cows weren't banished until about 1905. The final old woman was pensioned off, and the cow sheds carted away. It is said that the foundations of the last milkmaid's stall were broken up into a sort of rockery and put in Hyde Park for alpine plants to take hold. Milkmaids and prostitutes across the street from each other. The women who kept London going yet we know none of their names.

Near here lies the home of the Beefsteak Club, an all-male dining club which has met since the early eighteenth century. It is a place where men from the arts and politics rubbed shoulders, and disappointingly continues to meet at 9 Irving Street, just behind the National Gallery. Allegedly an ancient tradition is that all the waiters are referred to as Charles. How very egalitarian. God forbid we should be troubled with learning the names of staff. Nearly half the members of the House of Lords belong to private members' clubs, many of which are men-only. As long as the boys in power keep meeting on their own nothing will change. Would it help if women started their own clubs? Kathy Lette and I have decided if we ever did start one it would be called the Devil's Doorbell. The Devil's Doorbell is Australian slang for the clitoris. We think it's a marvellous name and perfect for a women-only place as most men would never be able to find it.

It is possible, of course, that I have gone too far with this idea. It does happen. My wonderful friend Pip Broughton keeps an eye on these things. She and I have been pals since university and still work together whenever we can. Today she is a very successful TV producer and director. So often over the years she has been my barometer of how far to push a thought. Years ago she directed a version of A *Midsummer Night's Dream* called *The Pocket Dream*, which I co-wrote and also played a part in, in the West End. It was a show where no joke seemed unwelcome. When we work together Pip always seems calm when I am agitated, clear when I am grappling to find the way. She is a leading light in my life.

During one rehearsal I suggested that perhaps I might fire a gun in the air and a rubber chicken would fall from the flies of the theatre. Pip looked at me and quietly asked, 'What is the Danish for rubber chicken?'

'Gummikylling,' I replied.

'Hmm,' she said, 'and gummikylling is the word I will always use in the future when you go too far.'

I must ask her if the Devil's Doorbell has a whiff of rubber chicken.

Trafalgar Square

I have just discovered the word 'absquatulate', which means to leave somewhere abruptly. When the Queen Mother died I learned the word 'catafalque' and in my head the two go well together. A catafalque, it turns out, is a sort of raised box used to put under the coffins of people too distinguished to lie on the ground. Her Majesty's coffin was placed on such a thing and on the morning of her funeral everyone kept talking about it on Radio 4. I wasn't really listening and thought someone said 'catapult', which seemed an odd choice for a royal funeral but a great way to avoid the traffic getting into Windsor. I think you could absquatulate with a catapult.

Today the bus is slow but I am in no hurry. My son has had a five-star review for his play in Edinburgh, which he has written and is starring in. My daughter Meg is busy on shift as an A&E doctor while Jesse continues to capture the world in blissful photographs. I want to tell everybody. Show all the pictures on my phone. But I keep quiet and just keep grinning at them by myself.

Trafalgar Square marks a low point in my parenting skills. For years I drove the kids through Trafalgar Square and pointed out Nelson atop his column. It was only after about a decade of this oft-repeated history lesson that one of them suddenly realised the guy at the top was not Mandela.

Behind Charles I on his horse is the National Gallery. Charles was a passionate and by all accounts knowledgeable collector of art. In fact, my favourite portrait, *Self-portrait as the Allegory of Painting (La Pittura)* by the Italian Baroque artist Artemisia Gentileschi, was probably painted somewhere around 1638–9 when Charles I invited her to London. The light in the painting is perfect and the portrait is as real as if she might sit on the bus beside me. She holds a very fine brush in her right hand while in her left are her palette and a small collection of brushes. She is wearing a green silk dress but she appears to wear it without a thought. A brown apron covers the dress and she has rolled up her right sleeve. Her dark hair is pulled back out of the way in an untidy bun from which great strands have come loose as she works. Around her neck hangs a chain with a small skull suspended from it, a memento mori. A sign of death to remind us all where we are heading.

I'm not much good at art myself. When I sat the practical exam for my art O level we had a choice of drawing a piece of rhubarb with its leaf still attached or the skull of a small deer. I chose the latter. When I was nearly finished my gentle Scottish art teacher stood behind me and said, 'Well, Sandra, that is an excellent depiction of some rhubarb.'

I wrote 'Rhubarb with leaf' across the top and submitted it. Got a B.

Not everyone is keen on the National Gallery. King William IV called it 'a nasty pokey little hole' and I am not mad about the place myself. Built in 1838, it's a strange sort of homage to the penis. I often walk into the National Gallery and see how long it takes to see art by any women whatsoever. If I take random turnings it's usually about half an hour. The history of art is too often one with a sign reading 'men only'. From the outset the National Gallery had an adoration of grand scenes from history where naked boys seemed so often to be de rigueur.

Women were barred from painting the male nude which rather limited their subject matter. Those women who couldn't resist the lure of the paintbrush had to specialise in what were seen as lesser categories – portraiture, still life and animals – but how extraordinary they were.

There was the seventeenth-century Rachel Ruysch, who was brilliant at flowers. She had ten kids and yet managed to achieve fame and fortune with her art. I also love the nineteenth-century French woman Rosa Bonheur who had to get permission from the Parisian police to wear trousers so she could muck about in fields and paint animals. Or how about the Venetian Rococo painter Rosalba Carriera, a miniature portrait painter to European royalty, or Elisabeth Vigée Le Brun, court painter to Marie Antoinette? Or, further back, someone Boccaccio wrote about when he glanced over famous women in art: Iaia of Cyzicus, known as Marcia, a Roman painter working about two thousand years ago. She was famous in her time as both a painter and an engraver of ivory. She was said to have worked faster and better than her male contemporaries and so made more money.

In all my schooling, no one ever mentioned any of them.

I give talks on these women. It is a futile game, the collecting, as it were, of female cigarette cards of history. There are just never going to be as many of them as men but still I try to spread the word for they reach out from their paintings and break my heart. I had one of these art encounters when I spent the weekend at Althorp, the stately home in Northamptonshire where Princess Diana grew up. I was the guest of Earl Spencer, Diana's brother and the current owner of the house which has been in the Spencer family for five centuries. It's a proper ancestral pile, which makes it sound like a pain in the arse that you inherit. Charles is a nice fellow and hosts an excellent literary festival once a year because, I suppose, these days the rich are not rich enough to keep their places up.

I don't know how many we were at dinner. Maybe thirty or so. I sat between the comedian Ken Dodd and the writer Julian Fellowes and marvelled at the male ability to monologue. I sat turning my head from side to side in a sea of anecdotage. Ken was genuinely fascinating and Julian was impressive in the self-belief that he was too. The house is extraordinary. Grand rooms lined with rich artwork and curtains which occasionally billow with the draught that the British aristocracy can't seem to live without. Find an aristocrat at home and you will also find wellingtons by the door, dog hair on your bed and a wind whistling through the conversation. Althorp is nice and clean, which is not always the case with a stately home. Debbie has been to many such a place with me to raise money for some charity or other. Everyone is always welcoming and cheerful but behind the scenes grand houses are often in a shocking state. We are usually shown to a room with an ancient bed where 'Great-Aunt Betty died', and from the state of it one can only imagine the death was recent. Deb is proud of her own northern working-class heritage. She always shakes her head and mutters, 'Heavens, look at the mess. We might not have had much but we were tidy.'

Because the houses often have generations of plunder and purchase, they are always worth a visit. Althorp has the most astonishing art you will find outside a national collection. The Picture Gallery is on the first floor of the west wing. Just saying the words 'west' and 'wing' gives you some idea of the size of the house. It features original Tudor woodwork and is where the ladies of the day would take a walk if they didn't fancy soiling their hems with nature. The walls are decorated with important and enormous paintings by mostly important men with enormous reputations like van Dyck. Charles Spencer explained that the windows of the gallery, which must have been twelve foot high, are specially built to swing open in the event of a fire so the giant paintings can be saved.

On the way to the loo, a fabulous painted face eyed me from an ornate frame. It was a woman and I thought I knew her. I stopped to look. Hidden away down a corridor, with no particular arrangement for her evacuation in the event of a fire, was a self-portrait of the Italian Renaissance painter Sofonisba Anguissola. Her talent was recognised by no less a fellow than Michelangelo, who encouraged and informally mentored her. She became a great portrait artist and van Dyck visited her when she was over ninety. He sought her advice and commented on the sharpness of her mind.

'You should hang Sofonisba near van Dyck in the main gallery,' I suggested to Charles. 'They ought to be together. They would have liked that.' He nodded. He is a good man who likes art, but I suspect she is still hanging outside the loo.

The actress Alison Steadman was also a guest that weekend. She is easy-going and unconcerned about soil on her hem, so along with my wife we went for a walk in the gardens the next morning. There was a chain across part of the path from which a sign was suspended, reading 'No Public Access'.

'Oh, we can't go down there,' said Alison.

'It doesn't mean us,' I said confidently. 'We're guests, not public.'

We wandered down the path until we came to a small lake. In the centre of the still water lay the island where we could see the stone plinth topped with an urn marking Princess Diana's grave. I never met Diana but performed for her once at Wembley on World Aids Day, and I saw her in the dark distance surrounded by protection officers. I thought, good for her, being here when few were paying attention to the terrible affliction of Aids.

'Could you do a couple of minutes about the importance of

condoms?' whispered the organiser to me as I stepped out on to the stage with Ian McKellen. Condoms are not my specialist area. I thought perhaps they should have asked Ian to do it.

After that I had to introduce the band Take That, who, with my usual zest for popular culture, I had never heard of.

The island where she rests looked overgrown and wild. Maybe that's nice. Her life was too controlled.

Out in the square outside the National Gallery is a pavement artist. The Italians call such men *madonnari* and they've been around since the sixteenth century. There was a time when London had no pavements. Up until the mid-eighteenth century there was nothing but dirt roads which edged right up to the buildings. A tiny alley by the Silver Cross pub called Craig Court stands as a tribute to the power of a man to effect change to suit his own needs. The story is told of Arthur Onslow, the speaker of the House of Commons, visiting the Earl of Harrington, who lived in Craig Court, one fine day in the 1760s. Having finished his business with the earl, Onslow got in his stately carriage, the driver headed off and promptly got stuck between the houses on either side. Indeed, so stuck that a hole had to be cut in the roof of his carriage, through which he was pulled to freedom. Onslow decided that kerbstones were needed so that even an idiot could see how wide a road was and the rest is paving history.

I sit for a minute and admire the square. It was also designed by Sir Charles Barry. Busy fellow. The Landseer lions stare out at me. Poor old Sir Edwin Landseer was literally driven mad by these bronze beasts. He seems to have been a sensitive chap. He had his first breakdown over a broken heart in the 1840s. From then he veered from one depression to another, not helped, it seems, by his abuse of alcohol and other chemical assistance.

Landseer was given to animal painting but the lions are

perhaps his greatest triumph. They are Barbary lions and they're all individual. Edwin was most particular that he got them right. Apparently he asked for a dead lion from London Zoo so he could sketch at will but, delivery times on deceased felines being what they are, it took two years for one to turn up. By all accounts it was delivered to his studio in St John's Wood Road by taxi, where the lifeless creature quickly began to go off and upset the neighbours with the smell.

I think about stopping in at the church of St Martin-in-the-Fields for some calm. I've been writing a new show and I am tired. A church was first commissioned to be built on the site by Henry VIII because he didn't like to see funerals of common people pass by his palace at Whitehall. I don't want to think about writing at all, but under the portico I come across a sculpture where a baby is emerging from the rough stone. I try to empty my mind. Engraved on the rock is 'In the beginning was the word . . .' and that leads me to think what word I would have started the world with, and then my brain fizzes and I wish I hadn't stopped here at all.

Regent Street / St James's

It is cold and rainy and so steamed up on the bus that the windows are entirely fogged. The result is an impressionistic wash of lights outside, so only the bus-stop announcements tell me where I am. Many passengers have taken to warm hats. Some funny, with comical ears added, while others have clearly been hand-knitted by a loving if myopic relative. I spy the first person I've seen on the bus reading a book. She is a young woman with curly dark hair and bright red glasses. I want to make friends immediately but she is quite rightly lost in what she is reading.

There appears to be gridlock in every street today. I don't think the British deal well with weather. Leaves fall in the autumn and the trains come to a halt. A splash of rain and car drivers lose the ability to move forward. One of the many things which baffled my Danish father was the fact that English houses seemed to have inbuilt draughts. I remember my English grandmother purchasing some kind of long sausage-dog pillow which lay in front of the sitting-room door to 'stop the draught'.

'Why don't you just get a door that fits?' asked my father.

My grandmother's house in winter was a trial. Each morning would begin with the curses of my grandfather, who in dressing gown and slippers pulled on some clanging lever on the boiler to shake the coal down and try to get the thing started again. Meanwhile my grandmother stayed in bed wearing a woollen jacket knitted for the purpose. During the day the two of them sat hunched in front of a three-bar electric fire, with two bars always the maximum permitted. My grandfather died watching television in front of that miserable fire. Granny called the police and then me.

'He'd just had a jam sandwich,' she was telling the officer when I arrived. 'Oh Sandi, he's dead. I can't think how it happened. He was only watching *Blankety Blank*.'

I know this part of the route so well. I have come to this street since childhood. I can sense us passing the old offices which still bear the sign for the Norwegian Railway where each summer my father would collect tickets for our boat trips home. I smile and think about the Lofoten Islands, where Debbie and I had our honeymoon. The islands lie within the Arctic Circle. I knew I had married the right person when I asked Deb where she wanted to go after the wedding and she replied, 'The Arctic.' We had the most wonderful time and loved the pragmatism of the people. We had nothing but fair weather but I asked a local man how bad it can get.

'Very bad,' he said. 'One winter my whole porch blew away.'
'Gosh,' I replied, 'what did you do?'
'Nothing. Who needs a porch in the winter?'

To my left lies Pall Mall, named after an Italian game a bit like croquet called *pallo a maglio*. It was popular with Charles II, who played it with his mistress in St James's Park. Down the road lies the Reform Club where a French chef, Alexis Soyer, held sway in the early nineteenth century. He was arguably the first celebrity chef and seems to have been a good guy. He tried to help the Irish suffering during the Great Famine when his 'famine soup' was served to thousands for free. He opened an art gallery in London and used the money collected from the entrance fees to feed yet more of the starving. During the Crimean War he joined the army at his own expense and advised them how to give every soldier a nutritious meal. His wife, Elizabeth Emma Jones (known as Emma), supported him in his endeavours. She was also a remarkable painter, one of the youngest ever to exhibit at the Royal Academy and hugely popular in her time. A popularity which she also used for good painting works for the abolitionist cause.

The rain is truly lashing against the bus now. There is a great rumble of thunder and the bus seems to shudder in echo. I think of Emma. She lived near here, at Charing Cross, and died in her home in 1842. Whilst pregnant she had received a fright during a thunderstorm. She went into premature labour and died of complications in childbirth. I know she's buried in Kensal Green Cemetery but I have no idea where her art is. Is it too much of a chance that there is a thunderstorm at this moment? That I think of her now? I don't know. I read somewhere that there are no accidents, just ideas trying to find us.

Past the Haymarket Theatre, where a group of tailors once rioted, so incensed were they by a play. How marvellous to get that emotional about theatre. I went to an event at the Royal Festival Hall where Lena Dunham was interviewed by Caitlin Moran. They are part of a new wave of feminism whose existence one can only applaud, but there were moments when I felt angry.

'Isn't it complicated sometimes,' said Lena to the packed audience, 'when a guy wolf-whistles at you and you feel both appalled and validated at the same time?'

Validated? What are we? Car park tickets? The young fans all murmured as if they were committing the sentence to memory while the older feminists wondered at the ground so hard fought for being so quietly given back. I shouldn't complain. The next wave of feminism is happening and the youngsters are doing wonders. I am just tired that each new burst of energy towards equality is necessary.

Men are accorded honour in all these streets. Past Jermyn Street, named for the earl Henry Jermyn. For students of London architecture, he is sometimes seen as the Father of the West End. Indeed, a green plaque in St James's Square hails him as the man who inspired the way the area developed. I get off the bus and wander down St James's Street to look for the window where George Brummell, nicknamed Beau, once looked down upon the world. He was the Regency period's arbiter of fashion and was said to have his boots polished with champagne. This very emblem of vanity was born in Downing Street, which seems appropriate as it too has become a symbol of narcissistic enterprise. There is a statue of him in Jermyn Street. I don't know why. If you look at all the statues across the country there are hundreds of men but only eighty of named women. Of those fifteen are fictional and thirty-eight are royal.

Beau Brummell, however, is immortalised in bronze. He died in 1840, penniless and quite mad with syphilis in Le Bon Sauveur asylum outside Caen in France. Caen, whose view was once said to have been painted with the blood of King Louis XIV.

I can only find one woman's ghost on Jermyn Street, but it is a good one. There used be a pub called the Rose Tavern at No. 96. Had you popped in during the early 1880s you might have found Fanny Cornforth behind the bar. Her face would look familiar because she was the model in so many paintings by

Dante Gabriel Rossetti. Her flowing reddish-blonde hair became quintessential of the Pre-Raphaelite period. She was Rossetti's muse if not his wife. Her life ended in dementia and she spent her final years in the West Sussex County Asylum in Chichester. Her glorious hair was finally laid to rest in an unmarked grave.

Lots of famous men lived on Jermyn Street, many of them called Thomas: the poet Thomas Gray; Thomas Wall, the ice-cream man; Thomas Lawrence, portrait painter – they all had homes here. I read that when Gray lived here, he 'dined generally alone, and was served from an eating house near his lodging'. That's sad. Odd that you can feel someone else's loneliness even though you never met.

I'm not sure why men of the same name seem to clump together. Perhaps there is something in the suggestion that employers mostly employ people who are a bit like themselves. Possibly the most startling fact in my TED Talk concerned the people who run the top hundred FTSE companies. At the time there were seven run by women but seventeen run by men called John. More men called John were in charge than women. As if that weren't enough, there were fourteen run by men called Dave.

Piccadilly Circus

Eros stands at the heart of Piccadilly Circus. He is as British as Brexit. Everything about him is wrong. In truth, the thing we refer to as Eros is actually the Shaftesbury Memorial Fountain. It was created as a tribute to the seventh Earl of Shaftesbury. Earl number seven seems to have been a good guy who had given away so much money to the poor that everyone felt the public ought to pay for a memorial. Money was raised and Alfred Gilbert was commissioned to create a statue not of Eros but of Eros' brother Anteros, the angel of Christian charity. No one thought of making an Eros statue as he was deemed frivolous and not at all commendable.

Anteros went up onto his perch in 1892 and there was some shock at his nudity. The fountain was a disaster, splashing passers-by, and the main people attracted to the memorial were vandals. The avant-garde aluminium from which the statue was made of proved a poor choice for the London weather and Gilbert lost a fortune on the commission. So it isn't Eros, it wasn't well made and no one really liked it. Gilbert hated it. He suggested the whole thing be melted down and the money given to the homeless. I think that about a lot of things.

Allegedly, Piccadilly is so named because in the early seventeenth century one Robert Baker set up a tailoring shop in the Strand where he sold 'picadils', a kind of lace collar popular at the time. So popular that he made enough money to buy the land near by. He built himself a mansion, but instead of respect he got the derision that only Londoners can muster. They called his place 'Piccadilly Hall'.

It was at Piccadilly Circus that London's first modern three-colour traffic light was installed in 1926. The idea of using lights to stop traffic in the street came from a nineteenth-century railway engineer called John Peake Knight. The very first one was gas-powered and manually operated, at the junction of Bridge Street and Great George Street outside the Houses of Parliament. The lights were not a big success. Everyone gave up on the idea when they exploded. A policeman was killed and some horses belonging to a passing cavalry troop bolted.

I look out at a shop window advising us all to 'Make every-day more extraordinary!' Below it a homeless man is sleeping. 170,000 people in the capital are without a home.

For a brief while the Georgians thought the world was coming to an end here. In spring 1750 many Londoners fled because they believed the end was nigh. There had been a couple of earth tremors early in the year strong enough to knock down a few chimneys. It's the sort of thing that sets off those who are already unbalanced into a frenzy. Some unwell military fellow walked up and down Piccadilly declaring it would all be over on 8 April, while bishops berated the populace for making God angry with their bad behaviour. Some people panicked and the streets became so choked with traffic hardly anyone could leave town. In the end 8 April came and went. The world carried on and the army man was sent to Bedlam. We should all beware which crazy men we follow.

I know all this but I don't know what good it does me. I think I have a very odd set of interests. My bucket list, for exam-ple, includes going to Fruita, Colorado, because on the first weekend in June each year they celebrate Mike the Headless

Chicken Day. Mike was a chicken destined for the cooking pot of the Olsen family who lived in Fruita. On 10 September 1945 Mrs Olsen sent Mr Olsen out to chop Mike's head off. Unfortunately, he was a poor executioner. Mike lost most of his head but kept one ear, his jugular vein and most of his brain stem. To the naked eye he looked headless. To Mike, life was still worth living. He refused to die and Mr Olsen, who I think felt bad, started feeding him with an eyedropper. Well, we all like a story about surviving against the odds, and soon Mike became famous. He was shown off at fairs and had his picture in both *Time* and *Life* magazines. Sadly, while on tour he choked to death in a motel in Phoenix. I don't know if it is a country song but it sounds like one. There is a very strange black-and-white photo on the Headless Chicken Day website where Mike appears to be being shown his own severed head.

Actually, that's about all I have on my bucket list because I learned a long time ago to be careful about what you want. I learned the lesson from John McCarthy. When John, Nick and I were sharing our Clapham flat, John worked for a shipping magazine, selling advertising space. He was no good at it at all, as the minute someone said they weren't sure about purchasing advertising space he agreed with them. The first month he worked for them he brought home a copy of the magazine. The front cover had a photograph of a large cargo ship with a strange goitre-like growth on the bow.

'What is that?' I asked.

'That,' replied John knowledgeably, 'is a bulbous bow.'

It became our nickname for him. Nick got him out of that dead-end job and soon we were all working at UPITN. For a brief while Nick was posted to Beirut and John was jealous. He too wanted to be tested in the field. When Nick was due to come home for leave John begged to be allowed to replace him, and off he went.

Lebanon was not a restful place and after a short while John called Nick to say there was trouble.

'Don't cross the green line,' Nick advised, 'and don't trust anyone.'

John is the most trusting person I know and he trusted his cameraman. It was a mistake and he was kidnapped. It was April 1986. Nick called me.

'It's Bulbous Bow,' he said, 'he's been taken.' And then my brother didn't speak again for months. He entirely lost the power of speech, so shocked was he at what had happened.

John was not released from captivity for five long years, not until 8 August 1991. I remember the evening well because, as chance would have it, I was at a fundraiser in a West End theatre organised by the Friends of John McCarthy when we heard the news that he was coming home. How we wept with joy.

Everyone was keen to know what he had been through, what he was thinking, and one of the things he told everyone was that while in captivity he had had a recurring image of freedom. The dream was that he was standing at the prow of an old sailing ship beating through the coastal waters of Britain. This was in the days when the BBC had a bit more money and someone decided to make this dream come true for him.

He and I were offered the chance to sail around Britain on an old wooden sailing ship, a 1911 Bristol pilot cutter called *Hirta*. We met the boat at the southernmost part of the United Kingdom, the small islands called the Minquiers which lie just over nine miles south of Jersey. There's nothing there except the country's southernmost public toilet and a lot of seagulls.

It was clear from the beginning that neither John nor I would get on with the ship's captain. He didn't like us and we found him ... well, tricky, but I had no time to think about that because the moment I boarded I became spectacularly unwell. Sailors will tell you that seasickness comes in two stages – in the first you think you're going to die and in the second you're very afraid you're not going to.

I did nothing but vomit for the first week of the trip. When at last I was able to make my way to the deck without losing my insides to the sea I found John standing at the prow of the vessel. It was the very spot where he had said he would feel freedom. He turned and smiled that charming smile.

'You know that dream I had? About freedom and this boat?' he asked.

I nodded, thinking that the fulfilment of this dream for John would make all my vomiting worthwhile.

John nodded. 'I think I've realised that I was mistaken.'

We both went silent and looked out to sea, knowing we had another three months of this hell ahead of us. I've told him, the next time he gets taken, dream about a cocktail bar in the Caribbean.

Beak Street / Hamleys Toy Shop

Beak Street was where the Italian painter Canaletto lived for a couple of years in the late 1740s. He would sell his paintings by placing adverts which read, for example, that his depiction of St James's Park was available to be viewed 'by any gentleman that will be pleased to come to his house'. He then gave the address: 41 Beak Street, where he lived with a cabinetmaker. I like Canaletto. If he was painting a view and thought a building he was looking at would look better somewhere else in his work, he just used his paints to move it. He was like a living Photoshop guy.

I've been to Grayson Perry's studio for coffee. He is an astonishing artist and I'm thrilled to be writing a piece for the catalogue of his new exhibition. Nice man who makes art relevant to us all. He has been making pots about Brexit. They were made by crowdsourcing ideas, phrases and even photographs via social media. There is a Leave vase and a Remain one. What I take away with me is the fact that both sides agree on liking Marmite, tea and David Bowie, and not much else. Great art, but he makes instant coffee, which shouldn't be allowed. I wonder if anyone ever complained about Canaletto's hospitality.

I didn't know what to take to the studio. The Dane in me requires a gift when you visit anyone. In the end I knitted him a rabbit. It took ages. I could have bought one in Hamleys toy shop. I love toys. Indeed, I like most games. The child in me is easy to delight. I like big toy shops. When I was about nine, for reasons I can't recall, my brother and I were asked to dress as old-fashioned soldiers in red tunics and white trousers to ride on a train made of Lego through the streets of Manhattan in the Macy's Thanksgiving Day Parade. The train, I think, came from FAO Schwarz, once the largest toy shop in the world.

I was feeling a little low as I walked past Hamleys. For some reason the driver of the first Number 12 which happened along had refused to stop and pick me up and I took it personally. It was early November and grey. A colleague called me to have a chat about her pay. She is a distinguished broadcaster who has discovered the most terrible pay disparity between herself and her male co-presenter. Despite his inexperience he is being paid so much more than her. I've had my own issues with this stuff and find it hard to be upbeat about a solution. The latest forecast is that gender equality on pay will be reached in the year 2235. I'll probably be a bit past it by then.

It is so boringly predictable that a comedian is actually depressed but there are dreadful black dog days of it. I could do with a laugh. My Achilles heel of laughter, the things that will make me laugh even on my deathbed, lie in two rather unusual areas: yodelling and amusing ways to die. No matter how sombre an occasion I will always giggle at yodelling. I realise I ought to have more respect. It is a fine rural tradition but even the name makes me snigger. It comes from the German *jodeln*, which means 'to utter the syllable jo' (pronounced 'yo'). How marvellously straightforward is that? I love the sound so much that for a long while I had fixed to my front door the small plastic head of an Austrian fellow in a traditional Tyrolean hat. He looked surprisingly cheerful for someone who had been beheaded, and acted as my doorbell. If you pressed his nose he yodelled and inevitably I could be heard inside, guffawing in response. Even the arrival of bailiffs would have made me laugh. One day I arrived home to find someone had stolen him and no doorbell on earth has ever made up for the loss.

Other than a good yodel I'm ashamed to say I am always amused by a good death. I think that if you are going to go you ought at least do it in sufficient comedic style to leave the rest of humanity helpless at the thought. It is not kind of me but an amusing shuffling-off into the next life makes me smile. Unable to find anyone who has yodelled themselves to death I am content to know the stories of, for example, the nineteenth-century American lawyer Clement Vallandigham who accidentally shot himself while trying to demonstrate that an alleged victim could have done so. It was an excellent defence. Clement died but his client was acquitted.

Along Regent Street neither yodelling nor entertaining demises seem available but there is at least a Christmas elf dressed in red, white and green, wearing a jolly hat and pointy shoes, who runs out from the toy shop and hugs me.

'I love you, Sandi,' she declares.

'Are you an elf?' I ask, despite the fact that this is clearly the case. She nods.

'Is it your dream job?' I ask.

'I'm only eighteen. I want to work in television production.'

'Stay being an elf,' I advise. I go off to find a friendlier bus driver thinking we could all do with more unexpected elf encounters.

Yesterday I took the car. I've bought a car which I hardly ever drive because I feel bad about it. It's a fantastic five-litre bright red Mustang convertible. I love it. It's a thing of beauty and I have wanted one ever since my American childhood. To me it seemed the ultimate symbol of success. Now I have it, however, I feel bad about the environment so mostly it just sits looking pretty outside my house. There's not a day goes by I don't think I really ought to sell it. Anyway, yesterday was a nice day so

I treated myself to a spin. I put the roof down and played the Beach Boys' greatest hits as I imagined myself cruising down to Malibu. I very rarely think I look cool. It's just not my style, but yesterday I felt good. I had stopped at some traffic lights by Waterloo Station when a great crowd crossed in front of me, heading to the South Bank. A shrill, posh voice pinged out from the crowd, declaring, 'Oh look, there's that lesbian!'

I put the roof back up.

I am seated anonymously again, on my bus, when a woman with bright turquoise hair gets on and sits down next to me. She immediately gets out her phone and begins playing a game in which she faces the daunting task of matching pieces of digital fruit to clear the board. She is utterly engrossed in the task and doesn't look up once. I wonder if I might die and she wouldn't notice. Would that be funny? Is it better to be noticed or not to be noticed?

The latest figures show that the average young person plays games on their phones or iPads or whatever for ten to twelve hours a week. When the game *Angry Birds* first came out it was reported that the world was spending five million hours a day playing it. In fact, David Cameron, while Prime Minister, was said to play it during Cabinet meetings. Perhaps that explains everything about his attitude to office. I know we'd all like to think those in charge are diligent about their duties but instead they are as feckless as the rest of us.

I wonder what other games one might play on a bus. Perhaps games could be invented which involved all the passengers but no phones. I can't think of one. My head is too full up. I spent quite a lot of this week mugging up on the theory of relativity for *QI*. It was not the topic we were going to be dealing with but it might have come up in a tangential conversation so I thought

I'd be prepared. Einstein's theory is the sort of thing I feel I ought to know but wasn't confident I could explain. Anyway, I developed a corking and simple explanation which involved playing ping-pong on a train. It took ages to get into my head and then the bloody subject never came up.

I once sat next to a spy at a dinner on board HMS *Victory* – which is quite a good sentence. It was Trafalgar Night and Deb and I had been invited to celebrate the occasion in Nelson's cabin. It was a rather jolly affair with a quartet of string players from the Navy playing background music and the whole thing culminating in the 'Parade of the Ships', when chocolate replicas of the vessels from the battle were paraded around the table complete with Maltesers for cannonballs. The spy told me a disturbing story about a scientist who used to make nerve gas at home and bring it in to the MoD on the Tube. I have no idea if he was kidding but he didn't look like a joker.

Oxford Circus Station

I've picked up a book from the outdoor book market on the South Bank. I don't know why I bought it, because I don't understand it. It's called *Pocket Ref*. It is, as the name suggests, small enough for your pocket. It was written by a man called Thomas J. Glover and clearly his intention was to provide some kind of easy-access reference book. Usually I love diving into such information. Thomas opens with a section on the 'Composition of Air'. It's not something I feel a need to carry in my pocket. I flick on to 'Dry Air Specific Heat at 20°C Constant Temperature and Various Pressures'. It is literally hot air. But then I move on to 'Automotive Trailer Wiring', with many useful illustrations should I find a boat that needs to be trailed behind my car; a table of 'Maximum Floor Joist Spans'; how to deal with 'Puncture Wounds to the Torso'; 'Canada and Mexico Postal Abbreviations'; and my absolute favourite, the 'Torino Asteroid–Comet Destruction Scale', which gives me a marvellous, clear understanding of my chances of being obliterated by something hurtling from outer space. In themselves all the pieces of the book are quite interesting, I'm just not sure what they're doing together. Mind you, my head generally feels like that.

Oxford Street lies on the route of an old Roman road. Lots of places I've passed carry rich men's names and this is no different. It was named after Edward Harley, second Earl of Oxford, who acquired the land in 1713. It's nighttime and I am in my best bib and tucker for an event. No one notices. There is something so comforting about the bus. How wonderful on a dark and wintry night to see the destination light in the distance and the Number 12 appear. The new 12s have a sort of peekaboo glass section at the back which curves up to the top deck. Makes the bus look like it's wearing an off-the-shoulder number.

A woman sitting next to me has been eating a bag of crisps loudly for the last ten minutes and spilling crumbs over my lap. I don't know why she doesn't notice. When I struggle to understand another human being I always take comfort in the fact that the two guys who were supposed to know the most about the human psyche, Carl Jung and Sigmund Freud, couldn't get on with each other. It was a bit like an intense love affair. Jung was younger and for a while he was besotted with Freud and kept telling everyone about him. There is a marvellous photo of the two of them on holiday together in 1908, crossing America like a pair of hobos. There are also snaps of them fishing, hunting and wearing seriously odd clothing on an Arctic expedition. Then it got weird. They fought. Freud was clearly dramatic as he fainted several times while Jung was having a go. Eventually, Freud wrote and called off the friendship. Jung wrote his final letter to his old mentor by typewriter but is said to have added the words 'The rest is silence' by hand at the bottom of the page. It's a quote from *Hamlet* about death. Good to see a Danish prince getting the last word.

I always look for Stanley Green when I get to Oxford Circus even though I know he's not here any more. He was a campaigner whose personal battle was against passion and peanuts. He seemed to believe protein was the source of all evil. Wearing a green cap and carrying a black protest sign with white lettering, for years he could be found marching up and down the streets around Oxford Circus. Before he took up his cause he had been, amongst other things, a gardener. I don't know what happened to him which led to his anti-peanut devotion. He sold booklets in which he also advocated sitting less. I remember them as being just seven pence each but he must have sold enough to keep going. He began in 1968 and carried on until he died in 1992. I admire Stanley's resolve. Passion is everything.

My father only mentioned my being gay once. It was after I had come out and the medical profession had reacted by drugging me. I was barely functioning, so my parents took me with them home to Denmark. In those days there was a ferry from Harwich in Essex to the Esbjerg on the west coast of Jutland. It took twenty-four hours and Papa always liked to spend the evening before dinner standing at the back of the boat watching the wash disappear away into the sea. It was something we had always done together. We were standing there silently enjoying the air, when he put his arm around me.

'You know this ... business ...' he said at last. I nodded. He squeezed me close. 'It's only made me love you more.'

Now that my father knew I had passion, nothing else mattered.

I feel he is with me on the bus and we motor along together.

How my father would have loved my amazing kids. My twenty-five-year-old son Ted has moved in with us. I love having him around. I used to worry that the kids might be affected by having two mums but actually I think it has been a source of pride. When Ted was about six he had a friend over for tea. I could hear them playing in the next room.

'What's it like having two mums?' asked the small friend.

I waited with hushed breath, not knowing how my boy might answer.

'It's fantastic,' he replied. 'Because if one of them is sick you still have another one to do for you.'

Good to know.

Margaret Street

I can't stop scratching my right hand. I have a condom scar on it. It itches sometimes, when the weather is on the turn. It is getting fainter as I age, which is not surprising as it happened forty years ago. I was in a play at university in which a retractable stage dagger was to be used. The wretched thing was cheap and, every time we used it, it made a great clunking sound. For reasons I can't fathom I was charged with subduing the thing into operational silence. I lived at my college, which was three miles outside the town. There were no shops and nothing in my room presented itself as suitable to dampen the dagger. Then I remembered there was a newly installed condom machine in the ladies' lavatories by the front door. The machine had been seen as a rather racy addition to the college, so despite the fact that the contents were of no use to me I knew where they were. I went down and purchased a pack of three.

My theory was that I could take the knife apart and use one as a sort of rubber sheath to soften the blade as it plunged back into the handle. It didn't work at all. Now I found myself with three unused condoms. I was young and didn't want anyone to think I might have a use for them so I went to flush them down the toilet. I tried one but it resolutely refused to flush. I now know that the brain is still developing in our early twenties and it is the only excuse I have for what I did next.

Back in my room I decided to set fire to the now annoying prophylactics. I held one of them in my left hand and set fire to

the top of it with my right. If you've never done this allow me
to issue a word of warning. Quite rightly, condoms are made of
non-flammable material. All that happened was that the end of
the condom separated itself from the body, flew into the air and
embedded itself in my right hand, just above the thumb. I've
never known pain quite like it. Naturally I was too embarrassed
to tell anyone or see the college nurse so it never really healed
properly. I must be one of the few lesbians in the world whose
hand bears such a scar. It is a tribute to foolishness which I carry
with me every day. Today it is itching. Something is changing.
Maybe it's the weather. Maybe it's me. I am arriving at work but
I don't want to get off. I just want to keep travelling.

I took the Number 12 because it carried me to where I needed
to go, but in the end I just enjoyed the journey itself and didn't
much mind where I got off. It is winter. My hands and feet are
freezing but I feel warm on the full bus. I haven't written half
the things I know about the places on the route because I can
hear my family telling me not to go on. No one else is that interested, Mum! Throughout the route I have struggled to pin down
history and that includes my own. What I remember and what
happened may not be the same thing.

I arrive at the BBC and it feels familiar. Of course it does, I've
worked here for years, but I also feel it at a visceral level. A professor of psychology called Dr James McConnell did some radical
research at the University of Michigan in the 1950s and '60s
which suggested that memories could exist outside the brain –
and even be transferred between organisms. He posited that all
kinds of cells contain a chemical memory trace, and not just the
ones in our head. It challenged everything we think we know
about memory and of course lots of people hate a challenge so
he was declared bonkers.

To prove his point McConnell enlisted the services of the
common freshwater flatworm. Flatworms are rather astonishing.

They have a centralised brain, and although they are rarely considered when selecting a pet, they can be taught to perform tricks. The training method is not great but if you use electric shocks you can teach a flatworm to respond to light cues and move, for example, to a particular part of a Petri dish. In other words, they can be trained to recall a behaviour and repeat it on cue. Add to this their incredible ability to regenerate themselves from pretty much any scrap of flesh. If you cut the tip of a flatworm's tail off it will only take two weeks for a brand-new flatworm to grow from this tiny piece. The new creature will be complete in every way, including having a brand-new brain.

So here is the thing. The new flatworm with the new brain still remembers how to move on cue. 'We didn't know what the tail would remember, if anything, for it had to grow an entirely new brain, new eyes, and almost an entire new nervous system,' McConnell wrote. The fact is the tail did remember. This upset so many people. Actually one guy, the American so-called Unabomber Theodore Kaczynski, was so enraged with McConnell and his research that he sent him a bomb. Perhaps we are all afraid of what we don't understand. Then again, maybe people just don't like being compared to worms.

I mention all this because I feel a connection to the BBC which is much more than just having worked there. It's not too much hyperbole to say I owe it my life. Back in the early 1950s my mother was working at Bush House, then the BBC's home for all international broadcasting. My mother is a redoubtable woman. She joined the organisation as a secretary but had no intention of remaining one. It did not take her long to become one of the first female studio managers, responsible for putting programmes on the air, making announcements and generally keeping an eye on things as broadcasts were happening.

My father was working for Danish Radio and was sent to the BBC for further training. Radio studios consist of a large plate-glass window between two rooms. In one half sits the studio manager with all the technical equipment and in the other the broadcaster with his or her microphone. I have no pictures of my mother at work but I do have one of my father in front of a BBC microphone which is practically the size of his head. My mother was engaged to a man called John but Papa swept her off her feet, and in 1952 they married.

My mother left the BBC because she was required to. Married women were not considered suitable employees in those days. She moved to Denmark where she didn't know anyone and didn't speak the language. Today pretty much everyone in Copenhagen has excellent English but back then she was isolated and alone. She learned the language and got on with her new life. I expect much of my resilience comes from her.

I love the BBC with my whole heart, although it has sometimes been a one-way street. After six years as a team captain on *Call My Bluff* I learned that I had been replaced. No one from the channel told me; I heard it from a member of the public who had read about it in the *Radio Times*. My wife also worked for the BBC. She began as a camera operator and then went on to be a lighting director. For many years she plied her trade at Television Centre. She gave up in the end, exhausted by misogyny and the battle to prove that a woman can turn lights on and off.

On the very last day that Television Centre was operating as a BBC facility I was filming a sitcom there called *Up the Women*, in which I played Emmeline Pankhurst. I was thrilled to be acting, thrilled to be in something so funny and even more thrilled because once again I had been allowed to park in the Horseshoe. People think actors do their work for the applause and recognition, but honestly a lot of the time it's for the parking.

Everyone knew the place was closing down and it had become popular to steal a sign or two bearing the familiar BBC font.

Using my ever-available penknife, Deb and I had taken down a couple of small signs and put them in the car. As we approached the security gate at the end of the evening we noticed a large sign that said 'All cars to be searched on exit'.

A wave of panic swept over me. Would I be arrested? What a way to end a long career.

'What shall we do?' I asked my wife.

'Smile,' she said.

I rolled down the window and did as she suggested. A fierce-looking guard looked up from his clipboard, smiled back and waved me through saying, 'Night, Sandi.'

The signs are in my office. One of them shows the way out.

Postface

I have in my time sailed around Britain, canoed across Africa and crossed both America and Europe not once but several times. Yet the 7.71-mile route of London's Number 12 bus stands equal to all those journeys. I cannot think of a trip with greater diversity or a more wonderful store of history. I had not realised until I really looked that there are hardly any women memorialised in this great city. Almost every street name and every statue stands as a tribute to a man, a white man, usually a rich one. Throughout the city, bridges were built and pavements laid just to make the passage of self-important men smoother. The travelling has unexpectedly given me new feminist purpose. There is so much work to be done for equality both in the improvement of the present and in the recollection of the past. I hope I have it in me to roll up my sleeves and get on. For someone who is not religious I am excessively preoccupied with my reason for being, with working out what good I can do with my life. I have no idea if I have made or will make any difference at all as I pass this way but so far, I guess, at least I looked up, I looked out, I looked those I travelled with in the eye, and sometimes I even got off the bus to join in. Maybe that's the best any of us can do.

Something has happened which makes me optimistic that change is possible. Over the years, as my public profile grew, I received various letters from my Cambridge college, Girton, asking me to speak at one thing or another. The hurt of what had happened to me still ran deep and I always wrote back and said I didn't think they would want to hear what I had to say. In 2013 Troy, still my friend, decided to try to broker some peace. We went to meet the new mistress of the college, Susan Smith. It had been thirty-five years since I had been put in disgrace yet still I found I couldn't even talk about what had happened to me without weeping. Over the next few years Susan and I met a few more times. By then I had been made an honorary fellow at two of the other women's colleges of Cambridge – Newnham and Lucy Cavendish. It is the highest honour a college can give to an outsider, but still my own alma mater was silent. I liked Susan and knew she wanted to put the past behind us.

Then in 2018 she wrote on behalf of the college to say the following year Girton was celebrating its 150th anniversary. To mark the occasion they were awarding five honorary fellowships and would I accept one?

'Might I say what I like?' I asked.

'Absolutely,' she replied.

It was one of the happiest days of my life. I did all the usual formal things – I planted a tree, had a Q and A with the students – but the bit which will stay with me is that in the moment of the fellowship being conferred Susan stood up and said, 'I am so sorry we failed you in the past.' I will be grateful to her for the rest of my life.

Troy, and her husband Glen, and Debbie were there. Troy was the unsung hero and I was getting the honour which didn't seem quite right so I used my acceptance speech to talk about friendship and loyalty and how she stood by me. In front of all the gathered dignitaries Deb and I gave her Danish candlesticks in honour of Portia's quote in The Merchant of Venice: 'How far that little candle throws its beams! So shines a good deed in a naughty world.'

Sorry is a powerful word and once the ceremony was over I

went out into the corridor and sobbed. Forty years of aching pain released by a single sorry. That night there was a dinner for more than 250 students to celebrate the contribution of the LGBT community to college life. A giant rainbow flag hung in the hall, and rather than sit eating I walked up and down all the tables of students and spoke to each one. The world had moved on, but not entirely. There were still those who were only 'out' at college and not at home, or who were afraid for their future. I tried where I could to give them comfort and courage. The night finished with wild cheering and foot-stomping. It was a joyous sound and soothed my heart at last. Perhaps if we are patient and wait long enough, things come right in the end. I hope so.

Acknowledgements

I have a ridiculous number of people to thank. Firstly, Lennie Goodings, who over the years has had to drag books out of me. Her patience has been astonishing and her friendship a real gift. I would never have written this if she hadn't been so determined. I am also grateful to Gill Coleridge, Susan de Soissons, Zoe Gullen, Meryl Hoffman, Josh Byrne and Cathryn Summerhayes for their support and advice. My kids Jesse, Meg and Ted and my grandson Arlo are, of course, everything to me and I will never cease to wonder that my wife Debbie, the love of my life, agreed to take me on. Finally I would like to thank my mother for having me in the first place.

Credits

17   Ruskin's concerns from Paul Dijstelberge, *Streetwise: A Cultural History Street by Street* (Armorica, 2018).

62   Details of the London Explorers' Club's visits from 'The London Explorers' Club', thelostbyway.com, 30 April 2005.

72   Philip Hammond's comments from 'Hammond: I reject idea millions live in dire poverty', BBC News, 3 June 2019.

73   Details of the workhouse outing from 'Feast Day for Camberwell Poor', *South London Press*, 25 July 1896; and 'Changing Times?', workhouses.org.uk.

145   Belzoni's '*personal charms ...*': *The Dictionary of National Biography*, vol. 4.

150   Dickens, '*of what is called the old school ...*': Charles Dickens, *Bleak House* (1853).

151   Entertainments at the Father Red Cap pub, from Mary Boast, *The Story of Camberwell* (Southwark Libraries, 1980).

153   '*The Femme Fatale ...*' from Brian McDonald, *Alice Diamond and the Forty Elephants: Britain's First Female Crime Syndicate* (Milo Books, 2015).

155   'Chalk Farm to Camberwell Green', lyrics by Lionel Monckton.

174   Robert Kennedy, *'Every time we turn our heads ...'*: Remarks before the Joint Defense Appeal of the American Jewish Committee and the Anti-Defamation League of the B'nai B'rith, Chicago, 21 June 1961.

178   Theresa May's comments from 'Statement from the new Prime Minister Theresa May', Downing Street, 13 July 2016.

182   Notice of the MS *Bergensfjord* sinking from 'Bergensfjord', simplonpc.co.uk.

295   James McConnell, *'We didn't know what the tail ...'*: From James V. McConnell, *The Worm Re-turns: The Best from the Worm Runner's Digest* (Prentice-Hall, 1965).

Sandi Toksvig was born in Denmark, brought up in Africa, then America and moved to the UK when she was fourteen. She has been on British stage, screen and radio for over forty years and was awarded an OBE for Services to Broadcasting. She is the mother of three children, married and lives in London.